Savannah's
Midnight Hour

Savannah's Midnight Hour

BOOSTERISM, GROWTH
AND COMMERCE IN A
NINETEENTH-CENTURY
AMERICAN CITY

LISA L. DENMARK

THE UNIVERSITY OF
GEORGIA PRESS
ATHENS

Paperback edition, 2022
© 2019 by the University of Georgia Press
Athens, Georgia 30602
www.ugapress.org
All rights reserved
Designed by Kaelin Chappell Broaddus
Set in 11/13.5 Adobe Caslon Pro by Kaelin Chappell Broaddus

Most University of Georgia Press titles are
available from popular e-book vendors.

Printed digitally

The Library of Congress has cataloged the
hardcover edition of this book as follows:

NAMES: Denmark, Lisa L., author.
TITLE: Savannah's midnight hour : boosterism, growth, and commerce
   in a nineteenth-century American city / Lisa L. Denmark.
DESCRIPTION: Athens : The University of Georgia Press, 2019. |
   Includes bibliographical references and index.
IDENTIFIERS: LCCN 2019041393 (print) | LCCN 2019041394 (ebook) |
   ISBN 9780820356327 (hardback) | ISBN 9780820356334 (epub)
SUBJECTS: LCSH: Savannah (Ga.)—History—19th century. | Savannah (Ga.)—
   Economic conditions—19th century. | Savannah (Ga.)—Economic policy—
   History—19th century. | Savannah (Ga.)—Commerce—History—19th century.
CLASSIFICATION: LCC F294.S2 D46 2019 (print) | LCC F294.S2 (ebook) |
   DDC 975.8/724—dc23
LC record available at https://lccn.loc.gov/2019041393
LC ebook record available at https://lccn.loc.gov/2019041394

Paperback ISBN 978-0-8203-6366-0

To William R. Wilson

CONTENTS

ILLUSTRATIONS

———•◆•———

FIGURES

TABLES

ACKNOWLEDGMENTS

In many ways, this book and my journey to its completion are about accumulating and honoring debts that were years in the making. However, I fear that there were too many people involved at some stage of this work or in helping me maintain my sanity as I pursued it to clear all my debts here.

The topic of this book was conceived, in part, as a result of tragedy and as a matter of convenience. I had just finished my first year of doctoral studies at the University of South Carolina when my mother was diagnosed with terminal cancer. Lacy Ford, my advisor, worked miracles that allowed me to keep my assistantship, continue my course work, and commute between Savannah and Columbia each week. As I searched for that ever-elusive original idea, I knew I needed something that would not require significant travel because my plan was to return home to help care for my mother. Fortunately, I stumbled upon that topic of convenience in Tom Terrill's New South seminar. As a native of Lowcountry Georgia, I readily interrogated the New South myth as it related to the region's so-called decline. I was amazed at the dearth of literature on Savannah as an urban community across the nineteenth century. From the start, Lacy supported my efforts in figuring out where Savannah fit.

It is hard to believe that two decades have now passed since I began this odyssey. There have been births, marriages, divorces, retirements, job security worries, other projects, and, sadly, deaths. My mother passed away before I completed my degree, but I give special thanks to Louise Denmark for instilling in me the belief that if I do my best, no one can take it away from me.

Frank Saunders joined me at the beginning of my journey, when, as a freshman, I walked into his office to ask advice on signing up for some history courses. He chaired my master's thesis and sat with me for hours reviewing my writing line by line. He also read the earliest manuscript versions of this book and challenged me with "why" questions on nearly every page. Unfortunately, Frank is no longer here to see the finished product, where many of those questions finally get answered.

I work with a wonderful group of teacher-scholars at Georgia Southern University. Four deserve special mention. Charles Thomas taught me
to look for the good in any situation and to enjoy life beyond the walls of
academe. Don Rakestraw has never failed to ask in person, over the phone,
or by email, "How's the book?" It is fitting that Don is a historian of diplomacy, for he can always be counted on to provide wise counsel even in
the most difficult situations. Don also organized the department happy
hours at Loco's, where colleagues became friends. On too many occasions
to count, Craig Roell has offered a sympathetic ear and helped me look
at things from a more humane perspective; his job is reminding me that
I can't control or fix everything. Anastatia Sims has been a mentor, a colleague, a friend, and a booster. In addition to being a model of connected
professionalism, she is a careful and conscientious editor. She's provided
me with sage advice and made me feel like I might be accomplishing
something important. As a Juliette Gordon Low scholar, Anastatia may
ask, "What would Daisy do?" I often ask, "What would *Anastatia* do?"

The best part of being in academe is engaging with students. They offer fresh perspectives and keep me on my toes. Discussions with students
helped me realize that Savannah's story is as much national as it is southern. During semesters in which the rest of my world seemed to be collapsing around me, my students made me smile and laugh and remem-
ber that the future is bright. I'd also like to thank the College of Arts and
Humanities at Georgia Southern University for its generosity, and in particular Dean Curtis Ricker, who mentored me through a truly crazy year
as interim chair.

It has been a pleasure to work with Mick Gusinde-Duffy, whom I met
by chance at a Southern Historical Association conference shortly after
his arrival at University of Georgia Press. He patiently listened to my excited ramblings about railroads, municipal finance, and debt. He asked me
to submit a proposal and periodically sent me encouraging emails nudg-
ing me forward.

I am indebted to the archivists and librarians at University of North
Carolina, Georgia Southern University, and Georgia Historical Society.
Georgia Southern's interlibrary loan librarian Cynthia Frost (now retired)
worked tirelessly to acquire books, maps, and microfilm for me. Sharon
Lee at the Kaye Kole Genealogy and Local History Room at Savan-
nah's Bull Street Library, Live Oak Public Libraries, introduced me to the
Thomas Gamble Collection, helped with locating maps, carried armloads

of books up and down stairs, and always greeted my arrival with a smile. Finally, Glenda Anderson, former director of the City of Savannah Municipal Archives, and Luciana Spracher, current director, are simply amazing. I have benefited from their encyclopedic knowledge of their extensive collection.

Portions of chapters 1 and 2 were previously published as "'But What a Pretty Thing a Rail Road Is!—We Must Have One of Our Own—Positively!': Savannah's Unique Rhetoric of Internal Improvements," *Journal of the Georgia Association of Historians* 28 (2009): 1–32. Portions of chapters 4 through 11 were previously published as "'At the Midnight Hour': Economic Dilemmas and Harsh Realities in Post–Civil War Savannah," *Georgia Historical Quarterly* 90 (Fall 2006): 350–90. They are published here with permission.

Family and friends have helped me through this process both directly and indirectly. Some, like my sisters Kathy Dasher and Susan Lott, were dragooned into proofreading and data entry duties. Jennifer Darby Speight also lent her proofreading skills to the earliest versions of this work. Cheryl Wells provided insightful comments on organizing and strengthening the introduction. Stacy Tanner found the most delightful ways of reminding me about my passion, usually by gifting me with something featuring a railroad, train, or tracks. Ashley Baumann has been amazingly patient and efficient in dealing with my myriad requests for the preparation of maps and photos contained herein. Jamie Credle offered me an opportunity to expand upon the history of the Savannah and Ogeechee Canal with an invitation to be part of the Harvest Lecture Series at the Davenport House. Nathan Miller, Steven Gibeault, and Michelle Hatch provided moral support in attending the lecture. Michelle also found herself drafted into reading a nearly final version of my manuscript and offering fresh ideas regarding the book's title and marketing. Gary Murphy, Kerri Ewing, Sean Holcey, Elizabeth Clarke, Peter Stubbers, Meghan McGreevy, and the rest of the Rail Pub Gang never read a line of text, but they introduced me to life beyond work and helped preserve my humanity and sanity.

For the last three years, Bill Wilson, my husband and my soul mate, has brought such joy to my life. He has been an unfailing source of comfort and support. His unshakable faith in my abilities remains a constant surprise. And he's absolutely right: happiness comes with marrying a history major.

Savannah's
Midnight Hour

The Ethos of Success

"Rain, rain, rain," recorded Savannahian Sarah Lawton in her diary throughout mid-June 1876.[1] Excessive heat followed the rains, and then in August came the yellow fever. As local authorities and benevolent societies organized relief programs, physicians and other health officials worked to contain the epidemic. Meanwhile, everyone waited for the first frost, after which the epidemic would subside. By November, when the Georgia Medical Society announced the epidemic over and Savannah safe, nearly a thousand people had perished.[2]

Thousands of Savannahians had left home to escape the epidemic. As they returned and debate raged about the causes of the epidemic and methods for future prevention, Savannah's municipal government faced a crisis of another sort: the city coffers were virtually empty. In January 1877 the city defaulted on its loans. As creditors, fearful of repudiation, initiated lawsuits, elected officials worked to negotiate a compromise. Exacerbated by other financial commitments along with a general taxpayer revolt and numerous court proceedings, the debacle resulting from this default would not be resolved until 1883.

Savannah was not the only city to find itself tottering on the brink of bankruptcy, nor was this a new phenomenon. In the 1820s, state governments used their borrowing power to fund various internal improvements. The willingness to fund these projects often failed to correlate with the ability to cover those debts. In response to the waves of defaults and repudiations, which followed in the wake of the Panic of 1837, several states revised their constitutions to restrict future legislatures from embarking on such "borrowing binges." Public aid, however, remained an important source for funding improvements, and municipal governments increasingly filled the vacuum left by state retrenchment.[3]

Local governments, the most active level of government in the nineteenth century, grew much faster than the federal or state governments and bore the heaviest financial burdens.[4] Rumblings of concern developed in the 1850s, and on the eve of the Civil War a number of cities defaulted on their loans. Yet boosters and advocates of active government continued to predict ultimate financial success, and borrowing continued apace.[5] The real crisis developed in the 1870s as overextended corporations, cities, and states defaulted on their loans and used innovative methods to frustrate creditor efforts to force repayment.

Municipal debt increased from $25 million in 1840 to $821 million in 1880, three times larger than state debts, which also increased noticeably. Between 1866 and 1876, debt increased by nearly 180 percent; between 1870 and 1880, overall municipal debt increased by $305 million. Iowa judge John Forrest Dillon, a prominent authority on municipal malfeasance, estimated that the total municipal debt in 1881 was $1 billion.[6] Dillon, an unyielding critic of what he considered extravagant municipal spending, lamented the trend in granting municipal and public corporations the power to issue commercial securities. Local governments, participating in what Dillon called "epidemic insanity," issued bonds "without much hesitation," fully expecting the burden "to fall principally on posterity." From his vantage point, these actions had "undeniably been attended with very serious, and it is perhaps not too strong a statement to add, disastrous, consequences."[7]

Often cities directly invested in railroads or guaranteed the principal or interest on railroad bonds. They also embarked on various infrastructural projects, especially related to water and sewer systems. Because expenditures far outpaced tax collections, city leaders became increasingly dependent on loans in servicing their debts.[8] They and their constituents seemed content to rely on these easily acquired loans as long as taxes remained low. As one legal commentator has noted, cities participated in "reckless aid to railroads" and engaged in "waste and excess optimism in local improvements."[9] Although municipal recklessness has often been associated with the South, in the two decades following the Civil War several municipalities throughout the country defaulted, including Pittsburgh, Memphis, Duluth, Mobile, Watertown (Wisconsin), and Elizabeth, New Jersey.[10]

Lenders had little sympathy for overextended cities, especially for what they condemned as unwise investments in defunct railroads or equally futile schemes. When municipal governments either could not or would not pay, creditors sought legal recourse.[11] Between 1865 and 1885, the courts were inundated with cases in which municipalities tried to avoid debt payment. Municipal defaults, bankruptcies, and attempted repudiations and compromises constituted the largest category of cases that appeared before the U.S. Supreme Court.[12] Though creditors had numerous legal remedies at their disposal, local political and judicial resistance and the inconsistent judicial procedures made collection difficult at best and at times impossible. Federal courts increasingly sided with bondholders, yet, with municipal officials motivated to avoid payment, even U.S. Supreme Court decisions could not guarantee enforcement.[13]

In his study of municipal defaults, Albert M. Hillhouse maintained that Savannah's situation was one of the rare cases in which a city's financial crisis could be blamed on an "act of God," specifically the tragic yellow fever epidemic. A cursory review of the timing, as well as the city's pleas for creditor leniency, certainly lends credence to such a conclusion. Upon closer examination, however, neither contemporary critics like Dillon nor historians like Hillhouse grasped that the crisis had deeper roots than the spendthrift proclivity ushered in after the Civil War or, in Savannah's case, the more immediate yellow fever epidemic. As in other municipalities across the nation, the financial crisis Savannah faced in 1877 was not merely the result of an "act of God," it was the result of decades of seemingly rational, human financial decisions.[14]

Over the course of a half-century, beginning in the 1820s and continuing into the early 1870s, Savannah's resourceful leaders had acted with energy, though not always with the greatest economic or technological acuity, to facilitate commerce, establish transportation links to the hinterland, and construct a more modern internal infrastructure. While contemporary critics castigated cities for their financial carelessness, especially regarding investments in worthless railroad schemes, this condemnation misses a crucial piece of the historical equation. Individuals and groups generally take risks in the expectation of benefit but with the understanding of some degree of uncertainty. This uncertainty is weighed against the potential positive and negative consequences.[15] Savannah, like so many cities, invested in various projects that ultimately proved worthless; how-ever, *some* projects proved remarkably successful. Borrowing sprees for in-ternal improvements (primarily roads, canals, and railroads) occurred pre-cisely because some of its previous investments had been successful.

Savannah's leaders and businessmen had long aspired to emerge from Charleston's shadow and have their city recognized as the Great Atlantic Seaport. Evincing a significant degree of pride, they enthusiastically and aggressively pursued this goal by investing in canals, railroads, and har-bor improvements. Savannah's antebellum leaders acted on the premise that the municipal government was responsible for facilitating commerce, which was based almost completely on the extractive economy of cotton, rice, and lumber.[16] In Savannah's case, this municipal entrepreneurship began largely in the absence of significant state activity and found inspi-ration in northern accomplishments, especially the Erie Canal. Optimism about the power of local agency pervaded both rhetoric and action. Rob-ert E. Wright, in *One Nation under Debt*, notes that, by the 1830s, "Amer-icans were world-renowned entrepreneurs, prepared to risk all on untried products, markets and techniques."[17] Savannah's municipal officials cer-tainly fit this description. While they had ties—sometimes reluctant—to plantation agriculture, they were widely traveled and chose to live in and focus their interest and energy on their city. Between 1825 and 1860, Sa-vannah's local government invested in an ever-widening number of proj-ects to improve the city's competitiveness with its primary coastal rivals—first Charleston and then Mobile.[18]

There was genuine enthusiasm for city and regional growth for the sake of pride and "manifest destiny." And there was a large degree of self-in-terest involved, especially for real estate speculators. Yet municipal entre-preneurs were also often astute businessmen who tied their success to the success of their cities.[19] George Rogers Taylor argues that while some in-dividuals might have invested to reap significant financial returns, more important was the expectation of "indirect benefits," or what he calls the "multiplier effect," whereby an investment in an internal improvement like a railroad was expected to have the potential of "greatly increasing the productivity of a whole area." For instance, producers would benefit from greater demand and therefore higher prices for their goods, consumers would "get more for their money," real estate values would increase, "mid-dlemen" and bankers would see an increase in profits, and cities would re-ceive greater revenue because of increases in taxable property. In essence, while investors might profit directly, the entire community gained advantages.[20]

As boosters worked to convince state legislatures and city councils to invest considerable sums in projects including canals, turnpikes, railroads, and harbor improvement, the line between public and private enterprise, a line always difficult to define, became increasingly blurred. Americans readily used governmental resources to fund transportation improvements. In addition to providing direct aid, local and state politicians demonstrated a decided preference for "mixed enterprise." Commonly this meant that public funding supplemented funds raised by private corporations.[21] While legislators vigorously debated the degree to which a project would benefit one locality over another, few questioned the legitimacy of state involvement in mixed enterprise.[22] The increase in both public indebtedness and the percentage of state and local expenditures devoted to various enterprises demonstrated that elected officials believed these ventures would benefit the public and contribute to the general prosperity of their people.[23] In looking at the increased reliance on credit, economic historian Edward Balleisen asserts that the willingness to use credit was a manifestation of Americans' optimism about their future, and the ultimate result was the creation of a national economy.[24]

Regional rivalries also played an important role in motivating cities to take an active role in promoting communication with their hinterlands. The intense competition for western trade between New York City, Baltimore, Philadelphia, and Boston and British North America (Canada) was the catalyst for New York's investment in the Erie Canal, which Governor DeWitt Clinton maintained would make New York "the greatest city in the world." To a certain degree, cities were acting on the fear of being the loser in a zero-sum game. The choice was simple: fail to act and watch their decay, or take decisive action that held out the potential for growth and success. This calculus not only explains the motivation for action but also the conflation of aiding private enterprise with working for the public good.[25]

The enormous and immediate success of the Erie Canal, completed in 1825, accelerated the pace of economic change. It also clearly demonstrated the impact that one well-placed, publicly funded project could have on determining the future for numerous localities. A defensive Philadelphia responded with investment in its own canal, while Baltimore and Boston built railroads.[26] These examples were not lost on other cities. States, cities, and towns actively competed for the commerce flowing from the hinterland.[27] Throughout the antebellum period, state governments built and operated canals and subscribed capital to private companies to build turnpikes and subsequently railroads. Municipalities also became heavily involved in financing these to compete with regional rivals. In 1830 only 13 miles of track existed in the United States. By 1840 that number had increased to 3,325, and it more than doubled between 1840 and 1850 to 8,879 miles. In the process of building canals and railroads, which contributed to the unprecedented expansion of the economy, municipal governments subsidized the transportation system that began linking farmers to markets and urban centers throughout the nation. Coastal cities pushed railroads into the hinterlands to gain access to western markets. The result was a growing network of railroads, which facilitated the creation of a national commercial network.[28]

The boom-and-bust nature of the American economy caused the investment pendulum to sway, but even during economic slumps local governments, taking the long view of financial risk, invested in various projects because of the potential they held for stimulating the local or regional economy. These vigorous activities and investments directly impacted their economy, the growth of their cities, and the prosperity of their people.[29]

Some of Savannah's larger antebellum investments included implementation of dry culture, harbor improvement, the Savannah and Ogeechee Canal, the Central of Georgia Railroad, the Savannah and Albany Railroad, the Atlantic and Gulf Railroad, and the Southwestern Railroad. Savannah's aggressive investment, in spite of some notable and expensive failures, seems to have had desired results. In 1860, after over two decades of spectacular growth, Savannah finally surpassed Charleston, its primary rival, in cotton exports.[30] The outlooks and entrepreneurial ethos that had characterized city leaders and boosters during the antebellum period continued in the postwar years. When the Civil War ended in 1865, leaders worked to revive the economy, return Savannah to its prewar prosperity, and extend its access to westward markets. Optimistic about swift recovery, they willingly pursued new projects.

The postwar context and the paltry income derived from its destitute citizens frustrated these efforts. Determined action to aid Savannah's physical recovery, build upon prewar expansion, and finance new projects quickly evolved into increased dependence on both long-term and short-term loans, the latter mostly to pay current expenses and service existing debts.[31] Acquiring millions of dollars in debt remained a risky venture, but given both real and imagined potential rewards of maintaining the city's good credit, facilitating its growth, and increasing its competitiveness, the risk seemed justified.

In the immediate aftermath of the war, political and economic realities had altered drastically. Resistance to Reconstruction put the interests of the South in direct conflict with those of the federal government. Due to the political instability occasioned by Reconstruction in Georgia, neither the city nor the state maintained consistent official representation in Congress. While Savannah survived the war physically intact and retained some of its reputation as an important southern port, it could not depend on that single distinction to return to its prewar commercial prosperity. As had been the case in the 1840s and 1850s, Savannah competed with old rivals like Charleston, Mobile, and New Orleans. It also faced new competition from Brunswick, an upstart port city to the south of Savannah, and Atlanta, the emerging railroad hub to the north; both rivals received support from many Georgians simply because they offered competition to Savannah.

In the half-decade after the Civil War, city officials continued a pattern they believed had been successful, a pattern that was national. They spent large sums of money, which they had to borrow, to restore Savannah's commerce and to meet emerging competitors. With the waning of Reconstruction in the early 1870s, city leaders, trusting that the new political environment would lend itself to Savannah's growth, embarked on a massive public works program to make their city more attractive to investment. They did so despite the economic hard times and a very lean city treasury. In addition to continued expenditures on the harbor and river, the municipal government funded a drainage system, street paving, construction of a new market building, and expansion of local public education. No one could legitimately claim that any of these projects were superfluous. The old market was near collapse; the city had been dealing with drainage problems long before the war; during heavy rains, unpaved sandy streets turned into impassable quagmires; and the existing offerings of public education were inadequate at best. However, the timing, unforeseen expenses, constant cost overruns, shoddy work, surprise bond requests, and the issuance of an unprecedented number of short-term notes provided the appearance of inept mismanagement of the city's finances or even, as some believed, corruption. In essence, Savannah's leaders had mortgaged the city's future.

Following the financial panic of 1873 and subsequent depression, the City of Savannah suffered increasing economic strain as it worked to satisfy the needs of its commercial and residential constituents as well as its creditors. Bond issues became more important in paying interest on past loans than in funding new projects. The financial strain ultimately became too great. While officials blamed the city's near financial collapse in early 1877 on a taxpayer revolt and the yellow scourge, the real culprit was a long-standing ideology of over-optimistic risk-taking for a goal that soon proved illusory.

Officials had spent much of the preceding half-century convincing themselves and their constituents of the rewards to be reaped from their aggressive boosterism. It seems that Savannah's leaders had instead harvested economic embarrassment, while its property-owning citizens suffered higher taxes. As Savannah sought to satisfy its creditors, and as the state instituted borrowing restrictions, the days of unrestricted leveraging of city credit to facilitate economic development came to an end.

The municipal default imbroglio certainly embarrassed Savannah. Yet, even as Savannah's municipal government muddled through the default crisis, the transportation system it had inaugurated put the coastal city in a better position than its two major rivals, Charleston and Mobile, to regain the prewar upward trajectory. In the two decades following the war's conclusion, Savannah's commerce recovered more quickly. It consistently outpaced Charleston and Mobile in cotton exports, sometimes by a two-to-one margin. Aggressive boosterism and the largess of the municipal government may not have fulfilled the leaders' promises of making Savannah the chief metropolis and grand seaport of the South. However, in its more limited objective of besting its historic urban rivals, the city's efforts did achieve relative success.

Savannah inhabits a complex place in the study of the U.S. South. Often it is included in the model of southern coastal decline, similar to that of Charleston and Mobile. Prior to the Civil War, as this thesis goes, these southern coastal cities prospered from their cotton-shipping monopolies, but the Civil War, along with the new political and economic circumstances, severely crippled this commerce and thus their efforts at full recovery. In this new, more competitive environment, they declined in economic and political importance. In their place arose hinterland cities of the "New South" like Atlanta and Nashville. These "New South" leaders accepted the predominant capitalist ideology, and they associated their individual success with the success of their cities. Due to favorable geographic, economic, and ideological circumstances, they were able to take advantage of changing postwar conditions.[32]

In this model, Savannah and its coastal counterparts fit rather neatly into the school of discontinuity or change associated with C. Vann Woodward's *Origins of the New South*. In its simplest form, this discontinuity thesis establishes the Civil War as the great historical divide in nineteenth-century southern history. Woodward and subsequent proponents claim that the Civil War destroyed the planter aristocracy and made way for a new group of urban-oriented leaders, who focused their energies on modernizing the South through agricultural diversification and industrialization. Woodward's thesis stood up for over a quarter-century before coming under sustained attack beginning in the late 1970s, and since then its challengers have been numerous.[33]

The diverse aspects of this debate often depend on one's perspective of the antebellum South. There seems to be an implicit assumption that the South was different from the rest of the nation. Those who focus on regional distinctiveness tend to see the South as existing outside the traditional narrative of U.S. history. In their eyes, the South is decidedly not part of the national experience. Southern slavery and later segregation and sharecropping can be used to explain how the region has been an impediment to national progress. More recently, however, a new generation of scholars has asserted that the entire premise of southern exceptionalism is a construct.[34]

This book seeks to place Savannah's development within the larger history of municipal finance, public policy, credit (with its intricacies and complex nature), and judicial readjustment in an urbanizing nation. Savannah certainly exhibited some distinctively southern characteristics and experienced similarly disruptive circumstances related to the vicissitudes of the cotton economy. At the same time, Savannah's leaders shared a larger urban outlook that reflected cities across the nation. In Savannah and elsewhere, municipal leaders believed that their cities needed to grow; otherwise they faced decline and decay. Savannah's fiscal experience, tied as it was to aggressive entrepreneurship in the antebellum and postbellum years, mirrors a larger national experience.[35] A history of Savannah's municipal decision-making regarding internal improvement investment over the course of the nineteenth century allows for a nuanced look at how the coastal city fits into both the regional and national narratives.

Savannah's fiscal difficulties were not unique. By the time Savannah defaulted on its loans in 1877, this fate had already befallen numerous cities. Bondholder impatience with Savannah's situation reflected a building resentment among creditors about the ability of states and municipalities to avoid repayment. Conversely, Savannah's leaders were aware of the relative success and failure of other cities in dealing with their own default crises, and they took these into account in their efforts to compromise and then negotiate Savannah's debt. The problem for both creditors and municipal debtors was the lack of a clear and decisive legal process for forcing payment. The default crisis of the 1870s and the murky legal standing of municipal corporations had the potential to make municipal bonds the riskiest of investments. But while state legislatures attempted to restrain the borrowing power of municipalities, they failed to create a clear legal process for municipal default and bankruptcy. Courts, nevertheless, generally backed the rights of creditors. As a result, municipal bonds came to be viewed as one of the safest financial investments.

Urban boosters often receive considerable attention for their efforts to convince elected officials of the advantages that would result from certain municipal-funded projects.[36] Frequently, historical narratives center on the rhetoric and tactics these boosters have used to cloak projects beneficial to them in the guise of economic development and public enterprise. In Savannah, elected officials, variously called councilmen or aldermen, were well aware that if they failed to create a favorable economic environment for business, business would relocate, and this would in turn decrease the urban tax base and mar the city's image. What separated individual boosters and municipal officials was power. Therefore, rather than focus specifically on booster rhetoric and demands, this book will focus on the degree to which municipal leaders internalized the rhetoric and carried out those demands. In Savannah, the mayor and board of aldermen had the political power and legal authority to carry out the desires of urban boosters, and they were committed to using the borrowing capacity of the municipal corporation to advance their corresponding interests.

The municipal corporation of Savannah became an aggressive economic developer in the 1820s when it invested in the Savannah and Ogeechee Canal. Though this project proved disappointing, when the next opportunity for significant public investment presented itself in the form of the Central of Georgia Railroad (also known as the Central Railroad or simply "the Central"), the city took a significant financial risk. The prosperity Savannah reaped from this highly successful railroad led to similar investments. In the process, the municipal government acquired an onerous debt—both an expected and an acceptable consequence.

Based on the perceived reasons for their prewar economic success, leaders assumed that local decisions and actions could achieve the desired successful and prosperous outcome. Savannah's leaders based postwar decisions on a tradition of success. Though the ideology that laid the basis for their decisions beginning in the 1820s was still valid in the 1870s, in Savannah's case the ability to match ideals with action diminished significantly. When debt crippled the city, municipal officials and the citizens who elected them had to deal with the repercussions and reconsider convictions that had been the foundation of municipal economic policy for half a century.

The choices city leaders made between the first, though less than successful, canal investment in the 1820s and the massive public works program in the early 1870s had three important results. First, efforts to promote internal improvements provided a foundation for a usable rhetoric. They had to be diligent to wrest money from conservative state governments, entice capital from planters focused on cotton, land, and slaves, and overcome traditional Upcountry Georgia animosity toward the Lowcountry. They were also more aware of decline because their own place in southern society was more tenuous. Second, investment in the Central Railroad and the Atlantic and Gulf Railroad, along with other less prominent lines, closely tied the hinterland to the city and the city into the larger market economy. The Central Railroad's success also stimulated railroad development throughout the state. By 1846, rail lines from Savannah and Augusta had connections to the state-sponsored Western and Atlantic Railroad at its terminus in Atlanta, all constructed in expectation of capturing western trade to the west of Georgia.[37]

In tying the city more tightly to the market economy, Savannah's decision to pursue more extensive links to the developing national market ironically restrained its ability to direct or control its prosperity and success. After the war, the railroads Savannah promoted to bring commerce to the coast became integrated into more coherent regional and national systems. These rail lines were intended to bring cotton to Savannah—as opposed to Mobile or Charleston. On the eve of the Civil War, Savannah could look with pride at its achievement, having for the first time topped Charleston in cotton exports.[38] However, these same rail lines also made possible the distribution of communication and financial services related

to cotton and credit, previously concentrated in the coastal port cities. A
growing number of merchants and bankers located in interior towns now
connected to the coast via rail assumed economic functions that had been
the province of coastal cotton factors. The railroad boom that the city had
helped foster reached its logical conclusion in the years after the Civil
War, and those same railroads ceased to serve their coastal masters.[39]

The third impact of the choices city fathers made in the forty years before the Panic of 1873 was crippling indebtedness. The successful Central Railroad venture gave the city the confidence to invest in other enterprises. This was also the case with harbor improvement and public works
projects. Beginning in the 1820s, Savannah's elected officials, taking the
long view of both direct and indirect benefits that would accrue to the
city, vigorously used the borrowing power of the municipal government
to fund a transportation network that tied the city into the developing
national economy. These were rational decisions made by individuals who
understood both the potential risks and rewards. On the eve of the Civil
War, Savannah's debt was substantial, but, with the city's commerce thriving, it also seemed manageable. Due to the outbreak of the war in 1861, it
is impossible to determine how the city would have fared.

In the years after the war, municipal officials continued to view growing public indebtedness as an acceptable risk. Only on the eve of the national economic panic did leaders realize that Savannah's treasury could
no longer sustain their efforts at expansion and improvement. The decision to scale back investment was not a decision in which municipal officials had much choice. Market integration, transportation changes, and
crippling indebtedness, not a lack of will or enthusiasm, limited the options still open to the municipal government.

This book is a study of the remarkably consistent economic decisions made by Savannah's leaders as they pursued a policy of aggressive municipal entrepreneurship. These policies had furnished Savannah's
commerce-related businesses with the ability to compete successfully
with traditional rivals before the war. Though Savannah suffered from
wartime and postwar political and economic disruptions similar to those
of its traditional rivals, it recovered more quickly and surpassed them.
Unfortunately for the city, as new rivals emerged, the overburdened municipality could no longer sustain its aggressive policies. This book ex-
amines the economic progress of the city and studies its people, whose
optimism for a bright future built on the foundation of past successes
was tempered by two things. First, they gradually realized that boundless

goals were no longer attainable with the establishment of just one more rail connection or just one more steamship line. Second, they recognized that their decisions and actions could not alone determine their future.

This book is structured chronologically, with chapter 1 providing a brief history of Savannah from its founding through the 1820s; the primary focus is on Savannah's ineffectual attempt to move out of Charleston's shadow with the failed effort at canal building. Chapter 2 covers Savannah's venture with the Central Railroad to protect itself from South Carolina's commercial hegemony; this success incentivized additional railroad investments and provided a blueprint for the future. Chapter 3 delineates the demographic and racial changes characteristic of booming city growth and details the challenges of wartime destruction. Chapter 4 surveys Savannah's herculean postwar efforts under Mayor Edward C. Anderson to revitalize the harbor, an economic project that was just one of many that clashed with Savannah's political goals during Reconstruction. Chapter 5 details the entanglement of municipal debt, municipal politics, and railroad territorial wars, which culminated in the election of John Screven, president of the Atlantic and Gulf Railroad, as mayor of Savannah. Screven's tenure as mayor is the focal point of chapters 6 and 7, as his administration embarked on necessary but costly infrastructural improvements. Due to unprecedented municipal expenditures and skyrocketing debt, his financial management became a major cause for concern. Chapter 8 discusses the return of Anderson as mayor in 1875, his administration's failed efforts at retrenchment, and the increased dependence on loans merely to service existing debts. Anderson's refusal to give up his mayoral post, the topic of chapter 9, created an exciting municipal campaign season, which was followed by a taxpayer revolt and then yellow fever. Chapter 10 analyzes Savannah's financial default and the efforts of Dr. James J. Waring to force the city to face reality as impatient creditors pushed for payment. Chapter 11 covers the final throes of the debt crisis, fear of bankruptcy, creditor efforts to prevent repudiation, legal maneuvering, and ultimate settlement. The conclusion evaluates the lessons Savannah learned and how municipal leaders opted to scale back on large projects to protect the city's financial reputation.

- • -

CHAPTER 1

"Far from This 'Ruin'"

CONFLAGRATION, PESTILENCE,
AND CANAL FEVER

Savannah came into existence as Georgia's first city in 1733, advertised as a philanthropic experiment with a military purpose. The Trustees of Georgia sent James Edward Oglethorpe, one of their number, to the new colony with the first settlers. They arrived in February 1733 and settled on the bluff overlooking the Savannah River. Over the next two decades, more immigrants arrived, but the colony struggled for survival, in part because of the various restrictions the Trustees placed on the inhabitants. In addition to forbidding the importation of rum and other strong drink, the Trustees restricted the disposition of property and prohibited slavery.[1]

Various malcontents, as Oglethorpe called them, clashed with the Trustees over Georgia's purpose and future. The Trustees wanted to prevent their worthy but poor settlers from becoming debtors. They feared that the colonists would be tempted to borrow money on property, had they control of it, to purchase slaves. The malcontents, on the other hand, wanted a chance at commercial expansion and to emulate their economically more successful neighbor—South Carolina.[2]

In 1752 when the Trustees' charter expired, Georgia became a royal province. Georgians welcomed the new and less restrictive status and began to develop a rice-based plantation economy dependent on slave labor, much like that of South Carolina. Georgia reluctantly and belatedly joined the other colonies in rebellion against Great Britain. In December 1778, the British attacked and occupied Savannah and much of the Lowcountry. Following its victory at Savannah, the British army moved into the Upcountry and took Augusta too. The next year a combined French and American assault on the coastal city failed. While control of the areas north and south of Savannah fluctuated, the city remained under British occupation until the summer of 1782, when the British finally evacuated.[3]

Following the Revolutionary War, Georgia experienced a rapid influx of immigrants, primarily from North Carolina and Virginia. These new arrivals settled in the area around Augusta, about 125 miles north of Savannah. With growing population in the Upcountry and the economic vacuum occasioned by the Loyalist abandonment of coastal Georgia, Savannah lost much of its wealth and influence.[4]

When traveler John Pope arrived from Virginia in the summer of 1790 and renewed his friendships with Joseph Habersham and Lachlan McIntosh, he noted the importance of the port. In a book about his travels published two years later, he predicted that Savannah would be a "place of Opulence, so long as human Nature shall require Food or Rainment [*sic*], or Commerce spread her Canvas to the Wind." Pope may have been swayed by the views of his more enthusiastic friends, for he confessed that he found Savannah too hot to go out and thus spent most of his time inside.[5]

Like Pope, George Washington, visiting a year later, remarked on the business of the port. Yet he too found Savannah rather unpleasant. He complained in his diary that the streets were sandy, which made walking "disagreeable"; furthermore, the houses were both "uncomfortable" and "filled with dust."[6]

The port may have caught the attention of observers, but the fledgling town, with two thousand inhabitants, failed to make a list of the hundred largest urban places in the nation in 1790.[7] It was certainly dwarfed by Charleston, its nearest sibling. The fourth-largest city in the United States, with 16,359 inhabitants, Charleston dominated Savannah commercially, especially in the export of rice and Sea Island cotton.[8]

By the mid-1790s, Savannah began to show small signs of growth. Via the four hundred ships arriving and departing annually, Savannah imported the likes of sugar, molasses, salt, and wine and exported lumber, indigo, grains, tobacco, skins, rice, and increasingly cotton.[9] In 1796, the city boasted $501,000 in exports. A fire in November 1796, which destroyed 229 buildings and did about $1 million in damage, briefly interrupted the recovery. Citizens quickly rebuilt, and two years later Savannah could boast 618 dwellings and 228 places of business.[10] Proportionally, Chatham

County had more houses valued at over $100 than any other county in the state.[11]

Although construction continued throughout the city, visitors remained unimpressed. When traveler John Davis arrived in 1799, he was oppressed by the weather and complained that there were "no two places on earth hotter than Savannah and Charleston." The sand also caught his attention. He described how he and his companion found themselves "ploughing through one or two streets of sand." He went on to observe that the streets were so "unsupportably sandy, that every inhabitant wears goggles over his eyes, which give the appearance of being in a masquerade."[12] Similarly, Frenchman La Rochefoucauld-Liancourt, who caught a fever during his visit, declared that he "departed with pleasure from this town, the climate, and the situation of the burning sand" where its inhabitants displayed a "spirit of disorder and anarchy."[13]

In the first decade of the nineteenth century, Savannah continued to suffer from its reputation as a small, dirty, and unpleasant place. The city council tried various systems to remedy the prevalence of filth. In the 1790s, it required all male slaves aged sixteen to sixty living within the city to clean the streets and carry the refuse to the foot of Whitaker Street for burning. The following decade, the city's scavengers removed garbage during the summer months to dumping grounds outside the city between White Bluff and Ogeechee Roads.[14]

Smallpox was a perennial concern. In 1802, there was an outbreak outside the city. Partly in response to this, local physicians established the Georgia Medical Society in 1804, and that year the city created a board of health. The following year, when smallpox reappeared within the city, officials removed all infected individuals to outside the city, posted guards, and commenced voluntary inoculations within the city. Over time, inoculations became compulsory.[15]

In spite of Davis's complaints about sand and heat and La Rochefoucauld's poor experience, the city was definitely reviving economically. In 1800, Savannah now with 5,146 inhabitants, was ranked twenty-first on the list of the nation's most populous cities. About half of Savannah's population consisted of slaves, who lived within the city and worked at a variety of jobs. A small number of free blacks worked as artisans and craftsmen. About four hundred white artisans lived and worked in Savannah; they constituted about 40 percent of the adult male population. The total population was small compared to Charleston's nearly twenty thousand.[16] Charleston continued to dominate the export market too, besting Savannah by nearly $8 million annually and exporting nearly double the amount of cotton as Savannah.[17]

Commission merchants facilitated the expanding business of Savannah's port. Many served as agents of commission houses in Charleston, Liverpool, and Glasgow. Although critics complained that they drained the wealth from Savannah, not all of this wealth left the city.[18] These merchants established businesses and constructed warehouses along the bay and on Johnston and Ellis Squares while they commissioned homes along West Broad Street and Broughton Street and around Reynolds Square.[19] The financial stature of the city received another boost when the Bank of the United States opted to establish a branch in Savannah in 1802 with Joseph Habersham as president.[20]

On the eve of America's second war with Britain, though Savannah's population continued to lag, it could boast a thriving commerce and a significant amount of residential and business construction.[21] It also continued to welcome newcomers. Of the 5,215 inhabitants, only one-quarter of the white population represented native-born Savannahians. Another quarter was foreign-born, mostly from Britain and France.[22]

According to historian Paul Pressly, to fill the vacuum in economic leadership occasioned by the end of the Revolution, Savannah, in contrast to Charleston, welcomed these non-southerners. These individuals viewed Savannah as a place of opportunity to engage in commerce and practice medicine and law. Some critics charged that such people sought only to make their fortunes before retiring or seeking more lucrative locations. Many, however, made Savannah their home, married into elite families, and further tied Savannah to the international web of commerce.[23]

Observers differed on their view of Savannah's commerce and future. Scotsman J. B. Dunlop, who visited in 1811, considered Savannah's trade "entirely in her infancy" but said that it had great potential for future growth, given its commercial advantages. British traveler John Lambert was less enthusiastic.[24] Already soured on Georgia's dearth of civilization (art, literature, science), which he claimed was "yet in the Gothic Age," he asserted that Savannah was "not likely to increase very rapidly" because the city's merchants were mostly adventurers hoping to do well in trade before moving on.[25]

Proving Lambert wrong, Savannah by 1816 was enjoying a flourishing economy. In January, the number of ships at one time docked at the harbor or at anchor at nearby Tybee reached a twenty-year high. Between March and June 1816, cotton shipments from Savannah totaled 76,582.

The port saw the arrival of 203 ships and the clearing of 191. In a three-month period, the value of native products exported from Savannah was more than all of New England. Items shipped through Savannah totaled $10,322,880 in 1816, only $4 million less than that exported by Charleston.[26] During this busy spring, Savannah and Augusta celebrated the launching of Samuel Howard's steamboat *Enterprise*.[27] Finally, the Treasury Department named Savannah as one of the eighteen branch locations for the recently chartered Second Bank of the United States.[28]

Within three years, annual exports had climbed to $14 million, a 600 percent increase since 1800.[29] With construction and the export market booming, Savannah's future looked bright.[30] Entrepreneurs plowed the wealth they derived from Savannah's expanding economy into new home construction. Arriving just in time, during Savannah's "most prosperous, boisterous years," was William Jay. He came to Savannah to design the home of banker and cotton merchant Richard Richardson. Richardson's friends and associates like Alexander Telfair and William Scarbrough were so impressed with Jay and his work that they too commissioned the young architect to design their family homes. William Scarbrough's home was completed in 1819, just in time for the visit of President James Monroe, who stayed there.[31]

Monroe's arrival coincided with the launching of another one of Scarbrough's investments—the steamship *Savannah*. In May 1818, the *Savannah Republican* notified readers that a subscription book would be opened for a "Steam-Ship Packet to run from this port to Liverpool." The Georgia legislature subsequently incorporated the Savannah Steamship Company to carry out that objective.[32]

The steamship company purchased a 320-ton sailing vessel and modified it with a steam engine.[33] The *Savannah* arrived in its namesake port from New York in April 1819. After making two trips between Savannah and Charleston, Captain Moses Rogers prepared to set sail across the Atlantic, bound for Liverpool. President James Monroe arrived in Savannah in time to tour the vessel and steam between Savannah and Tybee. The vessel departed on May 24, and twenty-nine days later the *Savannah* docked in Liverpool, having worked the engines a total of eighteen days.[34]

Liverpool citizens were "gratified and astonished" at the *Savannah*'s arrival. The writer for the *Chester Chronicle* declared that "more handsome specimen of naval architecture never entered a British port." In July, it departed Liverpool. After visiting Denmark, Sweden, and Russia, it embarked on its homeward voyage. On November 30, the *Savannah* docked in Savannah.[35]

Savannah's prestige in launching this venture, however, did not extend to the Savannah Steamship Company's long-term commercial success. In the end, despite its historic voyage (as the first steamship to cross the Atlantic), the *Savannah* failed to develop into a profitable enterprise. The vessel required more fuel than it could carry. Upon its return from its ten-thousand-mile voyage the engine was removed, and it became a sailing packet. For the next few years, the *Savannah* existed as a sailing packet between Savannah and New York before being lost along the shores of Long Island in 1822.[36]

By this point, the heady days leading into 1819 were a distant, if cherished, memory for Savannah and its aggressive entrepreneurs. Savannah's commerce, which had languished during the war, soared to new heights with the conclusion of hostilities. In 1816 Savannah exported over $14 million in goods—overwhelmingly cotton.[37] Easy credit heightened the optimism occasioned by high export prices. The Second Bank of the United States, which provided only the most limited control over its branch banks, expanded its credit. This easy credit intensified land speculation and borrowing to expand cotton production.[38]

The boom times went bust in 1819. The factors contributing to the Panic of 1819 began with European economic recovery from the Napoleonic Wars. By 1818, the continent reduced its dependence upon American food imports. More significantly, English manufacturers began supplementing American cotton with imports from India. With a glut in the Liverpool market, the price of cotton fell precipitously, and the rest of the economy tumbled with it.[39]

The Bank of the United States, curtailing its policy of fueling the economic expansion, embarked on severe contraction measures and called in its loans to redeem its notes, which created a chain reaction. With payment required in specie, panic ensued, followed by bankruptcies and foreclosures.[40] Two of Savannah's wealthiest merchants, Richard Richardson and William Scarbrough, suffered greatly. Savannah's cotton export trade languished, going from a high of $14 million in 1818 to less than half that in 1819.[41] Recovery took years and would be further complicated by local calamities.

The economic turmoil associated with the Panic of 1819 was minor compared to the two tremendous blows the city suffered in 1820. A disastrous fire, which started in a livery stable, tore through the city, consuming over ninety lots and four hundred buildings. One observer noted that the fire had "literally laid the city in ashes." The *Savannah Georgian* mourned, "Alas! Never did the sun set on a gloomier day for Savannah, or on so many aching hearts."[42] The fire gave the city a "desolate appearance," but its inhabitants once again began rebuilding with wood, though some who could afford to do so opted for brick.[43]

Before the year ended, however, Savannah experienced a major yellow fever epidemic. After first denying its existence, then assuring citizens of its confinement to strangers and those with bad habits, the city council finally admitted the obvious. Thousands fled the city. By the time the epidemic ran its course, nearly nine hundred people had succumbed to the disease.[44]

The dual tragedies of conflagration and pestilence inaugurated a decade of difficulty for Savannah as it fought against the tide of economic depression followed by stagnation. Savannah's population experienced a sluggish increase of slightly less than 4 percent in the decade of the 1820s. Indeed, Savannah during this time would often be characterized by outsiders as a lethargic, sleepy coastal port, not awakened to its own interests. Yet geography continued to bless the slumbering entrepôt—along with the numerous factors and merchants who called it home. The Savannah River, which stretched 180 miles in a nearly straight course to its headwaters, made Savannah the natural outlet for the expanding Georgia Upcountry. John Melish, who traveled extensively throughout the United States between 1806 and 1811, asserted that the Savannah River was "one of the most important in America."[45] Melish, who also wanted to promote British immigration, certainly exaggerated the river's national status, but it was important to Savannah's survival.

And here was the rub for merchants in neighboring Charleston, the bustling South Carolina coastal port. Charleston's citizens might like to think that the Ashley and the Cooper came together at their city to form the Atlantic Ocean, but the idea that they might stretch those rivers into the cotton-rich Upcountry was equally far-fetched, and they knew it. Farmers in Upcountry South Carolina, seeking the cheapest outlet for their cotton, readily used the Savannah River. As long as that river reached deep into the hinterland and flowed to the Atlantic Ocean, Savannah seemed assured of its continued survival, albeit on a much smaller scale than its older and more developed South Carolina sibling.

With the westward-moving cotton frontier, it was only a matter of time before the Savannah River would be the main artery of commerce.

Savannah's commerce, though smaller than Charleston's, was not insignificant. In 1820, admittedly a poor year for Savannah, the city accounted for over $6 million in exports compared to Charleston's nearly $9 million. An envious and imperialistic Charleston sought to gain control of Savannah's limited but valuable river commerce.[46]

Nature may have geographically handicapped Charleston merchants, but they had plenty of business acumen. In their first salvo, they bought a controlling interest in the financially struggling Steam Boat Company of Georgia, which held a monopoly on the river's steam traffic.[47] The company plied the waters between Savannah and Augusta, which handled Savannah's Upcountry trade; Augusta also served as the collection point for the South Carolina Upcountry.[48] Initially successful in this endeavor, the company rubbed it in. Charleston's merchant ships, taking freight from Augusta to Charleston, fired their guns in passing to remind Savannah of its place in the economic hierarchy of southern ports. One Savannah newspaper noted that it was a "knell to warn all good citizens of the Bay, that the 'glory had departed,' or was departing from our wharves and store-houses."[49]

The victory was only temporary. The company's monopoly came to an end following the 1824 U.S. Supreme Court decision in *Gibbons v. Ogden*, a case with a unique Savannah connection. Savannah native Thomas Gibbons, a Loyalist during the Revolutionary War, had emerged in the 1790s as one of the city's wealthiest citizens—a successful planter, attorney, federal judge, and local Federalist politician. He served as mayor of Savannah for three terms. In 1810, Gibbons moved to Elizabethtown, New Jersey, and went into partnership with Aaron Ogden, who had procured a monopoly from the New York legislature on steamship trade in that state. After the partners had a falling out, Gibbons began his own steamship ferry service along the same route. Ogden, facing what he considered illegal competition by virtue of his monopoly, sued. Eventually the Supreme Court, in *Gibbons v. Ogden*, overturned a New York State court decision and ruled that the New York license was invalid because the ferry service was being conducted on an interstate waterway. Federal power to regulate interstate commerce included the operation of steamboats. In striking down the New York law granting the steamboat monopoly, the Supreme Court's decision undermined a similar monopoly granted to the Steam Boat Company of Georgia.[50]

Even as Charleston merchants took advantage of their steamboat monopoly (as long as it lasted), they were formulating a new longer-term strategy. In 1821, the South Carolina legislature, at Charleston's prompting, awarded a no-interest $50,000 loan to developer Henry Schultz to establish the town of Hamburg on the Savannah River, opposite Augusta. It also exempted the town from state taxation for five years and granted it banking privileges.[51]

Charleston remained disappointed with the trade it captured, but Savannah fretted. The city's annual exports declined between 1822 and 1823 by nearly $2 million. The next year, Charleston exported goods worth over $8 million while Savannah could claim slightly over half as much.[52] Concerned Savannah merchants held meetings and petitioned the Georgia General Assembly to eliminate the steamboat monopoly. At the same time, Savannah's newspapers tried to put the best spin on the situation and consistently asserted that the city was "far from this 'ruin' of which we are so good naturedly reminded." Yet they knew they faced a greater challenge than Charleston did, since Upcountry support for Savannah remained weak at best. Indeed, some in Savannah believed that Upcountry politicians actively sought the ruin of their "wise, industrious and virtuous community."[53]

Savannah's boosters next turned to the possibility of a canal. In the 1820s, as canal fever swept the nation, Savannah became infected with a belief that a canal would provide exclusive access to the growing trade of middle Georgia. Exclusivity was important. Charleston's schemes may have proven unsatisfactory to its merchants, but they demonstrated the vulnerability of Savannah's complete reliance on the upper Savannah River traffic.[54]

Initially thinking in terms of immediately accessible hinterlands, Savannah pegged its hopes on a canal system connecting the state's major river systems to the Savannah River. Like South Carolina, Georgia had between the coast and the Black Belt a wide swath of territory known as the Pine Barrens or Piney Woods, with sandy soil not conducive to growing cotton or much else at the time. Rather than a region to be tapped, it was a "dull tedious monotonous ocean of pine barrens" to be spanned.[55] Two rivers—the Ogeechee and the Altamaha—spanned the region, and on these Savannah focused (see fig. 1).

The Ogeechee River begins in Greene County and winds southeast about 160 miles, eventually meeting the Atlantic Ocean sixteen miles south of the Savannah River. Navigable beginning at Louisville, Georgia, the Ogeechee drains nearly five thousand square miles. Farther south and west, and more important, the Oconee and Ocmulgee join to form

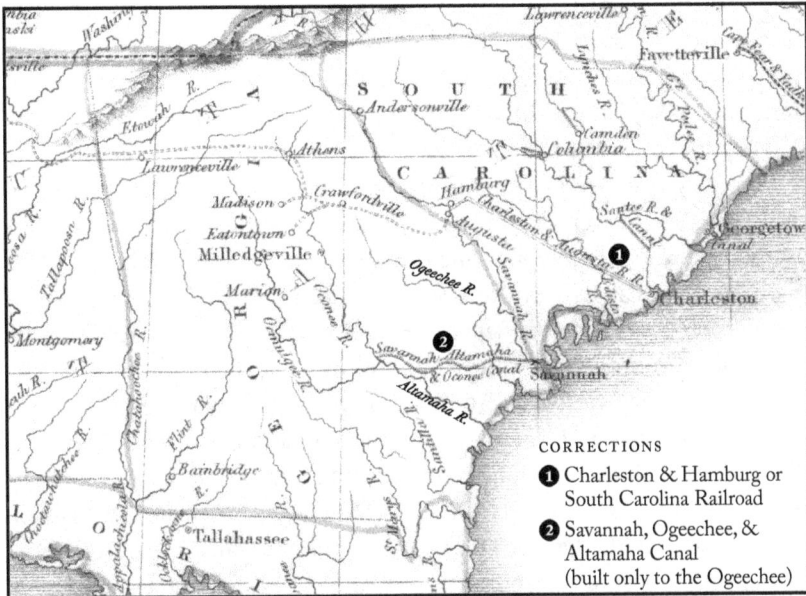

FIGURE 1. Map of southeastern railroads and canals, adapted from
T. G. Bradford, *United States, Exhibiting the Railroads and Canals* (1835).

the Altamaha River, which flows from this convergence seventy miles to
its Atlantic outlet a few miles north of Brunswick. Much larger than the
Ogeechee, it drains about fourteen thousand square miles.

Having decided that a canal was the solution to Savannah's transportation problem, the city's newspapers launched a campaign to generate
political and financial support for constructing a canal from the Savannah to the Ogeechee. The proposed canal clearly aimed at benefiting Savannah and the farmers along the Ogeechee. The rest of the state, however, saw little to be gained from it. To get the General Assembly to fund
construction, Savannah's leaders needed to make the case that the canal
would promote the welfare of the entire state. This would be a hard sell,
especially since Savannah desired a canal, in part, to divert trade from Augusta because Charleston had access to that city.[56]

Savannah faced a major obstacle in the form of sectional antagonism,
whereby communities viewed themselves as competing in a zero-sum
game. This obstacle was not unique to Savannah or the South. Aspiring
cities bent on imperial conquest of their hinterlands often faced a myriad
of competing sectional challengers.[57] For instance, rival regional aspirations undermined the failure of the Gallatin Plan for a national transpor-

tation system of roads and canals both before the War of 1812 and again in the postwar nationalist glow. At all levels the stakes were high, for, once transportation routes had been constructed, cities both feared and hoped they would "fix forever the opportunities for growth encouraged by distant places within the nation."[58]

One way boosters attempted to overcome the challenge of sectional rivalry was to "universalize" the advantages of pet projects.[59] Savannah's promotion of a sixteen-mile canal merged with grand schemes of building a series of canals from the Savannah River to the Tennessee River and the Mexican-Atlantic scheme that would connect the Savannah to the Apalachicola River.[60] More important was the plan's emphasis on the eventual connection to the Altamaha River, which would link the area drained by both the Oconee and Ocmulgee in addition to the Altamaha. The proposed sixteen-mile canal, along with state aid for river improvements, would make the Oconee and Ocmulgee navigable to the state's new capital at Milledgeville and the newly incorporated town of Macon. Lowering the cost of transportation, Savannah boosters contended, would benefit Upcountry producers by enabling them to get their cotton to the "best market."[61] Furthermore, construction of the canal would foster new settlements and towns along its path. As evidence of this certain eventuality, promoters pointed to the example of Rochester, New York, whose population had increased by over a thousand due to the Erie Canal.[62]

Emulating New York became an important aspect of both the desire for canals and their promotion. In following New York's path to success, Savannah would avoid the predicament of Philadelphia and Boston, which experienced a significant diversion of their western trade.[63] Savannah tried to convince the legislature that the proposed canal would be to "Georgia what the Erie Canal is to New York." Savannah could become the "New York of the South."[64]

In late 1824, Ebenezer Jenckes, a crafty dry goods merchant and turnpike builder, applied to the Georgia legislature and received the right to cut a canal from the Savannah River to the Ogeechee River. This was not the first time the legislature had granted such a right.[65] Generally, previous efforts had ended at that point. Since the legislature did not accede to Jenckes's other request, an appropriation of $100,000, the project might have ended there.[66] However, knowledge of the Erie Canal's success and Jenckes's determination, combined with a healthy sense of self-preservation, convinced some Savannahians that the time had come.

Jenckes made a pilgrimage to New York to meet with DeWitt Clinton, the man who turned Clinton's Ditch into a monument of progress. The "Father of the Grand Canal" advised his admirer that he could attract more "capitalists" if he extended the canal beyond the Ogeechee to the Altamaha.[67] After returning to Savannah, Jenckes continued to struggle with reluctant investors. Having failed to raise the necessary capital, Jenckes presented a second request to the General Assembly, this time for the right to extend his canal to the Altamaha, as Clinton had advised.[68]

Once again he appealed for state funds. With the bill before the General Assembly, Savannah's papers inundated the public with column after column of letters, editorials, and canal "facts," touting the ease with which a canal could be built and the advantages that would accrue to Georgia and Savannah. As "Bridgewater" noted, "No rational man can for a moment doubt the utility of a canal, connecting the Oconee and Ocmulgee Rivers with the Savannah."[69] This time Jenckes found a much more receptive legislative audience. The General Assembly approved the extension and authorized a loan of $50,000 in notes from the Darien Bank.[70]

DeWitt Clinton Jr., whom Jenckes had hired as the canal's chief engineer, submitted his report in February 1826. The report significantly raised Savannahians' expectations. In addition to projecting lower construction costs than expected, Clinton expounded on the potential benefits of the canal, which he claimed would be completed in 1828. A canal to the interior would allow farmers to choose between wet and dry culture. The climate, he wrote in a letter to Jenckes and his backers that was then published in the *Savannah Georgian* on February 15, 1826, would be "modified, for the swamps will be drained, the forests cleared and the country open to the sea breezes." If it could then connect with the Mexican-Atlantic Canal, the city hoped it would "become at no distant day the New York of the South."[71]

Within weeks of his published letter, leading citizens organized a public meeting and decided to try leveraging the power of a corporation to raise the necessary funds. The result was a newly formed company: Savannah, Ogeechee, and Altamaha Canal Company (SOAC), with Alexander Telfair as president. Jenckes transferred his canal rights and the state's loan to the newly formed company for $20,000.[72] Expecting this to be a significant step forward, one enthusiastic observer noted that it was time to "leave off talking and go to digging."[73]

Excavation began in November 1826, but the early optimism turned to disillusionment and impatience. The new corporation found itself challenged both in the day-to-day construction operations and in maintaining financial backing. Ultimately the city of Savannah stepped into the vacuum. In a deal worked out between Alexander Telfair, Planters Bank, and the Bank of the State of Georgia for matching pledges, the City of Savannah agreed to invest $7,000. The city council also donated city property through which the company constructed the canal.[74]

Initially the problems of acquiring and maintaining a productive and docile labor force plagued the company. Throughout the spring and summer of 1826, Jenckes and the other contractors advertised for slaves, promising "liberal wages."[75] The effort to hire slaves from owners is a reminder about the flexibility of slave labor. There were two basic systems for hiring out slaves. Owners could bind a slave to another individual, or they could allow slaves to hire out their time to whites. In both cases, the ultimate goal of the owner was to profit from his or her slave even if not directly involved or economically invested in the specific project. Owners could expect $10 per month for renting their slaves to the canal company. Contractors attempted to reassure owners concerned about the safety of their property with promises that the laborers would be working in "perfectly dry" areas.[76]

Seeking to capitalize on the canal's construction, northern contractors arrived in the city with Irish laborers, who were attracted by the promise of work and $13 a month. By one estimate, seven hundred Irish laborers passed through Savannah between 1826 and 1827.[77] Locals, never comfortable with large numbers of "strangers" in their midst, proved ready to believe the worst of these individuals—as was the case in December 1826 when the *Savannah Georgian* reported that white laborers along the canal were "committing acts of violence and riot."[78]

A local Catholic priest volunteered to investigate and proclaimed the "rioting" overblown. The men he found were in "deep distress" and close to starvation because the contractors from New York had absconded with their pay, totaling $700. The men had not been paid in four months. The Hibernian Society took charge of the situation, formed an investigating committee, and saw to the needs of the men. Within a few days, the laborers had been provisioned and were back at work.[79]

Although the company continued to employ whites, primarily Irish, slaves always outnumbered white workers except during the summer months. During the four years of construction, both the company and the contractors consistently demonstrated a preference for slave labor. Advocates for using slave labor touted its numerous advantages: It preserved the area's capital. Slaves were more "tractable," and, so the claim went, were better cared for and thus healthier than white laborers; those from the Lowcountry were "particularly adapted to the work of canalling" because both men and women were familiar with ditching and knew how to work with an axe.[80]

At the beginning of 1828, the *Savannah Georgian* noted the "zeal" with which construction of the canal was occurring. With a little less than five miles to go, the expectation was that they would "see boats running in its waters" in a few months. This optimism was misplaced. In November 1828, after months of silence regarding the progress of the canal, the ailing Savannah, Ogeechee, and Altamaha Canal Company applied to the General Assembly for additional funds to complete construction.[81]

While everyone sought to emulate the success of the Erie Canal, few seemed to recall the years of arduous construction preceding its ultimate success. Boosters, in an attempt to convince cost-conscious legislators of the economic viability of their projects, often provided extremely overoptimistic cost and time estimates. Thus, projects received limited funding, and construction became seasonal, piecemeal, and slow. As a result, the work of the boosters did not end with legislative approval of a project. They had to remain ready to motivate their elected officials to continue financial support for often decade-long projects in the face of public intolerance of delay.[82]

Mordecai Meyers, a director of the Bank of the State of Georgia, led the effort in prodding the legislature to further action on the canal. He waxed eloquent on the advantages of pushing the canal to the Altamaha. The "lonely and solitary" Pine Barrens would become productive and profitable. Surely over one thousand bales of cotton would make their way down the canal to Savannah. Capitalists, attracted by the port's advantages, would settle here. Oh, the tax revenue! Eventually, he confidently predicted, the waters of the Altamaha would be "mingling" with those of the Flint and Chattahoochee. Meyers also warned of the dangers of failing to "awake from our apathy and inertness." By this point, Charleston was building up a head of steam to construct its railroad to Hamburg. If successful, the elder sibling would gain a monopoly over Georgia's trade and produce. Savannah would sink into "decay and ruin"; "neglected and forsaken," it would be "annihilated."[83]

The Georgia General Assembly, like Savannah, remained at least mildly susceptible to the canal contagion coursing through the country. Seeking to emulate New York's success, states invested heavily in canal construction by issuing bonds, purchasing securities, and guaranteeing privately funded bond issues. In 1828, the General Assembly, noting the necessity of "giving facility to the commerce and transportation products of the different counties of the State," subscribed $44,000 to the stock of the company.[84]

Following this appropriation, news of the canal once again faded. The SOAC continued to suffer from numerous delays, and the populace succumbed to bouts of extreme impatience. In November, the impatient Georgia Assembly passed a resolution authorizing the governor to investigate the status of the canal. The subsequent report was surprisingly positive, though it noted the difficulties the company had faced in terms of inexperienced engineers and procuring enough laborers. Legislators continued to express confidence that it would be "the first successful trial" at "canalling in Georgia," which would eventually "diffuse wealth and prosperity even through the most remote and sterile sections of our State." Yet they also voiced their frustration at the "ignorance and miscalculations" that increased the cost of the project beyond anyone's expectations. Nevertheless, the committee predicted canal completion "within a very few months."[85]

In March 1830, a brief newspaper article, which included a detailed list of construction problems, estimated that the canal would be complete in another month, but that month turned into several months.[86] The canal finally opened in December 1830 to little fanfare. The article announcing its opening warned that if the canal were to stop at the Ogeechee, the large expenditure of money would be "wasted." The official "meeting of the waters" celebration occurred in late March 1831. Ironically, the opening of the canal occurred just days after the governor notified the attorney general to begin collection proceedings, with a view to rescinding the company's charter.[87]

Georgia's frustrating experience with the Savannah and Ogeechee Canal proved strikingly similar to that of other states. Expecting to achieve success comparable to the Erie Canal, states had borrowed large sums of money to finance canal construction.[88] In the wake of the Panic of 1837, some of those states defaulted on their loans, thus injuring both state and national credit.[89] In 1840, state debt totaled $17 million, 60 percent of that for canal and railroad funding. States including Florida, Mississippi, Illinois, Maryland, Pennsylvania, and Louisiana defaulted on interest payments in 1841 and 1842, and other states came close.[90] In reaction to these embarrassments, some states instituted constitutional restrictions on acquiring debt.[91] Compared to other states involved in the canal frenzy, Georgia's investment had been moderate. However, the misadventure made the already miserly state leery about future investments in such experimental ventures in internal improvements.

The canal project did not deal a mortal financial blow to Georgia or Savannah. The state, which enjoyed a surplus at the time, had invested relatively very little and could afford to watch it disappear. Savannah had created a debt to aid the canal, so it was on the hook for some time to come for a canal that was not profitable. The canal failed to deliver on even its most modest goals. It did not help Savannah extend, maintain, or defend its hinterland. In fact, by the time the canal was crawling to completion, South Carolina's railroad from Charleston to Hamburg was under construction and promised to give Savannah a great deal of trouble. Savannah's territory was indeed in danger of being poached by its older sibling. From this perspective, the city's first significant effort at fostering internal communication had failed.

In the most tangible sense, the municipal government lost its investment in the canal. Yet, more importantly, the failure proved beneficial to Savannah. Accepting the canal as a failure allowed Savannah to push forward in other areas. It did not sour the city on new technologies. It gave boosters and critics of internal improvements a more realistic view of what one could expect. Further, it gave them an understanding of the tangible and the intangible challenges they would face in the process of seeking public funding, especially from interior counties—often simply called "sectional jealousies."

Debate over canal funding in the General Assembly and more specifically Savannah's ambitions demonstrated the divisiveness of internal improvements projects. Upcountry aversion to funding these regional projects forced Savannah's boosters to develop arguments and at times exaggerate claims regarding statewide benefits. Boosters discovered a usable rhetoric for motivating the municipal government and even the state to invest public money in these enterprises. The canal provided the impetus for the city to begin looking outward and to the future, specifically to the development of the state's interior, and it laid the foundation for the movement to establish a much greater and ultimately far more successful enterprise. It demonstrated the city's acceptance of its responsibility to promote and facilitate commerce. The city council also acknowledged the necessity of borrowing money and creating indebtedness for the sake of promoting first the city's survival, then its status as an important entrepôt. Most importantly, it demonstrated the limited degree to which the state was willing to aid internal improvements. If Savannah were going to defend its territory, it would have to do the heavy lifting in the future.

CHAPTER 2

·◆·

"But What a Pretty Thing
a Rail Road Is!"

UNDERWRITING SAVANNAH'S
ECONOMIC GROWTH

In September 1833, the *Savannah Georgian* reprinted a letter from "An Old Engineer" first published in the *Augusta Chronicle*:

> But what a pretty thing a Rail Road is!—We must have one of our own—positively! How sweet to ride 100 miles, in the teeth of a north-wester (in the winter)—to Athens to breakfast (on wild turkey,) to dine at Mobile (on oysters or turtle soup,) and to sup at New Orleans (on shrimps) oh it is like sleighing that we hear the yankees talk about. It is like hanging to the tail of a comet. It would cure . . . consumption, if one hadn't to shut ones eyes and mouth to keep from being blinded and choked by the cursed smoke. How charming![1]

Clearly, the Old Engineer was not impressed with the railroad. He believed that it was nothing more than a passing fad—just like the canal fever of the 1820s. The Old Engineer's concerns were valid. Canal fever had left many a public treasury drained and governments wary of future contagions. Only time would tell if this new delirium sweeping the nation would yield the same result.

The Old Engineer, however, was a lone voice in the cacophony of boosters demanding that Georgia join the rest of the nation in rail development—before it was too late. It did appear in the fall of 1833 that Georgia had gone crazy over the idea of covering the state with rails. Newspaper editors made sure their calls for internal improvements found their place amid discussions of states' rights, tariffs, nullification, and Indian re-

moval. In 1833, as the Charleston and Hamburg Railroad (also called the
South Carolina Railroad) neared completion in South Carolina, some
Savannahians finally realized the threat this new transportation development posed.[2] Stretching from Charleston to Hamburg, across from Augusta, this railroad had the potential to drain the upland trade that had
been Savannah's by virtue of its natural waterways. Not coincidentally,
Savannah lobbied the legislature for a railroad to run to the center of the
state (see fig. 1).

In 1833, the legislature, succumbing to the fever while trying to satisfy local interests, chartered two railroads, the Georgia Railroad Company, slated to run from Augusta to Athens and beyond, and the Central
Railroad and Canal Company, slated to run from Savannah to Macon,
with plans eventually to cut westward over to Columbus. Like other cities in the throes of railroad fever, Savannah discovered that chartering a
railroad was easier than constructing one. Newspapers printed optimistic claims that capital to complete the work would "be found among the
native and adopted sons of Georgia," who would be moved by the noble
"spirit of Internal Improvement." However, lack of funding was an obstacle that stopped many a railroad in its tracks.[3]

In his study of Georgia's antebellum internal improvements, Milton
Heath argues that Georgia's government accepted the notion of constructive liberalism. However, as a result of the canal hangover, the state's
politicians proved reluctant converts to state-financed railroads until after both the Georgia Railroad and the Central Railroad began construction and demonstrated their economic potential. At points in 1833, 1834,
and 1835, both companies attempted to convince the legislature to provide
some type of state financing, but their efforts yielded only paltry funding for surveys and otherwise disappointment and frustration. Savannah,
in particular, found a number of formidable obstacles in its path, not the
least of which was opposition to the mere existence of a railroad emanat-
ing from the coastal city.

Savannah's representatives energetically lobbied the legislature for endorsement of various direct and indirect funding schemes. Like other
boosters, they touted the numerous and at times lofty economic advantages a railroad would bring the state. At the same time, however, they
crafted justifications that took into account the unique role that a railroad
from Savannah could play in Georgia's economic and political future.

The driving force in Savannah's efforts to establish a rail line was William Washington Gordon, son of New Jersey native Ambrose Gordon. Ambrose had served as a lieutenant of cavalry during the Revolution under Colonel William Washington Gordon, a nephew of George Washington. After the war, he and his wife Elizabeth Meade of Virginia settled near Augusta on a land grant and later moved to Savannah. When Ambrose died in 1804, the family sent eight-year-old William to New Jersey to live with his uncle Ezekiel Gordon. After schooling in Rhode Island, the young Gordon was admitted to the United States Military Academy in 1814, and he became the first Georgia graduate of that school. After serving less than a year, Gordon resigned his commission and returned to Savannah to study law under Judge James Moore Wayne, a future U.S. Supreme Court justice. After being admitted to the bar, he served the city council in various capacities, including clerk and legal advisor. Gordon participated in numerous civic-minded activities, including the Library Society and the centennial celebration of the 1733 founding of Georgia. He demonstrated an interest in internal improvements and was elected a director of the Savannah and Ogeechee Canal Company. In 1833, Gordon became a city alderman, and he served in that position until he was elected mayor the next year. He divided his time between local government and the state legislature, to which he was elected in 1835.[4]

When Gordon addressed the state house of representatives on behalf of railroad development, he pointed to the success of other enterprises, primarily northern enterprises, like the famous Erie Canal. "Shall we," he asked, "not emulate her example, and make our State what that system has made of New York?"[5] When southern economic developers looked at northern progress, it was something they sought to emulate.[6] Northern "ingenuity" was something to be admired: "their industry and perseverance" had led to profit and progress. While, as one commentator noted, southerners "establish only for present gratification," our "northern brethren look to permanent establishments." Therefore, "is it then surprising that we should be backward, and they in the condition of enjoying the fruits of their enterprise and industry? Is it surprising that they should have become capitalists, and we a people of expedients, and depending entirely on the seasons for bread and the means of buying clothing? What has Georgia done? Nothing."[7] It was not a matter of condition but of action, not a matter of region or circumstance but of choice. Georgia needed to imitate the "noble example of New York."[8]

In spite of the growing debate over slavery, a southern critique of northern capitalism as antagonistic to the South and southern economic growth remained in its infancy. Furthermore, that southerners sought to imitate northern economic success suggests that they believed they could apply northern experience to southern conditions and that southerners generally assumed a certain degree of similarity between the two sections. Far from accepting an agrarian critique of the North, southern urban boosters were aware of their own region's shortcomings in light of northern superiority, and they were willing to admit them.[9]

When southerners spoke of sectionalism and sectional animosity, often they were referring to the greater threats closer to home. Savannah's newspapers often complained of the "prejudice" against bills designed to elevate their city's economic status. Gordon openly denounced Upcountry politicians who allowed local and sectional feelings as well as their general antagonism against Savannah to cloud their judgment and outweigh their state pride.[10] As mayor of Savannah, Gordon was well aware of a simmering anti-Savannah feeling, which had existed since colonial times. While increases in population in the Upcountry had given that region political power, Savannah, because of its economic influence, could not be ignored. Even as late as 1830, it was the location of a branch of the much maligned Second Bank of the United States, and more importantly it was at the mouth of the Savannah River, the state's primary commercial outlet. Upcountry planters and farmers had long viewed themselves as victims of Savannah's river monopoly.

Also jealous of Savannah's river monopoly, South Carolina began construction on its railway from Charleston to Hamburg in 1831. Seeing the railroad's potential and excited at the prospect of constructing a line from their town to Augusta to take advantage of this new mode of transportation, citizens of Eatonton, in Putnam County—one hundred miles from Augusta—began planning a connection and received a railroad charter in 1832 for this purpose. Nothing came of it at the time, but it prompted others, especially citizens of Athens, to consider the consequences of such a scheme. Seeking to become the hub for a connecting Georgia railroad, Athens had joined Eatonton in calling on the Upcountry to build a 110-mile line to Augusta. Augusta, for its part, viewed these plans with a mix of anticipation and worry. Savannah, on the other hand, fretted.[11]

For profit-minded planters and farmers, a railroad from Eatonton (or Athens) to Augusta had much to offer. In addition to speeding transportation and reducing its costs, they would be liberated from Savannah's pernicious river monopoly. They did not seem to mind tying themselves to Charleston instead. Nor did they have any qualms about soliciting Charleston investment to implement their plans. In August 1833, in a well-publicized letter to the South Carolina Railroad, an Eatonton planter wrote: "I believe Charleston, and the Stockholders in your Company, have a deep interest at stake, in our enterprise. If successful, I have no doubt, it will enhance the value of your Stock, ten per cent, . . . besides throwing into the Charleston Market a large portion of the staple of this State, that would otherwise not go there."[12] The infamous Eatonton letter seemed to demonstrate that Georgia's interior planters were willing to sacrifice both Savannah and Augusta to their own interests.

If nothing else, this letter provided motivation for action. Savannah's two newspapers, the *Georgian* and the *Republican*, although on opposite sides of the political spectrum, decried the "apathy on the part of the State," since the Charleston enterprise had a direct bearing on the "preservation" of Savannah.[13] They also made dire warnings. If a railroad were established at Augusta, Savannah could very well "sink into a condition of a rotten Borough."[14] Already, Upcountry merchants were purchasing their goods in New York or Charleston. If its citizens did not act, Savannah would "inevitably fall, and fall to rise no more."[15]

In the spring and summer of 1833, Savannah's city council finally moved beyond hand-wringing and fretting and launched an offensive in internal improvements. If the Upcountry were to build a railroad to Augusta, Savannah would build one to Macon and then to Columbus. The possibility of a competitor railroad in Georgia did not sit well with the Upcountry. The Athens *Southern Banner*, in particular, while applauding the spirit of internal improvements in general, frequently reminded its readers how slowly the coastal city, obsessed with "their delusive and miserable schemes of River Navigation," had been to adopt the notion of a railroad.[16] It also alluded to the botched Savannah, Ogeechee, and Altamaha Canal Company project. While Savannah might "raise a grand chat about a mighty canal," what did they *do*? "They then go on to dig a ditch to Ogeechee, and . . . doubt whether they can keep it clean!"[17] If the state were to support any road, it should be the one seeking to connect with Augusta.[18]

Savannah's immediate motivation, Upcountry suspicions to the contrary, was survival. The threat already existed: South Carolina had a working railroad. A railroad from Eatonton or Athens would drain Georgia's hinterland trade to Charleston and destroy Savannah along with other

smaller towns in the process. Georgia's "wealth and resources" would become "tributary to the State of South Carolina, or rather to the merchants
of Charleston!"[19] There was also a long-term threat. Never ones to think
small, South Carolina also planned to tap Tennessee and other western
trade, a plan that, if successful, would bypass Georgia completely. Painting
an even more dismal picture, the *Savannah Georgian* warned that Georgia would be laid "prostrate . . . at the foot of haughty Carolina." Georgia
would be "bowing to her elder sister, sweeping by in splendid garments,
purchased by the gold of Georgia's citizens."[20]

There was an even greater danger. The *Georgian*'s legislative correspondent despaired: "We are sorry to believe that there are many who would
be glad to make Georgia commercially, as well as politically, subservient
to South Carolina."[21] It was the link between the economic and political power that the Old Engineer had failed to take into account. At any
given time, the notion of being economically dependent on South Carolina should have given many Georgians pause, but in the 1830s the prospect was downright disturbing.

South Carolina had only recently openly defied the federal government, nullified a federal tariff, organized for the state's defense, and actively sought support for its actions from its sister southern states, especially Georgia.[22] South Carolina's desperate actions followed more than
a decade of economic disruptions. Between 1820 and 1840, planters and
farmers on the make abandoned South Carolina for the more fertile western lands. While worn out lands and reduced cotton yields and prices
constituted the predominant factors in the state's decline, political leaders seized on the tariff as the primary culprit. They claimed that the tariff reduced British demand for American cotton because it taxed British
cloth imports and increased the prices for some other imported products.
In 1828, when Congress once again raised the tariff on a variety of items,
South Carolina led the South in the intensity of its protest.[23]

Unsatisfied with the lower import duties achieved in the tariff reform
of 1832, the state took decisive action. Following the prescription laid out
by John C. Calhoun in his anti-tariff "Exposition and Protest" document,
the state legislature called a convention, which subsequently declared the
tariffs of 1828 and 1832 unconstitutional and nullified them. This set the
stage for a standoff between the United States and South Carolina.

South Carolina's leaders expected that the other southern states—especially neighboring Georgia—would follow their lead; they were wrong.
While so-called nullifiers could be found on the southern banks of the

Savannah River, they were more vocal than numerous. An effort to hold a nullification convention in Georgia foundered. Chatham County refused to participate in the proceedings, and delegates managed only a series of anti-tariff resolutions. While Georgia's legislature criticized federal tariff policy, it officially rejected nullification as an option. When South Carolina, in spite of its isolation, refused to back down, Congress granted President Andrew Jackson the authority to use military force to collect tariff duties. Only a timely compromise by Henry Clay averted a more serious crisis.[24]

The nullification controversy, though political in nature, also had an effect on the pattern of economic development and internal improvements. Certainly the desire to compete with its older sibling Charleston may have been reason enough, but the fear of economic dependence on a state that had a clearly demonstrated propensity for radical and unilateral action gave greater impetus to Georgia to develop its own system of internal improvement, not only independent from South Carolina but also superior.

Since the 1833 effort, Savannah had been working vigorously to make the railroad to Macon a reality. Hoping that a favorable survey might demonstrate the viability of the railroad and make it more attractive to investment, the Savannah city council opted to fund the survey. In November 1834, with favorable report in hand along with estimated costs, William Gordon attempted, once again, to convince the state legislature of the need to support the enterprise.[25] When the legislature demurred, Savannah took more decisive action. Seeking to prompt enough investment to subscribe the 7,500 shares to elect a board of directors, the city council authorized a subscription of 5,000 shares and began preparations for borrowing the necessary sum. The council specifically asked Macon to subscribe the other 2,500 shares, which it refused to do.[26]

After failing to entice Macon into investing in the enterprise, Savannah decided to go it alone. Although the city treasury was not in the best condition, especially with the burden of dry culture contracts, cotton prices continued to be high as was optimism about the economic potential of the railroad. The initial outlay would be tremendous, but city leaders believed Savannah would derive much wealth from the railroad in the long run. As one editorial promised, the railroad would "elevate our city to that rank, which, as the principal natural outlet of one of the most fertile States of the Union, she is destined[,] with but a moderate exhibition of the spirit that is abroad in our land, one day to attain."[27] City officials concurred and undertook a tremendous economic burden. The council authorized the mayor and finance committee to negotiate a $500,000 loan for its investment in a company that as yet had not constructed a single mile.[28]

Later that year, Savannah finally received a little cooperation from the state. The legislature, whether for economic or political reasons, opted to provide both the Central Railroad and the Georgia Railroad with indirect public aid in the form of banking privileges. In the first years of railroad building, some state governments, though reluctant to provide direct aid, granted railroad companies these banking privileges, which made it possible for half of a company's capital to be devoted to banking. It was believed that investors viewed banks as more appealing because they expected them to issue dividends more quickly. Additionally, these companies could issue notes up to three times the banking capital. These notes provided funds needed for construction projects. The banks could then issue dividends to stockholders long before a railroad was completed and running profitably.[29]

In March 1836, the long-awaited occurred: the Central Railroad and Banking Company received the necessary capital, formed a corporation, and elected a board of directors and president. William Washington Gordon, mayor of Savannah and first president of the company, made the victory speech. He told Savannah, "Now the destiny of Savannah for weal or woe is in your hands." He then offered a toast to "our Enterprize—It began with the proper spirit: it cannot fail of a certain magnificent result."[30] Gordon's faith was not misplaced. Throughout the lean times following the economic panic of 1837, Savannah maintained its support of the Central Railroad.

The railroad had been under construction for only a few months when the nation's booming economy stumbled, partially righted itself, and then fell into a long depression.[31] The economic exuberance that propelled the funding of the Central Railroad had pervaded the nation in the early 1830s. Urban and agrarian entrepreneurs had borrowed money to expand their operations or purchase new western lands. As exports of cotton, grain, and wheat flowed out of the nation, foreign capital flowed in, particularly to cotton factors. The price of cotton rose, which fed soaring land and slave prices. Banks, not immune to this optimism, fueled this investment with easy credit.

Yet things were not quite right. Americans had only recently weathered Andrew Jackson's war against the Second Bank of the United States and the Specie Circular that required that public land be paid for in gold or silver, which created uncertainty on both sides of the Atlantic. A poor harvest in England subsequently drained investment from the United States and led to a mild decline in the British demand for cotton. Then, as news spread of broker failures in London, Paris, and the United States, real unease set in. One paper observed that the nation was "in the midst of one of those spasms [to] which the United States seems to be periodi-cally exposed." After a period of volatility between March and April 1837, banks from New York to New Orleans suspended specie payments in May and called in their loans. Banks across the nation followed their ex-ample, which precipitated a further panic.[32]

The nation experienced a brief recovery in 1838 before the economy stumbled again in 1839, this time in part due to a cotton glut in the Liver-pool market. By the end of the year, the price of cotton had fallen to half its 1836 price. The panic and subsequent cotton crisis ushered in a half-decade of depression.[33]

Private and public moneys that had been pouring into internal im-provement projects dried up. As states and cities groaned under the weight of their loans, debates raged over the wisdom of their financial choices, and some states considered repudiation a legitimate option. Con-struction on railroads like the Montgomery and West Point Railroad in Alabama came to a halt. Most railroad construction in Louisiana halted; projects in Michigan and Illinois were scaled back; several companies de-faulted on their loans.[34]

Unlike less fortunate companies, the Central Railroad continued con-struction in spite of the pinch. The company by no means made it through the period unscathed. By the end of 1839, stockholders, suffering from the tightness of credit, found it difficult to make their final stock payments. The continuing decline in cotton prices further exacerbated the situa-tion.[35] Though many so-called improvement banks went under between 1836 and 1840, the Central Railroad's bank carried the financial burden, al-lowing the company to weather the early years of the economic crisis. By 1839, the railroad began carrying more of the load. Having eighty miles completed, the company benefited from passenger, cotton, and freight traffic. Traffic was so good that the company purchased additional rolling stock.[36]

The company dealt with income shortfalls in a variety of ways, includ-ing reducing expenses, absorbing banking capital, issuing railroad tickets as scrip, and paying contractors in bonds.[37] To demonstrate confidence in the future of the Central Railroad or, more likely, to prevent a decline in the confidence of the bank, the city council announced that it would receive Central Railroad bank notes for the purchase of city lots.[38]

Disease, heavy rains, and flooding further complicated construction.[39] Gordon, who became president of the company in 1836 at the age of thirty-nine and devoted six years of his life to building Savannah's railroad, submitted his last report on the condition of the railroad a few days before his death, likely from yellow fever. Disease remained a constant concern, and its prevalence was one of several factors in the company's evolving labor decisions. The canal project had made use of both Irish and slave labor, and so did the directors of the Central Railroad to varying degrees.

Initially the company opted for Irish workers, who constituted the bulk of the thousand men who went to work grading the line. At the time, the agricultural demands of the region already engaged most slave labor. Thus Irish labor was more plentiful, apparently cheaper, and viewed as the easiest option.[40] It is also likely that the choice of using Irish labor heavily only in the initial phases of construction was based on the calculation that, as the construction moved into the interior, slave labor would be more readily available.[41]

The use of Irish labor involved a certain degree of risk. In 1837, on hearing rumors that the company was unable to pay its workers, 150 Irish laborers threw down their shovels and marched on Savannah. Father Jeremiah F. O'Neill, a local Catholic priest, went out to meet the laborers, returned with a committee to negotiate, and managed to defuse the situation.[42] Two years later, more labor disturbances, primarily between Irish laborers from Kerry and Cork, convinced some of the contractors to shift entirely to slave labor. Planters, likely feeling the pinch because of the declining price of cotton, benefited from the company's timber purchases, and this likely made them more willing to rent their slaves to the company.[43] By the close of 1839, most of the five hundred workers were slaves.[44] Usually each slave cost $15 to $20 per month, and the company paid planters both in cash and in stock. The increasing dependence on renting slaves also gave the Central Railroad more flexibility when it needed to adjust its financial tack during the latter period of construction.[45]

The directors believed they were justified in choosing slave labor, especially as sickness and fever began overtaking the workers in 1839. L. O. Reynolds, the chief engineer, opined that if more of the force had been white, "sickness and mortality" would have been worse, as the few white

employees had been very sick.[46] Echoing the engineer on the canal project, Reynolds asserted that slave labor was "perfectly adapted to the construction of works of internal improvement."[47] By the end of the following decade, the company had ended its contract system and switched to
the direct hiring of slaves. During the next decade, the Central Railroad
purchased its own slaves, and on the eve of the Civil War the company
owned $40,000 in slave property.[48]

In 1843, a decade after its inauguration, the railroad was completed to
Macon, and Savannah began to reap the benefits. As the Central Railroad
extended its rails and influence throughout the state, it brought the products of the Upcountry to the port at Savannah, and with this came prosperity. Emerging from Charleston's shadow, Savannah's leaders gained
enormous confidence in the future success of the city and were therefore much more willing to invest heavily on the expectation of continued
growth and progress.[49] Over the next two decades, following the city's investment in the Central Railroad, cotton flowed into Savannah, and the
value of the company's stock increased. Savannah paid off its debts by selling the increasingly valuable railroad stock.[50]

The Central of Georgia Railroad and Banking Company, unlike so
many other railroad schemes, became a success story. The city's half-
million-dollar investment in this railroad benefited Savannah and expanded its market. Between 1833 and 1861, the Central Railroad joined
in the successful integration of the state's railroad system, which led to
the creation of Atlanta, a true child of the railroads. Savannah's participation, indeed leadership, in the expansion and integration of the antebellum economy laid the foundation and set the benchmarks that New
South leaders in the 1880s sought to surpass.

More immediately, the Central's success and Savannah's rise in economic status reinforced the conviction that railroads held the key for continued economic growth. Both the Central Railroad and the city continued to invest in additional feeder lines, like the Southwestern Railroad,
which ran from Macon into western Georgia. Cotton flowed into the
Georgia port, and Savannah began closing its cotton gap with Charleston. It finally overtook its elder sibling in cotton receipts in 1860.[51] Although Charleston dwarfed Savannah in population, its population fluctuated, with a decrease between 1830 and 1840 and again between 1850 and
1860. Savannah's population increased over the same period by over 200
percent.[52]

When it came to the question of increasing the city's dependence on loan-financed projects, the Central became the touchstone. Savannah's municipal leaders willingly accepted the risk of a heavier debt burden because they believed such projects would ensure Savannah's continued growth and prosperity. Having been immensely successful with its first capital venture, throughout the 1840s and 1850s the city enthusiastically continued this pattern and aggressively undertook more bond-funded projects, including the expansion of a dry culture system to eliminate yellow fever, construction of a parade ground, lighting extensions, street paving, and harbor improvements, the last with the help of federal funds. The municipal government also invested in several more railroads, hoping to continue the trend initiated by the success of the Central Railroad.[53]

In addition to cities' own ambitions, their fear of rivals intent on garnering trade incentivized additional railroad investment.[54] Like Savannah, the younger city of Brunswick, eighty miles south, aspired to become a major coastal hub. To that end, in 1835, a group of citizens applied to the General Assembly and received a charter for the Brunswick and Florida Railroad Company, later renamed the Brunswick and Albany Railroad. The company's charter authorized it to construct a line to the Flint and Chattahoochee Rivers. Unlike the thriving Central of Georgia, the Brunswick company floundered until 1852 when it drew the interest of northern investors, who raised enough capital to begin construction.[55]

Savannah initially responded dismissively, claiming that the line would never be built, that it posed no threat to the older city, that it might actually benefit Savannah, or that it would not be a profitable enterprise until it reached the Gulf. Rhetoric aside, Savannah's leaders viewed the Brunswick and Florida as a serious threat. While Savannah's papers continued to deride the project as a Yankee enterprise, its citizens went on the offensive and resurrected a long-dormant project of their own: the Savannah and Albany Railroad.

Chartered by the General Assembly in 1847, the Savannah and Albany Railroad was projected to run from the Savannah River westward to the Flint River at Albany. The company accomplished little beyond various amendatory acts and the official commencement of construction to maintain its charter.[56] Confronted with the new threat from Brunswick, aggressive boosters moved quickly to revive the enterprise and elected a new board of directors, with Savannah native Dr. James P. Screven as president.[57]

Dr. Screven's father, John Screven, had arrived in Georgia from South Carolina before the Revolution and settled in Liberty County. After the

Revolution, the elder Screven purchased plantations on both sides of the Savannah River and became a successful rice and indigo planter. He also owned a place on Betz Creek on Wilmington Island and a residence on St. James Square (now Telfair Square). John and his wife Hanna welcomed their son James Proctor into the world in 1799. James attended South Carolina College at Columbia and studied medicine at the University of Pennsylvania, where he graduated in 1820. After two years studying and traveling in Europe, he returned to Savannah, practiced medicine, and participated in local politics. In addition to his election to city council, he was a founding member of the Board of Health and helped supervise the early river dredging operations. In 1835 Dr. Screven retired from medicine and moved with his wife and children to Nonchalance on Wilmington Island to attend to his planting interests, and he purchased additional properties on the Savannah and Ogeechee Rivers. By all accounts, he met with success. In 1850, he was the largest producer of rice in Beaufort County.[58]

After a little over a decade of Screven engaging in these agricultural pursuits, Savannah lured him back into its urban environs. Once back in Savannah, with his family ensconced in a residence on Reynolds Square, he again engaged in local politics and was elected an alderman. Screven remained in the city during the yellow fever epidemic of 1854 and assumed the duties of acting mayor.[59] Of more consequence to the economic development of the city, Screven became involved in the Savannah and Albany Railroad project, was elected company president, and devoted the remainder of his life to this enterprise.[60]

With local subscriptions of $27,000 and rumors of a potential $2 million investment from Belgium, Screven lobbied the city council, of which he was also a member, to subscribe $500,000 to the new enterprise. The council, eager to counter the latest challenge to its coastal dominance, voted to fund the costs for an immediate survey and authorized the mayor to invest $500,000, pending approval of a citizens' meeting. Conveniently forgetting the derisive language used to criticize the Brunswick enterprise, local boosters optimistically predicted that the Savannah and Albany Railroad would secure for Savannah "her ultimate supremacy as the Great South Atlantic City." The road promised to open the region of southern and western Georgia, Alabama and eventually all of the Gulf Coast.[61]

The citizens' meeting, held in November, resolved that Savannah had to "preserve at all hazzards [sic] . . . the position which nature has assigned to her as the eastern terminus of any great thoroughfare connecting the

Atlantic and the Mexican Gulf." Although there were two competing resolutions regarding the investment, the difference related to route choice,
with both agreeing that the city should subscribe $1 million, not the orig-
inally requested $500,000.[62] In the end, the municipal government voted
to subscribe $500,000 provided that others subscribe the first $500,000.
Screven, in an effort to demonstrate his confidence and commitment to
the "enterprise," promised to invest $80,000 to $100,000 and to devote at
least the next two years of his life to the endeavor.[63]

Though local officials recognized the risk involved in such an investment, they believed that Savannah, with aggressive action, would be
able to "repeat the experiment" of the Central Railroad by exchanging
the stock of the railroad for its own bonds. A meeting of citizens, in a
nearly unanimous vote, ratified their council's actions.[64] Savannah's officials and vocal railroad boosters fully expected that the municipal government could service this enormous debt in a similar fashion to that of the
Central. By 1853, Savannah's municipal government owned a majority of
the stock in the Savannah and Albany Railroad even as critics accused the
city of using the railroad to destroy the "Brunswick enterprise." By early
1854, the newly named Savannah, Albany and Gulf Railroad was making plans to construct its depot on the eastern side of the city and had requested that Savannah subscribe another million dollars.[65]

For nearly four years, these competing railroads vied for capital and
support. In the end, the state stepped in and offered both struggling companies a proposition neither was in a position to turn down. The state approved the incorporation of the Atlantic and Gulf Railroad, which was
envisioned as a trunk line, extending westward from a junction of the
two roads. To further encourage cooperation, the General Assembly authorized a subscription of $500,000 in the company as soon as $600,000
could be raised from other sources. When the enticement of this state aid
failed to sufficiently motivate potential investors, Savannah once again
stepped in with a $200,000 subscription. With the added confidence Sa-
vannah's investment provided, the company managed to raise the required
amount, and the state kept its bargain.[66]

Unfortunately, the newly formed Atlantic and Gulf Railroad proved
no better able to consistently mobilize sufficient private backing than the
Savannah, Albany and Gulf Railroad or the Brunswick and Florida Railroad. Perennial financial problems and route squabbles further plagued
the company.[67] Savannah, already heavily invested in the enterprise, con-

tinued to sink money into it, including an endorsement of $300,000 in the company's bonds.[68]

As war clouds approached, the Savannah, Albany and Gulf Railroad had reached Thomasville, and the line to Bainbridge was under construction. The Savannah, Albany and Gulf Railroad and the Atlantic and Gulf Railroad were consolidated under the Atlantic and Gulf Railroad in April 1863. Construction continued into 1864, after which about sixty miles of line were destroyed, along with the depot in Savannah.[69]

Expecting prodigious returns on these investments, the city carried a bonded indebtedness of $2 million by 1861. The meager dividends from the city's investments, however, did not come close to meeting the annual interest on the loans. For instance, in 1856, Savannah received almost $45,000 in dividends but spent over $80,000 on interest payments alone. By 1860, the gap between those numbers had widened further. The decreased income of slightly over $24,000 from dividend payments did not come close to covering the interest payments, which exceeded $140,000.[70]

Tax revenue failed to close the gap. Between 1850 and 1860, the amount of taxes the city collected more than doubled from $54,373 to $175,268. Despite annual increases in the amount and breadth of taxes, receipts always fell well short of needs. In 1856, Savannah collected slightly over $100,000 in taxes, but its expenditures totaled almost $800,000. In 1860, there was a similar difference of over $500,000 between the tax receipts and city expenditures. Citizens commonly complained about the increasing rate of taxation prior to the war, and some naysayers made dire predictions about the dangerously high debt burden.[71]

Yet, because the Civil War precluded a demonstration of the danger of being addicted to loans, the past became a blueprint for the future. Looking to reestablish the city's premier position among seaports, officials who had participated in the antebellum system, which generated the economically thriving decade of the 1850s, perpetuated the same system in the postwar years. After the Civil War, desperate to generate revenue to revitalize the city's economy and to pay off its antebellum debt, Savannah continued the trend toward dependence on loans.[72] The city council issued bonds with the intention of promoting the city's commerce by creating an economic atmosphere that would facilitate economic development and encourage population growth. It was commonly accepted that the city had to continue growing; economic stagnation and competition from rival cities would bring about its decline. In short, Savannah's economic survival depended on continued development. The relatively easy process of issuing bonds initially facilitated the zealous efforts to strengthen the city's competitive edge by funding its revitalization projects.

Cities recognized that debt represented a risk but also provided them with opportunities. Savannah, like so many other cities, proved willing to assume the role of aggressive actor and "underwrite and promote their economic growth" in this fashion.[73] However, this general optimism had a tendency to mutate into what latter-day critics called "over-optimistic recklessness and extravagance."[74] City officials seemed unaware, or at least unwilling to recognize, that much had changed in the first half of the 1860s. Consequently they pursued strikingly similar policies without comprehending the tremendous risks.

CHAPTER 3

—— •◆• ——

"The Worst Whipped and Subjugated You Ever Saw"

SECESSION, WAR, AND DEFEAT

The building of the Central Railroad and the reviving economy brought other changes to Savannah. In addition to cotton, people flowed into the city. Between 1830 and 1860, the population more than tripled, going from 7,303 to 22,292, with most of this growth occurring in the 1840s. Central Railroad agents traveled north to recruit skilled engineers and laborers for construction and other employment. Soon thousands of laborers, many of them Irish, arrived in Savannah to take advantage of the opportunities.[1]

By the end of the antebellum period, this immigration had changed Savannah's demography. The three thousand Irish accounted for 70 percent of the foreign-born population, 23 percent of the white population, and about 15 percent of the total population. By 1870 these numbers had not changed significantly. The city counted thirty-six hundred persons of foreign birth, approximately 15 percent of the total population. The Irish remained the largest group, constituting 60 percent; Germans accounted for another 21 percent.[2]

Generally these immigrants lived in poorly constructed housing on the eastern and western edges of the city: Gilmersville, to the east of Habersham Street; and Yamacraw in Oglethorpe Ward on the west, bordering the Central Railroad depot, the canal, and the river. These wards had higher than average populations, suffered from housing shortages, and contained an overabundance of liquor shops.[3]

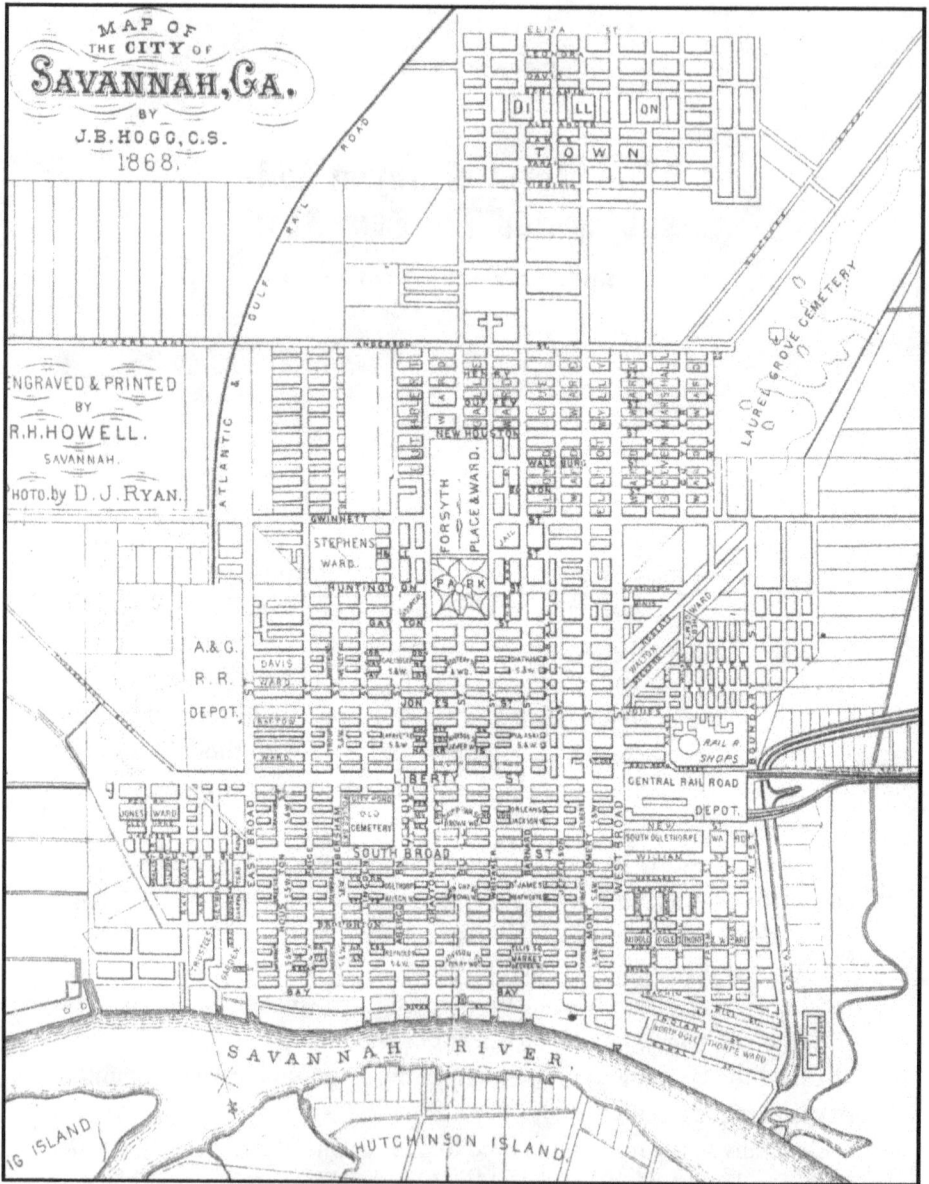

FIGURE 2. Map of Savannah by J. B. Hogg, 1868, from F. D. Lee and
J. L. Agnew, *Historical Record of the City of Savannah* (1869).
Courtesy of Kaye Kole Genealogy and Local History Room,
Live Oak Public Libraries, Savannah, Georgia.

Irishmen could be found scattered throughout the various trades, especially as carpenters, tailors, and blacksmiths. The great bulk, however, worked as unskilled common laborers; they were employed in railroad construction and maintenance, handled freight for the railroad, and worked at the wharves. Increasingly they sought employment as domestic servants, previously the province of slaves and free persons of color.[4]

The influx of foreign immigrants transformed the contours and patterns of employment. The vast majority of immigrants experienced competition from slaves and free persons of color for both jobs and housing. Urban African Americans, both slave and free, generally worked as common laborers, while a lesser number labored in semiskilled or skilled trades. They lived in every section of the city but particularly on the eastern and western fringes. By 1860, there were 725 free persons of color and 14,807 slaves in Chatham County, with most of the latter working on the numerous rice plantations surrounding the city.[5]

In Savannah proper, the total number of African Americans was much smaller; at 8,400, they constituted about 37 percent of the city's population. By the 1870s, the total number of African Americans in Chatham County rose to 24,581, while in the city itself the population swelled to 15,166, comprising about 46 percent of the population. Therefore, while the African American population increased significantly in the postwar years, the foreign-born population did not see a similar increase. During the antebellum period, African Americans and immigrants competed for employment and living space. Yet immigrants enjoyed one important privilege that was denied to all African Americans—the franchise.[6]

During the 1840s, the Irish population developed into a significant factor in municipal politics in part because of enthusiastic participation and in part because Savannah had a healthy two-party system. Irishmen became an important voting bloc, albeit a volatile one. They also tended to vote Democratic at a time when the Democratic Party advertised itself as the party of the workingman. The contribution of the Irish to municipal Democratic victories resulted in a system of patronage in the form of city jobs and employment in public works projects. The Irish received other less obvious benefits as well. Officials and police often overlooked their illegal trade with slaves and lack of business licenses. The Whigs clearly considered the foreign-born element an unsavory lot. Throughout the pages of the *Savannah Republican*, the Whig political organ, the Irish commonly received blame for the bulk of the political corruption in the city. Some of the charges leveled proved accurate, but in many cases the problem was exaggerated.[7]

Even after the collapse of the Whig Party in the 1850s, Savannah continued to experience active political contests. Local politics centered on the enforcement of Sunday hours and various blue laws, restriction of liquor sales, and maintenance of law and order. Due to the participation of various immigrant groups throughout most of the 1840s and 1850s, Democrats remained in power. However, the culture clash and perceived threat to the good order of society from the so-called foreign element prompted the brief appearance of the Know-Nothing Party. Mostly composed of former Whigs looking for a convenient political organization, this nativist party experienced some popularity in the mid-1850s.[8]

In the second half of the 1850s, Savannahians became increasingly concerned about the great national question of slavery. As was typical of the Deep South, in spite of the city's diverse population and the unusually large percentage of northern-born residents, anti-abolitionist sentiment and heated rhetoric dominated. Although the Irish continued to vote Democratic and Unionist, by the time of Lincoln's election many segments of the city's population had joined in the frenzied agitation for secession, and Savannah developed a reputation as a fire-eating hotbed. After Lincoln's election, a crowd, estimated at three thousand, attended an anti-Union rally in the city and enthusiastically resolved not to submit to Lincoln's election.[9]

William Freehling, in his second volume of *Road to Disunion* (*Secessionists Triumphant, 1854–1861*), suggests that Savannah railroad leaders may have played a significant role in South Carolina's hasty decision to move forward with secession. As the South Carolina legislature was debating a bill to delay a state secession convention, secessionists attempted to engineer a "public outcry against a delayed convention." In what Freehling calls an "amazing coincidence," the Savannah and Charleston Railroad (or Charleston and Savannah Railroad) had been completed only two weeks prior, and several Georgians celebrating the railroad's completion just "happened to be in Charleston on the night of the legislature's decision." A few of them joined their Charleston hosts at a public gathering at Independence Hall. Here Francis Bartow, scion of young Savannah, told listeners not to put off the storm that was to come. Meanwhile Henry R. Jackson, another Savannahian, at a different Charleston gathering, told his audience that "Southern Civilization . . . must be maintained at any cost." These public guarantees of support by leading Georgians solidified South Carolina's stance. The next day, Charleston's secessionists told the legislature in Columbia, "Georgia will be with us."

With this, according to Freehling, the "race toward revolution became irresistible."[10]

In December 1860, following South Carolina's lead, Georgia called a convention to decide the issue of secession, and in early January Savannah elected three pro-secessionist delegates.[11] When Georgia voted to secede, the city celebrated in grand style. Following the creation of the Confederate States of America, the Georgia secession convention reconvened in Savannah. Here the convention delegates wrote and ratified a new state constitution. Even in advance of secession, Savannah became the site of Georgia's first official act of rebellion, the seizure of Fort Pulaski on Cockspur Island.[12]

Following the firing on Fort Sumter, Savannahians patriotically gave men, money, and supplies to defend their infant nation. With the outbreak of war, editorial overtures encouraging Savannahians to meet and defeat commercial challenges of other seaports such as Charleston and Mobile were silenced. In their place came calls for solid patriotism, self-sacrifice, and endurance.

Some believed that Savannah could benefit from secession. Boosters had often touted the merits of opening direct trade with Europe and reducing southern economic dependence on the North. Secession made this opportunity seem all the more possible as Governor Joseph Brown dispatched a representative to Europe with instructions to establish a direct connection with Savannah. Immediately following the outbreak of war, Savannah made a brief bid to become one of the blockade-running hubs for the Confederacy. This effort reached its height with a singular success in November 1861, when Edward C. Anderson, piloting the *Fingal* from England, slipped through the Union blockade and landed at Savannah with Enfield rifles, cannons, uniforms, and medical supplies. Following this, the Union navy's blockade became more effective, thus strangling Savannah's efforts. Aspiring to break the blockade, Savannah's shipyards constructed three ironclad gunboats: the *Atlanta*, the *Georgia*, and the *Savannah*. Though touted far and wide as a significant threat to the Union navy, they neither challenged the Union navy nor contributed significantly to the defense of the city.[13]

The Union navy systematically tightened its grip on the coast and cut off Savannah from its defenders at Fort Pulaski. With the use of the innovative rifled cannon, it forced the surrender of the fort in April 1862. Fearing an imminent invasion, leaders talked of burning the city rather than letting the Yankees have it. Local leaders had to accept the reality that Savannah had become expendable and would be sacrificed to protect

Augusta. Both the Confederacy and the Union navy began the process of obstructing the Savannah River to prevent their enemies' passage. With Union forces so close to the city, most Savannahians spent the rest of the war less concerned about direct trade than about invasion.[14]

The Union blockade and the capture of Fort Pulaski stifled the city's economy. Citizens suffered from food shortages and extravagant prices for what was available. Disease was prevalent. City services strained to keep up. By 1864, several women, having reached their breaking point, began raiding local stores for food and supplies.[15] The end, however, was longer in coming than many thought, and it came from a different direction. In November 1864, news of General William T. Sherman's advance, possibly toward the sea, alarmed citizens. Some fled, but many who had no means to leave stayed to face the Union onslaught. In late November, as the situation deteriorated, help from outside seemed slim. With the Confederate army unable to stop the federal advance, Richard D. Arnold, Savannah's mayor, issued a call for "all men of every age, not absolutely incapacitated by disease" to report for the city's defense. Citizens, having read the sensationalist press accounts of the horrible fate of many interior towns, prepared for the worst.[16]

On December 17, 1864, General Sherman, with his forces on the outskirts of Savannah, ordered General William J. Hardee, commander of Confederate troops in Savannah, to surrender the city by December 20. Even though Hardee officially refused, he was already planning to evacuate the city. During the night of December 20, after the last of Hardee's troops crossed the Savannah River, city leaders surrendered Savannah to General John W. Geary. By 7:00 a.m. on December 21, federal troops were marching through the streets of Savannah.[17]

Though left to the mercy of the Union army, Savannah was quite fortunate. In his surrender order, Sherman had provided for liberal terms if the city were surrendered peacefully. Sherman, who had received word of Savannah's surrender while stuck in the mud in Romerly Marsh, arrived in Savannah on December 22 and sent President Lincoln a telegram giving him Savannah as a Christmas present. The war was over for the people of Savannah.[18]

Due to the ravages of war, many of those citizens were in a desperate condition by the time the Union army arrived. The first federal troops entered Savannah to find a mob gathered in the streets, breaking into stores and houses. Union soldiers easily quelled the violence and restored order. Beyond this initial outbreak, citizens reportedly remained "quiet and well disposed." While likely relieved that their city had been spared

Sherman's fiery wrath, they did not welcome the invading army. Sherman commented that they were so well-behaved because they "are the worst whipped and subjugated you ever saw." He astutely observed that their actions were due mostly to the despair they found in defeat and occupation.[19]

Many civilians, black and white alike, quickly became dependent on the Union army for the basic necessities. Thrown together by circumstances, city officials and the military worked together to relieve the suffering of the poor. In addition to military aid, Savannah also received help from sympathetic northerners.[20] As it appeared that victory for the Union was near, northerners began to envision a return to peace. Some viewed the situation in Savannah as an opportunity to demonstrate that the Union was not the evil beast the Confederacy portrayed it to be. This was especially necessary in the wake of Sherman's recent infamous march. Savannah gave the Union a chance to "show the Southern people that we cherish no malice, and are ready again to give the hand of fellowship." Federal policy, at least in Savannah, changed from punishment and retribution to benevolence. Savannah was, according to the *New York Times*, to become "a standing illustration before the Southern people of the brotherhood we would extend to all of them, if they would but cease resistance of the Constitution and the laws."[21]

Whether they regarded the army as a source of humanitarian aid or simply a conquering foe, Savannah's inhabitants for the most part were pragmatic about the situation. One manifestation of this attitude was the outcome of a citizens' meeting held shortly after the surrender. This meeting, closed to all Union officials, published resolutions that officially recognized that the city of Savannah was under the authority of the United States. Looking to the future, the attendees believed that it was in Savannah's best interest to "seek to have peace by laying down our arms and submitting to the national authority under the Constitution, leaving all questions ... to be adjusted by the peaceful means of legislation, conference and votes." By submitting to reality and "burying by-gones in the grave of the past," they planned to use their "best endeavors once more to bring back the prosperity and commerce" once enjoyed by the city. While many still hoped for an ultimate and miraculous Confederate victory, most citizens resigned themselves to accept the current reality.[22]

The sense of defeat, despair, and helplessness of the white citizens was thrown into bold relief by the feeling of joy and celebration that swept the city's African Americans upon the army's arrival. If there were those in the community concerned that their slaves would rise up against them, they had little to fear from the freedmen, who generally behaved "admirably." In their joy, they took "no advantage of their freedom in any way in their conduct to those who ill treated them in former days, except that they leave them for the sake of obtaining remunerative employment." Many were merely thankful that the day of freedom had arrived for them, and they were specifically thankful to General Sherman, to whom they flocked, expressing their "manifest joy."[23]

Slavery, the cornerstone of southern social and economic relations, was dead. However, battlefield defeats and constitutional amendments did not eradicate the old ideology of white supremacy. The "quiet and respectful" demeanor with which African Americans accepted their new stations failed to assuage the anger of many whites. Most slave owners believed they had been good masters, but even the most loyal of slaves often left the kindest of owners for a taste of freedom. Whites seemingly believed that prewar paternalistic acts of kindness, generosity, and even respect would continue. When Sherman marched into the city and the new freedmen forgot "their place," shock quickly turned to anger.[24]

Even as many whites reacted with indignation, others mentally accommodated themselves to the new order. Denying that the new situation was to their disadvantage, some, claiming slavery had been a drain on their finances, expressed relief to be rid of their human burdens. Whether they were distraught or relieved over the end of slavery, all whites were concerned about the destruction of the old social order. Freedom for all changed the rules for everyone.[25]

Slaves had longed for the day when they would be free of their masters. With their liberation, freed blacks sought tangible ways to demonstrate this freedom. Initially they defined freedom in terms of doing things that were forbidden during slavery, but they also began to separate themselves physically and socially from their former masters. Freedpeople made education, which was officially denied them under slavery, a high priority. For many years prior to the Civil War, Savannah's blacks, aided by religious institutions like the First African Baptist Church, struggled to educate themselves in Sunday schools and other clandestine schools established in violation of Georgia law. Shortly after Savannah fell to Union forces, freedpeople formed the Savannah Educational Association (SEA). Aided by the Freedmen's Bureau and northern philanthropic societies like the American Missionary Association, the SEA established a fund to open a school for African American children. By January 10, 1865, less than one month after their liberation, they opened a school in the former slave market. As the number of students attending school swelled, freedpeople established other schools in the city and on the sea islands.[26]

Labor was another area freedpeople sought to redefine on their own terms. For African Americans, slavery was hard work for the benefit of others. Therefore, with freedom came new choices—of either not working or working for themselves. For ex-slaves, returning to work, as whites discovered, did not mean returning to the master-slave relationship. Blacks either left their former masters or demanded fair wages for their labor.

Between the diametrically opposed goals of southern whites and blacks were northerners who had been baptized in the ideology of free labor, and they were anxious to demonstrate to black and white southerners its superiority.[27] White southerners remained skeptical about the virtues of free labor. Alternatively, northerners had to convince freedpeople that free labor simply meant the freedom to choose one's employer, even if that employer had been a former master. In the close confines of Savannah, as blacks sought to define and maintain their freedom and as whites worked to circumscribe that freedom, avoiding violence became increasingly difficult. This huge flood of refugees complicated the adjustment to new circumstances and strained the resources of the city and the federal army. Punitive manual labor and northern charity provided only temporary measures in alleviating the symptoms of a deeper problem.[28]

With the need for a more permanent solution, Savannah and the coastal sea islands became the focus for significant changes in federal policy. In early January 1865, Edwin M. Stanton, secretary of war, visited the city to meet with General Sherman and find a solution to the refugee problem. Stanton met with twenty local black leaders, including ministers, barbers, sailors, and pilots. Stanton lectured the freedmen about certain responsibilities that came with their new freedom and then "gave them a hearing." Garrison Frazier, a Baptist minister, the spokesman for the group of black leaders, was diplomatic in his responses to Stanton's queries regarding their treatment by Sherman. Stanton was reportedly surprised at their intelligence. Demonstrating remarkable patience with Stanton's patronizing tone, they were determined to get one point across—that they should be given land on which they could receive the benefits of their labor.[29]

In light of this meeting and the desperate need to relieve the city of the growing number of freedpeople, Sherman, after further consultation with Stanton, issued Special Field Order Number 15. Also called the "Sea-

Island Circular," it gave blacks "possessory titles" to the land on the sea islands abandoned by Confederates. This encompassed the abandoned rice
fields along the rivers and "30 miles back from the sea" to the St. Johns
River in Florida. Though given no deeds, the freedpeople received assur-
ances that the government would honor its commitment to them. In early
February, General Rufus Saxton, inspector of settlements and plantations,
in charge of the land distribution program, met with one thousand freedpeople and distributed thousands of acres. According to optimistic estimates, approximately forty thousand blacks relocated to the sea islands of
Georgia and South Carolina, including many who already owned property in Savannah. After its creation, the Freedmen's Bureau took control
of the land distribution program.[30]

While some whites expressed satisfaction that the city had been relieved of what they considered the "idle masses," others protested. They
believed that the federal government's policies threatened the entire social order and that only determined resistance could save it. This resistance
would take many forms over the next nine years. Yet, even as white conservatives in Savannah grappled with the forces of Reconstruction and
sought to turn back the clock, they worked to revive their city and cultivate an image of economic progress.[31]

CHAPTER 4

"Artery of Wealth and Prosperity"

RAISING REVENUE AND
REVITALIZING RIVER NAVIGATION

The Union army's occupation of Savannah in December 1864 brought the Civil War to an end for its citizens. While the military and political future of the Confederacy had yet to be determined, most of the city's inhabitants focused on the much more immediate and demanding problems of economic recovery and revival. Though Savannah had escaped the type of physical destruction that befell Atlanta, Charleston, Columbia, and Richmond, its major railroads were badly damaged, the harbor was closed, and many of its citizens depended on the U.S. military for the basic necessities.[1]

Savannah's leaders divided their attention between the fractious political situation occasioned by Reconstruction and putting their financial resources toward economic recovery. While economic stagnation and competition from other coastal cities such as Mobile, Charleston, and New Orleans certainly jeopardized the city's future, so too did the potential political changes contemplated by the federal government. Savannah's political and economic futures, leaders believed, could be safeguarded from "degradation and ruin" only by maintaining conservative local control as the nation worked through Reconstruction. Economic opportunity, they reasoned, would return once political issues had been resolved.[2]

They based this optimism on the assumption of a quick and speedy Reconstruction as outlined by President Abraham Lincoln and subsequently implemented by President Andrew Johnson. However, in reaction to increasing southern intransigence and a rising tide of southern white vigilante activity, northern Republicans, who controlled Congress, neutralized Johnson, and, seeking tangible change in the South, they launched a much more thorough and punitive Reconstruction. Stubborn white southern resistance prolonged the period of political turmoil and delayed the process of economic recovery. For nearly five years, Savannah's conservative leaders supported Georgia's recalcitrant political stance and fought to maintain home rule even as they strove mightily to promote the city's economic revival.

Unable to wait for the indefinite conclusion of the Reconstruction process, and convinced that delay would be detrimental to Savannah's future prosperity, the municipal government aggressively spearheaded the quest to resuscitate the city's flagging economy. Even as municipal leaders struggled to meet prewar financial obligations, maintain minimum services, keep taxes low, and present an image of economic progress, they risked even greater financial strain to fund harbor improvement. Prioritizing municipal expenditures on dredging the river increased the financial burden under which the city struggled and left scant resources to carry out other municipal responsibilities. Leaders' actions, based as they were on past experience, public enmity toward local Republicans with economic connections, and an optimistic vision of the post-Reconstruction future, were successful only in the short term, and that success was much more political than economic.[3]

The individual tasked with managing these priorities was Edward Clifford Anderson, whom citizens elected mayor in December 1865.[4] Anderson's family had put down roots in Savannah prior to the Revolution when his grandfather George Anderson, a sea captain and New York native, bought a plantation southwest of Savannah. He and his wife had three children, John, Mary, and George. His namesake became a successful planter and merchant, extending the family's holdings to three plantations. The young George married Elizabeth Clifford Wayne, sister to James Moore Wayne, the U.S. Supreme Court justice, and Edward Clifford Anderson was their ninth child. While Edward's older brother, the third George of the family line, became a successful merchant and bank president, Edward grew up knowing that his father expected him to manage the family's plantations. Edward, however, had different plans; he wanted a life at sea.[5]

In 1833, young Edward pursued his own dream and joined the U.S. Navy. While resisting his father's efforts to lure him home, Anderson grew increasingly dissatisfied with his naval career, the slow promotion

FIGURE 3. Edward Clifford Anderson, circa 1870s.
Courtesy of City of Savannah Municipal Archives.

process, and his frequent transfers, usually at the request of his superiors. After nearly a decade at sea, he married Sarah McQueen Williamson and a few years later took temporary leave in an attempt to satisfy his father, who gave him management of Lebanon Plantation southwest of Savannah. Anderson discovered that plantation management did not suit him, and he resumed his naval duties for another few years before returning home for good in 1849. Although his family owned interest in three working plantations, Anderson chose to live in Savannah and become part of a growing number of philanthropic organizations associated with the emergent urban South, including the Massie School, the Georgia Infirmary, the Benevolent Society, the Savannah Port Society, and Chatham Academy.[6]

Anderson also participated in local politics. In 1854, the citizens of Savannah elected him mayor on the former Whig/American Party/Know-Nothing ticket, locally called the "Law and Order" ticket, on a platform of police reform. He served one term, angered citizens with his overenthusiastic enforcement of the city's blue laws, and subsequently lost to Democrat James P. Screven. In spite of their political differences, Anderson like Screven enthusiastically supported Savannah's path of aggressive municipal entrepreneurship. As mayor of Savannah, he had supported the city's endorsement of the Savannah, Albany and Gulf Railroad's bonds, was appointed a board of commissioner for the Atlantic and Gulf Railroad, and subsequently became a director of that company.[7]

During the Civil War, Anderson, piloting the CSS *Fingal*, as noted above, managed to elude the Union blockade, bringing Enfield rifles and uniforms into the Savannah port. Upon his return, he commanded Savannah's coastal batteries. After the war, he served in Georgia's first Reconstruction convention and ran again for mayor of Savannah in 1865.[8] Though disappointed with the elections' outcome in 1865, a landslide victory for the rebel candidates, John Hayes, editor of the *Savannah Republican*, described Anderson as an honest man; aside from his political views, Hayes had "no fault to find with him."[9] Anderson was elected mayor and, at fifty-one, assumed the office for the second time.

The newly elected city council took office in mid-December, only a month after the U.S. military returned control of municipal functions to the city council. This proved a mixed blessing. Local officials regained political control, but the expense of maintaining the city fell completely on the shoulders of a nearly bankrupt municipal treasury. When Anderson took the reins, he found but $2,000 in the treasury, a decrease of $62,000 since September 1862. The city's debt had ballooned to more than $370,000.[10]

Given the destitute condition of the population, now swelled with an influx of freedpeople and returning veterans, the recently installed city council concluded that taxes, even at an increased rate, would be entirely insufficient to carry on the city's normal functions, much less pay the city's prewar debts and stimulate economic recovery. Ultimately the council opted to issue bonds to fund the city's debt and maintain essential services.[11] Cities commonly resorted to short-term, high-interest loans from local banks to cover cash shortfalls prior to revenue collection, in the expectation that future taxation would pay for these loans. In Savannah, these short-term loans were commonly called mayors' notes.[12] Councilmen believed that the city's desperate postwar economic circumstances exacerbated by the political chaos of Reconstruction were temporary restraints. Once they were overcome, they could focus on investment in the future.

Over the next two years, city officials worked to erase the physical reminders of the war's destruction and to project an image of recovery and growth. With its treasury regularly exhausted, the council funded improvements and repairs through the use of loans; therefore, recovery and growth were more of a facade than real. That paying off loans and interest on loans absorbed 50 percent of the city's expenditures in 1866 and 1867 seemed of little concern, for council members were confident that the poor financial situation would be short-lived. Once Savannah recovered lost ground and surpassed its prewar economic successes, these burdensome financial obligations would seem insignificant. In spite of this optimism, political and economic recovery was not quick.[13]

In the interim, to pay for the interest on these loans, the city council depended on various revenue streams, including property taxes, dividend taxes, income taxes, and specific taxes. Property taxes, which constituted 40 to 60 percent of the city's receipts, provided the most significant source of income. Over the next two decades, the municipal government—to the consternation of property owners—gradually increased this ad valorem tax from 1 percent to 2.5 percent. Specific taxes included taxes on gross sales, incomes in excess of $800 annually, commission profits, and various business transactions. Professional licenses, badge fees, and market stall rentals provided additional funds.[14]

A final source of revenue came from ground rents. Of feudal origins, ground rent was the interest, generally 5 percent, on the unpaid balance of the purchase cost of a city lot. Instituted in 1790, it allowed the city of Savannah to "sell" property to citizens who could not afford the entire purchase price. Purchasers of city lots could pay for the lot outright and receive a fee simple title. However, if purchasers could not pay for the property in full, they could agree to pay, commonly in perpetuity, the interest on the remaining balance. It was advantageous to the property owner, in this case the city, because it allowed for a consistent income. Until 1878, these city lots, as they continued to be called, were not subject to taxation; the city neither assessed them for taxation nor recorded the property in the assessment books.[15]

Savannah's economic mainstay was commerce, and the rebuilding of its transportation system became the primary focus for economic recovery. As citizens put the devastating year 1865 behind them, many signs indicated that the city was indeed recovering. Following the end of military control, commerce returned and, with it, confidence in the city's future. In 1865, the city's two main railroads, the Central Railroad and the Atlantic and Gulf Railroad, which were vital to the city's commercial prosperity, began reestablishing their routes. By 1866, both railroads were partially restored and had resumed delivery of products to Savannah, where reestablished steamship lines carried goods northward and abroad. As a result of the railroads' efforts, the port exported almost 257,000 bales of cotton, worth close to $12 million during 1866, a 30 percent increase over the pre-

ceding year, and imports nearly doubled.[16] The gradual reestablishment of
the rail lines, however, highlighted one of the glaring deficiencies in Savannah's recovery—the harbor.

During the early days of the Civil War, Savannahians had hoped their
harbor would become an important blockade-running hub. Instead it became a source of military vulnerability. In 1862, following its capture of
Fort Pulaski, the Union navy tightened its grip along the coast, and the
Confederacy reversed the decades-long progress made in river and harbor
improvement by sinking vessels, cribs (framed timber filled with rocks),
and piers to prevent the enemy from reaching farther inland. By the end
of the war, the river was almost impassable.[17]

Without an adequate harbor and a navigable river to serve as the
city's "artery of wealth and prosperity," Savannah's leaders feared the city
would lose its competitive edge and never recover its share of trade and
commerce or sustain its position among old and new rivals. The reconstruction of the railroads would do the city little good unless sufficient
water transportation existed to ship products to other markets. Unlike
the Central Railroad and Atlantic and Gulf Railroad, however, the river
was not a private corporation. Therefore, the task of its repair fell to the
public sector. Attempting to spur leaders into action, Savannah's newspapers purposely overstated Charleston and Mobile's own recovery efforts,
which were limited. Norfolk, a more viable threat, was moving to reestablish trade with Liverpool, and many feared that Atlanta would choose
to ship its goods via the Virginia city. Rumors also surfaced that Atlanta
planned to invest in Savannah's rival Brunswick as a new site for direct
trade with Europe.[18]

Harbor improvement was a familiar subject in Savannah. Since the
1820s, the city had been involved in the removal of obstructions such as
sunken vessels and maritime remnants of the Revolutionary War. Natural disadvantages were also challenging. Vessels traveling the twenty-four
miles to Savannah encountered a narrow channel with extremely low
draught at certain points. The river also had serious problems with silt
buildup and shoaling, and it was subject to extreme tidal currents. Finally, various small islands divided the main river into narrow and shal-
low channels, thus reducing the flow in the main channel fronting the
city.[19]

During the 1850s, city initiative and generous federal expenditures
overcame these impediments. In 1852 the federal government allocated

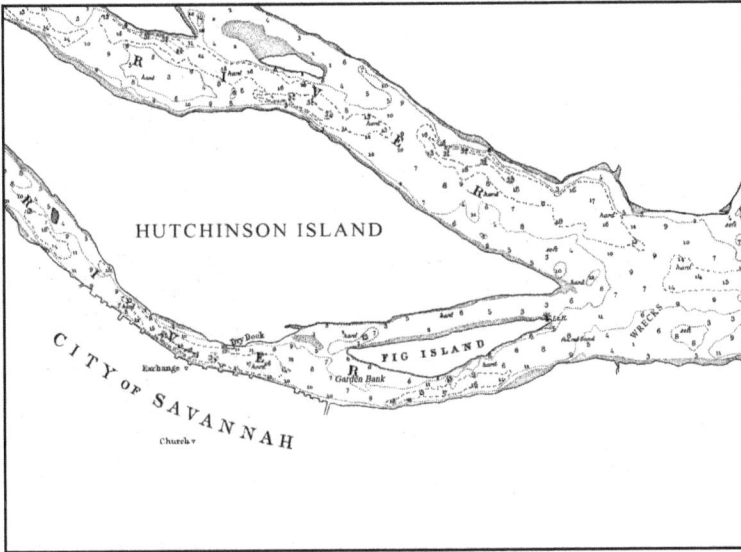

FIGURE 4. Navigation chart of Savannah River, approaches to the city
of Savannah including front and back rivers, by U.S Coast Survey, 1851.
Courtesy of National Oceanic and Atmospheric Administration,
Office of Coast Survey, Historical Map and Chart Collection.

$40,000 for Savannah's harbor improvement. When government engineers estimated that an additional $200,000 would be necessary to complete the dredging to make the river navigable for the largest ships, city fathers refused to wait for the federal government and risk losing what had already been gained by previous work. Fully expecting the federal government to reimburse the expenditure, the council borrowed $160,000 to continue the dredging. Savannah's faith was not misplaced; the federal government ultimately appropriated an additional $161,000 in 1855, which allowed work on the harbor to continue into 1860. The deepening of the river allowed more ships to sail directly to Savannah's wharves. In 1859 and 1860 the number of vessels leaving the city for foreign ports grew by over 90 percent. Even more staggering was the 142 percent increase during the same period in the amount of tonnage clearing the port. By 1860, Savannah ranked as America's second-largest cotton port, due in great part to its extensive rail connections and river improvement. In that year, it finally surpassed Charleston in number of cotton bales exported.[20] It was with this success in mind that some of Savannah's leaders, particularly Mayor

Edward Anderson, became obsessed with harbor improvement in the immediate postwar years.[21]

Following Savannah's surrender in December 1864, General Sherman designated Savannah as a military depot and initiated the earliest postwar improvement of the harbor. At the time torpedoes and log piers filled with cobblestones and live oak obstructed the river below the city. The Union navy's efforts opened the channel for vessels of limited draught.[22] Heavier vessels loaded part of their cargo at the wharves and picked up the remainder eight to ten miles below the city. Large merchant ships also anchored south of the city and lightered their cargo. This process was inefficient, time-consuming, and expensive, which translated into higher freight rates, thus reducing the competitive edge Savannahians sought.[23]

Looking to make the harbor adequate for Savannah's postwar commercial needs, in late 1865 the city council received permission from the U.S. Treasury Department to make contracts for the removal of river obstructions.[24] As the council began contract negotiations with various companies, Savannah's old rival, the Brunswick and Albany Railroad Company, represented by Henry S. Welles, presented a claim to the Treasury Department for the iron plating on one of the sunken vessels in the river. The company charged that the Confederate military had taken the iron without the company's consent.[25] The Treasury Department launched an investigation and instructed Savannah to exempt that particular vessel from any contract the city might make for wreck removal. To complicate matters further, Welles applied to the Treasury Department for his own contract to raise and remove other vessels. The Treasury Department granted Welles the contract to raise obstructions considered to be of monetary value, from which his profit would be derived.[26]

This new development disappointed and angered local officials. First, the department's action took control of the improvements out of the city's hands. Second, basing Welles's payment on the proceeds from the raised vessels incentivized the removal of the most valuable vessels first, without regard to the channel obstructions, thus working at cross purposes with the city's navigational needs. Finally, the council had also made plans to form a similar contract with private parties, using the proceeds of the vessels as compensation.[27]

The council sent a committee to Washington, D.C., to protest Welles's contract. Though the Treasury Department refused to nullify the contract, the department did modify it to include removal of all items obstructing the river. It also required Welles to pay $5,000 from the proceeds of the sale of the salvaged material for the purpose of dredging the channel. City officials remained dissatisfied because the contract failed to place a priority on any particular obstructions.[28]

Already displeased with the particulars of the arrangement, Mayor Anderson and other city officials found constant fault with Welles's work. They charged him with ignoring the work of removing obstructions from the main channel in favor of the removal of more valuable vessels. They bombarded the Treasury Department with numerous complaints about Welles's "want of due diligence" and "unnecessary delay." Welles, of course, denied all charges.[29]

City leaders gave up any hope that Welles would open the main channel adequately or that the federal government would take active measures to ensure that he did so. Ultimately the frustration with Welles's work, the perceived unreliability of the federal government, and strong pressure from Mayor Anderson prompted the city council to dredge the river at its own expense.[30] Given the postwar context, leaders did not expect the cooperation and aid of the federal government in the immediate future. However, drawing on their experience from the 1850s, they did hope for reimbursement when the political situation was resolved.[31]

The council's decision to have the city bear the financial burden of harbor improvement demonstrated its belief in the importance of, and dependence on, commerce. The city's success and its financial survival depended on the business the river brought to Savannah. Aldermen knew that tax receipts would not meet current expenses, yet they believed that harbor improvement should "take precedence over every other project" because it was absolutely necessary for increased business and "enlarged public prosperity." The hundreds of thousands of dollars spent to reopen and revitalize the city's commercial lines seemed well worth the cost and risk.[32]

The council issued bonds to purchase a dredge and sent Anderson to New York to procure it. Although the dredge and additional equipment, including a tug steamer and dumping flats, cost more than expected, Anderson optimistically predicted that the equipment would pay for itself within three years. As if to second Anderson's claim, the Commissioners of Pilotage, who bore responsibility for removing navigational impediments, claimed that the dredge, after only a short time in operation, had achieved a miraculous twenty feet at high tide in some locations. The *Daily News and Herald*, which sporadically complained about river navigation, admitted that the dredge worked better than expected and predicted it would profit taxpayers with increased business. It proudly published reports of various large ships safely arriving and departing and gloated that Savannah's harbor received over $9,000 more in receipts than Mobile. Anderson echoed the paper's sentiments in his annual report, stating that the dredge had "realized the most sanguine expectations." He also predicted that the equipment, which ultimately cost over $72,000, would "speedily and surely accomplish all the ends that induced its procurement," by improving Savannah's competitive edge in making it the new port for western, South American, and West Indian trade.[33]

Such predictions were certainly overoptimistic, but the combined efforts of Welles and the city did yield positive results. Subsequent reports from the Commissioners of Pilotage indicated that the main channel was flowing better. River traffic, a more tangible measure, increased so much that the busy harbormaster requested an assistant deputy to help him with his duties. By 1868, the city's import and export statistics showed marked increases over previous years. The tonnage of coastwise vessels entering the harbor from the coast more than doubled from 168,748 in 1865 to 440,204 in 1868. Until the dredge had been put into operation, ships drawing seventeen feet or more were unable to access the wharves. With the spring 1869 departure of the *Hannah Morris*, which drafted seventeen feet, the city could point to solid proof to the contrary. By this point, only New Orleans exported more cotton than Savannah (whose exports were nearly double those of Charleston).[34]

As willing as they were to take credit for improvements in the river, Savannahians were equally certain to blame Welles for any problems. From 1866 to 1870, Welles worked under contract with the Treasury Department in a process and at a pace that displeased city officials. The city spent an inordinate amount of time, energy, and funds trying to influence the Treasury Department to pressure Welles toward speedy completion of his work or to discredit his work in the expectation that the department would revoke the contract for noncompliance. To make up for its lack of direct political representation, the city council, with civic groups like the Savannah Chamber of Commerce, dispatched several committees to Washington to present Savannah's side of the case. Interested citizens also renewed contacts with northerners who were willing to use their political influence on the city's behalf. In response to these numerous complaints, the Treasury Department appointed agents to supervise and review Welles's work. Various agents admitted that the work was progressing at a less than satisfactory pace, yet they found no major fault with Welles and accepted his reasons for delay.[35]

Although Welles complained that the only goal of the city leaders was to embarrass him, such was not entirely the case. They remained primarily concerned with the harbor's reputation and its impact on commerce. For instance, an *Insurance Monitor* article labeled the Savannah River "a notorious graveyard." The *Savannah Morning News* attempted, albeit unsuccessfully, to counter the *Monitor*'s charges by publishing articles boasting that the river was in the best condition since the war. Certainly Savannah's harbor was comparable to those of its southern rivals. In addition, with boats equipped with "skillful pilots, captains and engineers ... seldom an accident occurs." But the facts were otherwise. Those directly involved in the city's commerce became increasingly frustrated and impatient with the number of accidents in the harbor due to navigational difficulties. These mishaps harmed the city's reputation among shippers, and this negative reputation translated into monetary loss.[36]

Welles remained in the Treasury Department's good graces in spite of incessant complaints. However, the legal system ultimately did what Savannah could not do. Early in 1870 the Treasury Department voided Welles's contract because the department was informed that it did not have legal authority to have made the contract in the first place. The city had never accepted Welles's work as adequate, but the end of Welles's contract with the government left the city completely on its own to repair the harbor.[37]

The city's dredge, though lauded for its work, could not solve all the navigational problems of the river. Officials also discovered, as Welles had, that harbor improvement was not a simple matter. One of the problems was the seasonal nature of Savannah's commercial activity. The safest time for harbor work was when traffic was slow. However, the decline in shipping traffic occurred during the summer months, the unhealthiest time of the year. Welles complained that he had lost several men to the "miasmic" diseases, and many of his employees refused to work during those months.[38]

Another impediment was the temporary nature of the repairs. Even though the city's dredge remained in constant operation, positive results were ephemeral. Some areas required constant dredging. From the beginning, councilmen had no illusions about the permanency of improvements. John Stoddard, chairman of the Commissioners of Pilotage, cautioned that work could not be "discontinued for any length of time without serious detriment" to the harbor. In spite of the enthusiastic report in 1867 that the dredge had achieved a seventeen-foot depth at "the Wrecks," which allowed even the largest vessels to pass safely, future reports noted more retrogression than improvement. Committed to the protection of Savannah's commercial interests, the council continued to pour money into a project it knew could never result in permanent success.[39]

The cost of river improvements thus became a constant drain on the city's treasury. By 1869, almost three years after the inception of dredging, the city had spent $125,000 on dredging operations. While ships drawing seventeen and a half feet could, at times, reach Savannah, the channel was still crooked, subject to frequent shoaling, and required constant attention. Additionally, many vessels still had to lighter their cargoes, and ships still ran aground frequently. In early 1871 the *New York Times* commented that, while a great deal of shipping went on at Savannah's port, it was to be "regretted that the accommodations are so poor, as half the time the ships lie in the mud, and are barely floated at full tide."[40]

The state's political intransigence also retarded Savannah's commercial progress. Without representation, Savannah had to depend on northern congressmen to introduce legislation favorable to the city. The introduction of these appropriation bills, while they raised the city's expectations, often failed to pass. Even as they fought the power of the federal government in an effort to turn back the tide of Reconstruction, Savannahians looked forward to the restoration of normal relations. They hoped that when the lingering animosity dissipated, the federal government would be as generous to Savannah as it had been before the war. Given the increase in violence in the state and Governor Rufus Bullock's request that the federal government return Georgia to military rule, Savannah would have to be patient and persistent.[41]

In early 1870, after Edward Anderson left the mayor's office, having declined to run for reelection, the city government funded his sojourn to Washington in yet another failed effort to convince Congress to reimburse $125,000 and appropriate an additional $75,000 to continue the harbor improvements. Furthermore, to Savannah's dismay, Congress appropriated funds for both Charleston and Mobile, neither of which, Anderson groused, had attempted to finance their own improvements. Although Savannahians sometimes seemed to disassociate political divisions and economic goals, Anderson recognized the futility of his actions as long as Georgia remained at odds with the federal government over Reconstruction and had no congressional representation.[42]

Anderson understood the political handicap and the delicate balance that had to be struck. The issue of harbor improvement demonstrated the incompatibility of the city's political and economic objectives. The dual goals of political home rule and economic stimulation through harbor improvement came into constant conflict. While tenaciously and even at times violently opposing the federal government's Reconstruction policies, Savannahians attempted to wrangle funding for harbor improvement from that same body. In spite of the obvious necessity of federal aid, Savannah's Democrats were loath to give their Republican representatives any credit. During the brief period in 1869 when Georgia had Republican representatives in Washington, they sought funding for river improvement. Yet Anderson, the most enthusiastic proponent and activist in pursuit of harbor improvement, refused to allow his economic goals to dictate his politics. Thomas Robb, the Republican collector of the port at Savannah, aggressively advocated federal funding for Savannah's harbor. Like Anderson, Robb was motivated by political and economic concerns. As collector of the port, Robb obviously saw the need to clear the river for navigational purposes. At the same time, he hoped that his support for government funding would ameliorate political tensions in the city and reduce the personal insults heaped upon him. Anderson, though he liked Robb personally and respected his business acumen, refused to overlook their political differences, at least publicly. He stated that he would rather see the river "dwindle to a little rivulet" than compromise his politics. Conservatives, therefore, looked forward to the end of Reconstruction so they could get on with the business of economic revival without appearing to sacrifice their political principals in the process.[43]

Once Georgia was readmitted to the Union in late 1870, Savannah's officials vigorously renewed their efforts to obtain federal reimbursement for the city's expenses. They discovered, however, that returning to the Union and reestablishing conservative Democratic political representation did not guarantee immediate success. The city's persistence, however, eventually paid off. At the end of 1872, Congress appropriated $50,000 for improvements to the city's harbor. In comparison, Charleston received $38,000 and Mobile $75,000.[44]

The 1872 appropriation of $50,000 was significant in that it was the first major federal allotment since before the Civil War. Still, the sum—half of what had been expected and a quarter of what the city needed—was a disappointment. The *Savannah Morning News* complained about the "il-liberal spirit" of the Congress and the bias for northern and western states. It never seemed to occur to the newspaper editor that the North and the West had not waged a four-year rebellion against the federal government. This frustration over the small amount stemmed not merely from concern about the harbor. Officials had hoped that the allotment would come in the form of a direct payment to replenish the destitute city coffers.[45]

By the time the federal government assumed control of harbor im-provement, the city had made progress on the river, but navigating the channel remained problematic and even treacherous. Groundings or ac-cidents due to shoaling and obstructions were common. Editorials in the *Savannah Morning News*, expressing growing frustration with the situ-ation, pondered the wisdom of spending so much money to make im-provements that were only temporary. Yet other editorials complained about the loss of trade that would result if the city discontinued all im-provements. Lamenting the situation, the editor predicted, "Savannah may bid farewell to all hopes of building up a foreign steamship trade, as owners will not send their vessels to a port where such accidents ... are so frequent."[46]

In the summer of 1872, with $50,000 at its disposal, the U.S. Army Corps of Engineers resumed responsibility for harbor improvement. Having been unsuccessful in gaining direct federal reimbursement to aid its ailing treasury but still desiring to benefit from federal funding, the city tried to establish a continuing role for itself in the project and profit from its investment in its dredging equipment. When Colonel Quincy A. Gillmore, superintending engineer of the coast defenses for the Engi-neers, advertised for proposals for dredging the harbor, the city prepared to lease its dredge to J. S. Kennard, who had supervised the city's dredg-ing operations, provided he won the dredging contract from the govern-ment. By October, the government had contracted with Kennard to be-gin work with the city dredge.[47]

The city's contract received significant criticism. One critic opined that the price paid by the city was too high. Besides putting the city under the direct authority of the federal government, a circumstance still distasteful to many, the municipal government also had to pay a heavy bond for the "honor." By one estimate, the project would cost the city at least $7,000 annually. City officials dismissed this criticism and began work under the new contract, only to prove the critics correct.[48] Expenses outran receipts and forced Savannah to discontinue many of its dredging projects. No matter how badly it needed a competitive river, given the status of its finances, the council resolved that the future of harbor improvement would be left at the discretion of the federal government.[49]

Such a policy was easier to adhere to as long as the federal government was forthcoming with even paltry funds. When the Corps of Engineers spent the 1872 appropriation, all federal work on the harbor stopped. The city had to choose between financial retrenchment and its desire for continued improvement. Ultimately it chose the more aggressive approach and resumed its own dredging operations even as it pushed even harder for the meager federal funding. Because the federal government chose to provide what Savannah considered meager appropriations for the improvement of the harbor, work continued in an unsystematic and haphazard manner for most of the decade.[50]

Justifying huge city outlays became even more difficult following the Panic of 1873. The city's commercial success became dependent on the ability of its agents to convince a Congress gripped by "retrenchment mania" to make the necessary appropriations. The council's decision not to pursue an independent course of harbor improvement as it had in 1866 and 1867 also reflected a new understanding about the city's limited resources. Between 1866 and 1873, the city spent nearly $200,000 on harbor improvement, including the purchase and maintenance of the dredge and associated equipment and payment of the commissioners of pilotage.[51]

In the spring of 1874, in an effort to increase federal funding, Anderson once again traveled to Washington. By now he had become quite familiar with the challenging process and was therefore not surprised to find Georgia's two senators, Thomas Norwood and John B. Gordon, more concerned with other issues and singularly uncooperative. While Gordon demonstrated nominal interest, neither he nor Norwood attended the Georgia delegation meetings regarding the matter. In addition to the lack of response he received from Georgia's representatives, Anderson faced an even greater challenge in trying to loosen congressional purse strings.[52]

Anderson observed that, besides fellow Democrat Alexander Stephens, the most helpful of Georgia's representatives were the Republicans. With Reconstruction winding down, Anderson's attitude toward cooperation with Republicans had softened somewhat. Thanks in part to the work of Andrew Sloan, the Republican representative from Savannah, Congress added another small appropriation of $50,000 to continue work on the harbor. Though the city lost its dredging contract to a Philadelphia company, which further delayed work, city leaders persisted and were later rewarded with two additional appropriations for the year, totaling over $200,000. Following this generous allotment, the federal government appropriated sums much closer to those appropriated in 1872 and 1873. Ultimately, government operations were doing exactly what city operations had been accomplishing—at federal expense. Savannah's boosters certainly desired greater generosity from the federal government, but they came to recognize that they could exert only so much influence. Especially after 1873, they began to accept that the city did not and could not completely control its economic destiny. Until the federal government decided to commit large sums of money to effect a more lasting solution to the problems of the river, improvements would be limited. The port would remain competitive with those of the other southern coastal cities, but Savannah would not become the Great Atlantic Seaport.[53]

City officials, having borrowed to invest in harbor improvement and similar projects, found little solace in a more generous federal government when their own finances were in an alarming state. Expenditures on harbor improvement put a severe strain on the city's treasury. While this was one of the more high-profile projects, it was neither the only nor the largest of the city's expenses.

In the five years between the end of the Civil War and the beginning of 1870, municipal expenditures increased by 200 percent, jumping from just over $396,000 in 1866 to over $1 million in 1870. During the same period, tax collections failed to keep pace, increasing at a rate of only 26 percent. In 1867, the city collected $238,488 in taxes, and 1870 tax revenue increased by just $100,000, a small sum compared to the increase in expenditures. The council made up the difference by issuing bonds and mayors' notes. In any given year, the mayor would issue these notes on the scale of $10,000 to $50,000 a month. Beginning with its first postwar loan in January 1866, the municipal government became almost totally dependent on bond issues and short-term loans, not only for large projects but also ultimately for normal city operations.[54]

During Edward Anderson's 1865–69 tenure in office, he had survived several attempts by the Republican-controlled state legislature to remove him and his entire board of aldermen—the city council—for political intransigence.[55] Conservatives in Mobile and Charleston were not so fortunate. Both cities experienced much more chaotic situations, drifting from military control to Republican control. In those cities, economic policy much more quickly became entangled with political factionalism and racial politics.[56]

As Anderson aggressively fought to maintain conservative political control of the city, he vigorously pursued the improvement of the harbor. Between 1865 and 1869, he had presided over a massive, 90 percent increase in the city's expenses. The city devoted 20 to 30 percent of its annual income just to pay interest on its loans. Expenditures for the police department, fire department, dry culture, city beautification, street paving, and public schools also increased. However, Anderson had managed to keep the funded debt of the city from a concomitant increase. Anderson and his board of aldermen had worked to balance their concerns about rising expenses with the need to protect Savannah's credit and facilitate the city's recovery. As had been the case for many decades, Savannah's leaders quashed their uneasiness and took the long view. Aggressive risk taking had yet to fail them.

When Anderson left office in 1869, the city was over $2 million in debt, but that was only $10,000 more than when he had entered office four years earlier. Anderson remained disturbed by his administration's fiscal record, but the city's growing reliance on bonds and massive spending increases would be eclipsed during the tenure of his successor.[57]

CHAPTER 5

"Knocking It into 'Smithereens'"

RAILROAD RIVALRY, MUNICIPAL POLITICS, AND THE PUBLIC CREDIT

During Edward C. Anderson's 1865–69 tenure as mayor of Savannah, the political landscape had witnessed dramatic change. Control of reconstructing the South passed from President Johnson to Congress. The passage of Black Codes and the election of former prominent Confederates to public office, manifestations of continued southern intransigence, convinced northerners that the federal government needed to take a more activist approach toward effecting tangible and lasting change in the South.[1]

Democrats maintained political control of Savannah even as the city became a center of Republican activity. Though the Republican Party showed early promise, by 1868 it was riddled with factionalism as some African American leaders, like Aaron A. Bradley, refused to accept the dictates of white Republican leaders. Yet, in the fall of 1868, with the presidential election looming, the Democrats remained fearful that the factionalized Republican Party might prove victorious. Tension and anxiety finally erupted in Election Day violence and a so-called insurrection in the Ogeechee district on the outskirts of Savannah a month later. The uprising, precipitated by the overzealousness of Chatham County's sheriff, forced Anderson to request military intervention.[2]

The election for county magistrates and constables in April 1869 provides an example of the new political situation on the coast. Prior to the election, the *Savannah Morning News* provided a breakdown of the county districts. The report implied acceptance of what it foresaw: that several districts would elect African American magistrates and constables.

On the day of the election, the reporter expressed disappointment at the lack of excitement at the polls; there was no violence, no charges of fraud or rumors of voter intimidation. In the districts closest to the city center, out of twenty-four offices, African American candidates won only three. In the Seventh District, which encompassed the islands, referred to as the Skidaway District, African Americans won all three available positions.[3]

The political calm boded well for the fall municipal election and the Democratic Party. The head of the party's municipal ticket in 1869, however, was not Edward Anderson, who opted not to stand for reelection. When he stepped aside, he knew his likely successor would be fellow Democrat John Screven, the president of the Atlantic and Gulf Railroad, the son of Anderson's previous political nemesis, James Screven.

James's son John was born in 1827. Educated early near Philadelphia, he subsequently attended Franklin College (University of Georgia). After he was "invited by the faculty not to return," he received private tutoring at home and studied law. Like his father, he set off on a grand tour of Europe, but he remained only a short time. Homesick and physically sick, he returned to Savannah and was admitted to the bar. At his father's request, though, he gave up law practice to see to the family's large planting interests. His successful management of the family's plantations enabled the elder Screven to pour his time and energy into local politics and railroad construction. However, like his father, John had interests in Savannah, and after his father's death in 1859 he stood for election to the legislature and succeeded James as president of Atlantic and Gulf Railroad. At the outbreak of the Civil War, John Screven, commissioned as a colonel, supervised the erection of fortifications around the city and the obstruction of the Savannah River. For much of the war, however, he attended to his duties as president of the Atlantic and Gulf Railroad before raising several companies for the defense of Savannah in 1864. After the war's end, he worked to revive his railroad, which had halted in the middle of southern Georgia in 1864.[4]

Following a divisive debate over the process of nominations, John Screven, as expected, received the Democratic nomination for mayor.[5] The citizens' nominating meetings had chosen Screven in part because he was less objectionable to a wider cross section of citizens (including poor people, immigrants, and African Americans) than Anderson. Also, he did not carry any taint from the 1868 Election Day violence or the Ogeechee insurrection.[6]

FIGURE 5. John Screven, circa 1870s.
Courtesy of Savannah Yacht Club.

While Reconstruction politics may have partly prompted his nomination, Screven never explained his motives for seeking the mayoralty. It is likely that his railroad interests were paramount, not the city's political woes. In September, John Stoddard, an Atlantic and Gulf Railroad director, congratulated Screven on his nomination, believing that the company would be "highly advantaged" by Screven's mayoral nomination and expecting that it would raise the company's stock value. This, he opined, combined with a good crop, would definitely "put us out of harm's way." Though Screven assured Edward Anderson that the only reason he accepted the nomination was to keep the city out of Radical hands, Anderson groused that while Screven might appear sincere, he knew that Screven had worked hard to secure the nomination "at all costs."[7]

Although Screven seemed well suited to the task of managing the city, his predecessor remained doubtful. Screven's political acceptance boded well for continued Democratic control of the city, but his position as railroad president, which he continued to hold, created the potential for significant complications.[8] Screven's nomination and the 1869 municipal election must be viewed in the context of the highly explosive environment of Reconstruction politics, railroad competition, and the Upcountry's intensified resentment of Savannah and the Central Railroad.

Anderson was not alone in his concern about the consequences of Screven's expected election. Thomas Robb, the Republican port collector, believed Anderson would be more persistent in pressuring the federal government about harbor improvement. Additionally, he was concerned about the effect Screven's election might have on the city's commerce, given the growing animosity between Savannah's two major railroads.[9]

James Waring's support for Anderson was even more surprising. Dating back to seventeenth-century South Carolina, the Waring family had southern roots running as deep as those of the Screvens and much deeper than those of the Andersons. James's father, William Richard Waring, was born in 1787 in South Carolina, graduated from South Carolina College, and studied medicine in Charleston before advancing his medical studies at the University of Pennsylvania. He served as surgeon of the Eighth Regiment Infantry, stationed in Savannah, during the War of 1812. Rather than return to South Carolina, he chose to stay in Savannah.[10] He was elected to several terms as a city alderman beginning in 1818 and served as mayor of Savannah from 1830 to 1832.[11] He remained engaged in the study of medicine, authored "Report to the City Council of Savannah on the Epidemic Disease of 1820," and served as attending physician at the Savannah Poor House and Hospital.[12] Like his colleague Dr. Screven, he championed Savannah's commercial development. He served as a director of the Steam Boat Company of Georgia and was an early investor in the Central Railroad.[13] In 1831, he was one of Savannah's representatives to the internal improvements conventions held in Eatonton and Macon.[14]

William Waring's son James Johnston Waring was born in Savannah in 1829 and attended school in Philadelphia. Educated at Yale, he followed in his father's footsteps and pursued a medical degree from the University of Pennsylvania. After his graduation in 1852, he spent a year at Bleckley Hospital in Philadelphia before holding positions in Dublin and London. His grand tour of Europe ended in 1856 when he returned to the states, married South Carolina native Mary Brewton Alston, and settled in Washington, D.C., in partnership with his uncle, William P. Johnston. There he was elected professor of physiology and obstetrics at the National Medical College.[15] When the war began in 1861, he returned to Savannah, where he was arrested on suspicion of being a spy; he was

FIGURE 6. James Johnston Waring, circa 1880–88.
Courtesy of Georgia Historical Society.

subsequently released, though rumors and suspicion among Savannahians persisted.[16]

In 1861 Waring received an appointment as surgeon in the Provisional
Army of the Confederate States and was assigned to duty in North Carolina. The following year, he narrowly avoided a court-martial for desert-
ing the wounded under his care (he had actually been arranging for the
transport of the wounded at the time he was found absent). An embit-
tered Waring returned to Savannah, taking up residence at 3 Perry Street
(on the corner of Perry and Bull).[17] Immediately after the war, he bought
Sedgebank Plantation, located east of Savannah, from the MacKay family and built a store on the northeast corner of Whitaker and State Streets.
That same year, he was elected alderman.[18]

Waring, who had ties to the Republican Party and had put up bonds for various politically active freedmen, had clashed with Anderson several times.[19] Anderson had been surprised when Waring attempted to convince him to join a fusion ticket with respectable Democrats and Republicans. In a public letter, Waring renounced his "Radical" connection and asked citizens to support a respectable ticket composed of men "who desire to see this town prosperous." In part, his inclination to field an opposition ticket arose from his lack of confidence in John Screven. Anderson too feared that Screven's real motivation had less to do with political aspirations than with the recent rivalry between the city's two major railroads, a rivalry that thus far had been very costly to Screven's company. More than Reconstruction, it provided the backdrop to municipal politics.[20]

The Atlantic and Gulf Railroad suffered less wartime destruction than the Central Railroad. Yet John Screven faced more significant obstacles in the postwar management of his company, especially in acquiring the capital needed to restore the line and extend it to the Gulf. On the eve of the war, the railroad, having built into some of the poorest regions of southwestern Georgia, had yet to show significant profit-making capacity. Unlike the Central, which could expect reasonable income from the reconstruction of its main line, the Atlantic and Gulf Railroad would remain unremunerative until it moved farther west than Thomasville, to capture western trade, and to the south, to siphon off trade from Florida. Given the company's significant existing debt, Screven had to work hard to convince already cautious lenders that his railroad was a sound investment.[21]

Screven eventually obtained a $500,000 mortgage from northern investors on the main line from Savannah to the town of Screven and financed the reconstruction of the main line and its extension westward toward its original destination on the Gulf. By October 1866, as the Central Railroad was completing its main line, the Atlantic and Gulf Railroad had completed a new Florida branch.[22]

Initially, the only common area served by both railroads was Savannah, with depots on opposite sides of the city; the roads did not even connect within the city.[23] Although the main lines did not compete with each other directly, the Atlantic and Gulf Railroad's extension to Bainbridge, Georgia, put that railroad into direct competition with the Southwestern Railroad, a feeder of the Central Railroad and a line in which both the Central and the City of Savannah had invested.[24]

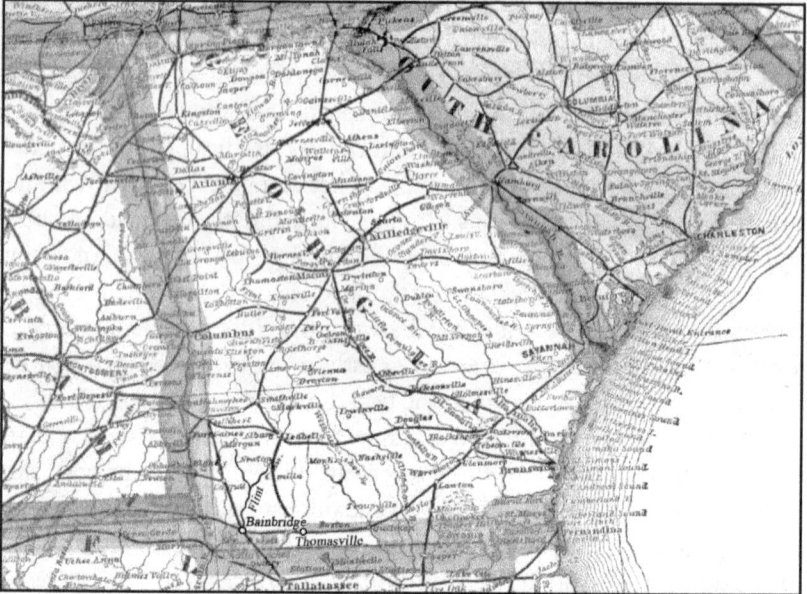

FIGURE 7. Map of Georgia railroads, from *The American Union Railroad Map of the United States, British Possessions, West Indies, Mexico and Central America* (1872). Courtesy of Library of Congress, Geography and Map Division.

In 1868, the Atlantic and Gulf completed its line to Bainbridge on the Flint River. To further its reach in that region, the company contracted with various steamers to collect cotton along the Chattahoochee, Flint, and Apalachicola Rivers to be delivered to Bainbridge. As incentive for shipping products to Savannah via the longer Atlantic and Gulf Railroad route, the company offered low rates. Hoping this new arrangement would make their town an important cotton transfer point, Bainbridge boosters enthusiastically supported the company's venture. Although the all-railroad Southwestern-to-Central-Railroad route was still the fastest, the introduction of reduced rates offered by the Atlantic and Gulf railroad-steamboat combination proved popular enough to divert a portion of the cotton crop to the rail-water route. Shipments to Savannah reached fifteen hundred bales per week. The editor of the *Albany News* attributed the success of the new route to both the reduced rates and the willingness of farmers of western Georgia to accept and use the "laudable competition" to the Central-Southwestern rail combination.[25]

Certainly, Screven's company had done very well with rebuilding efforts. The directors sought to fulfill the antebellum objectives of connecting with Pensacola, Florida, and Mobile, thus linking the grain-growing region of the West with the South Atlantic coast. More importantly, they would be linking Savannah with New Orleans via the Atlantic and Gulf Railroad. In great rhetorical flourish, Screven compared his railroad's advantage to Georgia with that of the Erie Canal to New York. Though these advances initially increased the indebtedness of the road, Screven maintained that the potential justified the cost.[26]

While Savannah merchants also expected to benefit from having two railroads connecting far into the interior, the Central Railroad directors regarded these developments as troublesome. The Atlantic and Gulf Railroad's use of steamers in the area around Bainbridge threatened to siphon off trade from three feeder lines in which the Central Railroad was heavily invested: the Southwestern Railroad, the Muscogee Railroad, and the Mobile and Girard Railroad, which usually carried cotton from their rail heads to Macon and then to Savannah via the Central Railroad.

The Southwestern Railroad, the most directly affected, refused to surrender its traditional market and began lowering its rates to compete. The Atlantic and Gulf Railroad responded in kind, and the resulting rate war was on. In one morning, the price for shipping a bale of cotton dropped from $5.50 a bale to $1.50 a bale. While some shippers complained about the lack of a uniform system of rates, farmers, who previously had few choices in type or cost of transportation, benefited from the competition.[27] The rate war had a ruinous effect on the rail companies, however.

William M. Wadley, president of the Central Railroad, was known for his aggressiveness when dealing with competing lines. Unlike Screven, Wadley was not a native of Savannah or the South. Born in New Hampshire and trained as a blacksmith, Wadley had traveled south looking for an opportunity in railroad construction. He arrived in Savannah in 1834 and found employment building bridges before the Central Railroad hired him. Working his way up through the company ranks, he became superintendent of the railroad in 1849. After a short time supervising the construction of Georgia's state-owned Western and Atlantic Railroad, he returned to the Central Railroad in 1853. Wadley left the Central Railroad again in 1857 to supervise the construction of the Southern Railroad of Mississippi. During the Civil War, the Confederate government recognized his skills in railroad management by appointing him chief of its new Railroad Bureau. During his brief stint in this capacity, he antagonized local authorities and railroad managers by promoting greater centralization and even nationalization of the rail system. During the summer of 1865, Central Railroad directors opened negotiations with Wadley, and by the end of the year he was at the helm of the war-ravaged road. After becoming president of the company, Wadley applied himself to the task of rebuilding the railroad. The Central quickly completed its main line and reestablished its feeder lines into the Black Belt. To eliminate "ruinous competition," Wadley aggressively purchased or leased potential rivals.[28]

Expecting to negotiate with Screven, Wadley initially restrained the Southwestern Railroad and refused to authorize the company to invest in steamships to compete with the Atlantic and Gulf Railroad.[29] However, as the water-rail route diverted more trade from the Central Railroad, Wadley felt pressure to take action. The competitors knew the situation was untenable and sought a compromise. In a so-called "gentlemen's agreement," the companies set a fixed rate on cotton and agreed to end the rate war. Yet within a month, Screven denounced the agreement as unjust, charged the Central with violating the terms, and pulled out of the agreement.[30] When Screven ended the freight-sharing agreement, Wadley reversed his decision, and the Central Railroad backed the Southwestern and Muscogee Railroads' efforts to arrange exclusive contracts with steamers. Another rate war ensued, this time encompassing steamship lines.[31]

To further solidify its position and give it greater flexibility, the Central Railroad officially leased the Southwestern Railroad, which controlled the Muscogee Railroad. It also increased its investment in the Mobile and Girard Railroad and extended it to the Chattahoochee River to waylay some of the freight being sent to the Atlantic and Gulf Railroad terminus at Bainbridge.[32]

The Atlantic and Gulf's alliances challenged the Central's dominance in central Georgia too. Even before the opening salvo of the rate war, the Atlantic and Gulf Railroad had aligned itself with the state-funded Macon and Brunswick Railroad, touted by its supporters as a line with the potential to compete with the Central Railroad.[33] The railroad was slated to cross the Atlantic and Gulf Railroad fifty-one miles from Savannah and about forty miles from Brunswick. Such an alliance directly threatened the Central Railroad's main line from Macon to Savannah.[34] The Central Railroad parried this new threat by endorsing $250,000 of Macon and Western's second mortgage bonds on the condition that the Macon and Western, which ran from Macon to Atlanta, could not enter into any contract with any other company for carrying freight to the Atlantic except by consent of the Central.[35]

The Central's reaction to this competition, while logical and consistent, evoked Upcountry resentment. Farmers viewed every Central Railroad move in defense of its territory and its interest as further evidence of the company's desire to create a giant, statewide monopoly. The *Columbus Daily Sun* scolded the Central Railroad; in going after the Atlantic and Gulf it became an even more "odious and oppressive monopoly." The *Bainbridge Argus* saw an even greater threat: the company's actions threatened to "defy the wishes of the people of the state."[36]

When Screven's company initiated this territorial conflict, the more financially vulnerable Atlantic and Gulf Railroad did not possess the funding, power, alliances, or influence to maintain a long rate war. Two months after the completion of the Bainbridge extension, even as Screven enthusiastically touted the success of the road, the company's financial situation should have given him pause. Extending its lines over 150 miles had increased the company's funded indebtedness to $1,841,200 and floating indebtedness to $512,524. Yet Screven brushed the debts aside, noting that this postwar restoration expense was to be expected. He dismissed investor reluctance as the result of "deep rooted distrust" in any southern securities. The company's own delicate financial situation could not be at fault. With a second mortgage, the company was mortgaged to the hilt.[37]

This was the company's financial situation when Screven initiated the war with the Central Railroad. He had acted in an all-too-common manner in mortgaging the entire railroad in expectation of future success. Already heavily in debt, the company plunged ahead with a scheme that threatened the most powerful and financially solid railroad in the state. Screven's strategy may have been based on the understanding that much of a railroad's cost is fixed and therefore does not change immediately as a result of traffic changes or a short rate war. The company could use the short-term cash from any rate wars to pay the interest on its debts. In addition to reduced rates, the company's use of steamboats provided a geographic advantage. Additionally, Screven expected the anti–Central Railroad feeling among farmers in that region to increase support for his route. In spite of these advantages, the Atlantic and Gulf Railroad was in no condition to sustain a long rate war. With feeder lines spreading out across the state, the Central Railroad propped up the Muscogee and Southwestern Railroads, which took the brunt of the financial hits, and made up for its financial losses elsewhere. The notion that the Atlantic and Gulf Railroad could count on the loyalty of shippers, who disliked the monopolistic practices of the Central Railroad, was also ill-founded. The lowest price, no matter which company offered it, prevailed. Due to the rate war, the Atlantic and Gulf Railroad's already slim profits evaporated.[38]

After Screven rejected yet another compromise negotiated by Mayor Anderson, who owned stock in both companies, the Central found another method of eliminating the threat posed by the Atlantic and Gulf Railroad.[39] The Central's board members knew that the municipal government was carrying a huge debt burden and looking for a way to improve its situation, for the Central Railroad was also a banking company that had provided short-term loans to the municipal government. The investment in the Atlantic and Gulf Railroad constituted one of the city's heaviest financial burdens.

In late December 1868, as officials struggled to meet the city's financial obligations, the Southwestern Railroad, in which the city held stock, made a proposition that seemed to offer deliverance from the financial woes of the past three years. With financial backing from the Central Railroad, the Southwestern offered to purchase the city's stock in several railroads, including the Atlantic and Gulf Railroad, the Augusta and Savannah, and the West Point Railroad, and to assume the onerous interest payments. The Central Railroad directors, the driving force behind the deal, made their intentions clear: they expected the news to force the Atlantic and Gulf Railroad into accepting its previous price-fixing terms, thus ending the rate war. In a letter to city leaders, the Central Railroad asserted that the Southwestern's stock purchase would bring an "amicable and just settlement of the present unhappy and ruinous competition on the part of the Atlantic and Gulf Railroad for business legitimately belonging to the Southwestern Railroad and Central Railroads." Looking beyond the current situation, the directors requested that the city council refrain from "fostering other conflicting lines, and for the purpose of rendering the line now in existence not only self-sustaining but profitable, disclaiming all antagonistic feeling, and desiring to contribute as far as possible to the commercial wealth and prosperity of Savannah."[40]

Acceptance of the offer would reduce the city's debt by over $1 million and relieve the city council of "depressing anxieties," not to mention allow Savannah to "recover the faculty of promoting the material and moral improvement of our City." Mayor Anderson exhorted the aldermen to accept the proposition. They needed little convincing. Most of them welcomed the timely offer, though they took exception to the Central Railroad's attempt to restrain the government's future investments. The act authorizing the transfer addressed this presumption by asserting that the city government was not "bound by its action to refrain from aiding any other line of Railroad that it may deem worthy of such support."[41]

Despite city council's minor note of defiance, the Central Railroad's confidence in the outcome was not misplaced. Within a week of the council's actions, Central Railroad, Southwestern Railroad, and Atlantic and Gulf Railroad representatives adopted a settlement regarding rate differences. Screven disliked the new arrangement and believed the compromise unfair because it cut the Atlantic and Gulf Railroad out of the profitable Columbus and Eufaula business in western Georgia. The Central Railroad victory, however, was only partial. It may have worked out an agreement with the Atlantic and Gulf Railroad, but massive opposition to the stock transfer prevented both the Central Railroad and the city from reaping the fruits of the deal.[42]

Opponents of the stock transfer saw the action as more than merely a potential threat to the Atlantic and Gulf Railroad. For it was not simply another Savannah railroad. They feared that if the Central Railroad gained control of Screven's company, it would be able to destroy the fledgling Macon and Brunswick Railroad and undercut efforts to establish Brunswick as a port to compete with Savannah. When the Macon and Brunswick had applied for state aid in 1866, its promoters successfully played on the prewar animosity toward the Central Railroad. They hyped the Macon and Brunswick Railroad, with its terminus at Brunswick, as a "competing line to Savannah." The popularity of providing competition to the coastal city and the Central convinced the Georgia assemblymen to endorse $10,000 in Macon and Brunswick bonds for every mile it had already completed and the like for every additional mile.[43]

In the summer of 1868, as the Central Railroad and its subsidiary lines battled the Atlantic and Gulf Railroad, the Macon and Brunswick successfully attracted investment to complete the road to Brunswick. Until then, the Macon and Brunswick Railroad planned to use its connection with the Atlantic and Gulf Railroad to transport goods to Savannah. If the stock transfer deal succeeded, the Central could prevent any connection with the Macon and Brunswick. The Macon and Brunswick Railroad, cut off at its origin and deprived of an outlet, would be worthless. The *Columbus Daily Sun* published an editorial expressing its outrage. It maintained that the Central Railroad, already "the most powerful monopoly in the South," had, with this stock purchase, struck at both their rivals, the Macon and Brunswick *and* the Atlantic and Gulf Railroad.[44] Even the *Savannah Morning News* admitted that the Central Railroad could cut off the Macon and Brunswick Railroad and "dispose of its most formidable antagonist, by knocking it into 'smithereens.'"[45]

Georgians did not necessarily begrudge Savannah in trying to ameliorate its heavy debt. Yet they feared that the purchase of the city's stock would, by giving the Central Railroad control over the Atlantic and Gulf Railroad, allow this "odious and oppressive monopoly" to reestablish dominance over the trade of central Georgia and "drive all opposition," including the Macon and Brunswick Railroad, from the territory. The controversy over the stock transfer reawakened the animosity, or what the *Savannah Morning News* termed "unjust prejudice," between Savannah and the Upcountry that had characterized much of their antebellum relations and often centered around the Upcountry's resentment of the Central Railroad and its perceived monopolistic stranglehold on the hinterland.[46]

In the antebellum period, most farmers had initially welcomed the railroads that pushed into the interior. The iron horse reduced handling and transportation costs. With cities and towns competing for railroad connections, one could expect competition to keep shipping costs down. Railroad companies viewed competition differently, especially after they experienced significant losses in rate wars. While rate wars benefited planters and farmers in areas of competing lines, the companies attempted to make up for this loss in areas served by only one line. To maintain a consistent and predictable profit, they responded with gentlemen's agreements, pooling, traffic-sharing and rate agreements, and consolidation. These activities resulted in a rural backlash against the railroads.[47]

In the face of nearly universal criticism, the *Savannah Morning News* defended the council's actions as being in the best interest of the city and the state because the interests of Savannah were "identical with those of the State at large." Critics remained unconvinced, fearing that Savannah's actions would help the Central Railroad establish a monopoly and, by abandoning the Atlantic and Gulf Railroad, destroy the Macon and Brunswick Railroad.[48]

Castigating the "iniquitous scheme," the *Albany News* announced its astonishment that Savannah's elected officials "could be influenced to sell out the best interests of their constituents . . . to the great Central monopoly."⁴⁹ The *Columbus Daily Sun* worried that the "giant monopoly" would, if not stopped, "swallow up all railroad enterprises in the country." Columbus, in southwestern Georgia, may have emphasized the dangers of monopoly in general, but the real concern was its own survival. The Central Railroad's takeover of the Muscogee Railroad had already injured the town. The *Daily Sun* feared that if the Central Railroad prevailed, Columbus might become "more of an insignificant way station" than it already was.⁵⁰

Macon was equally concerned. A contributor to the *Macon Telegraph* cautioned that the Central Railroad would "crush all the efforts to provide the interior with a new line of communication to the coast." The attempt to get control of the Atlantic and Gulf Railroad demonstrated "a desperate spirit of monopoly" that was "dangerous to all interests" of the entire state. Believing itself to be the primary target of discrimination, Columbus maintained its determination to "fight against a monopoly and sustain a competitive line to the Central Railroad."⁵¹ Others made more dramatic predictions. A letter from "Sleepy Hallow" warned of a "great monied railroad monopoly" that, if not checked, would eventually rival the power of the state government. The *Milledgeville Union* opined that many Georgians believed that the Central Railroad had been "too grasping, too selfish, and too monopolizing for the good of the country, or for the good of the city [Savannah] either." The editor advised Savannahians to "endeavor to remove this deep-seated opinion" as it would "greatly enhance their popularity and their interests."⁵²

To prevent the execution of the stock transfer, a few Southwestern Railroad stockholders, who were also heavily invested in both the Macon and Brunswick Railroad and the Atlantic and Gulf Railroad, sued for an injunction against the Southwestern Railroad and the Central Railroad. In January 1869, Judge Carlton B. Cole of the Superior Court, Macon Circuit, granted the injunction on the grounds that the purchase was a "violation of the franchises of these companies, and of general public utility and convenience." The Savannah city council and the Central appealed the decision to the Georgia Supreme Court.⁵³

Although the city remained confident, Cole's injunction meant that the complainants could hold "it over the heads of the city and the railroad companies" until the Supreme Court convened later in the year. In practical terms, the injunction restricted Savannah's municipal officials and the Southwestern Railroad, to which the stock had already been transferred, from casting votes at the Atlantic and Gulf Railroad stockholder meeting in February 1869. This prevented the Central from forcing a change to the Atlantic and Gulf Railroad's board of directors. For the municipal government, the injunction proved more detrimental; it prevented *both* railroad companies from paying interest to the city.[54]

In spite of the threat of the stock transfer, the Central's attack on the Macon and Brunswick Railroad, and the company's declining incomes, Screven and his directors remained defiant. Temporarily out of the Central's clutches, Screven used his annual report delivered at the stockholder meeting in February 1869 to defend the company's decreased receipts. Not surprisingly, he blamed the Central for starting the rate war. As consolation, he bragged that the Atlantic and Gulf Railroad had forced a significant reduction in the Central Railroad's revenue.[55]

Less sanguine stockholders criticized Screven's course. Gazaway B. Lamar, a banker, cotton merchant, and former financial advisor for the Confederate government, chastised Screven for placing the Atlantic and Gulf Railroad in competition with the Central Railroad, and he predicted it would "ruin the Road."[56] Though Screven retained enough support for his reelection and that of his board of directors, several directors and stockholders privately expressed concern about the situation. Stockholder William H. Tison wrote to his business partner, large Central Railroad stockholder William Washington Gordon Jr., that "Screven and his board of directors" were "not railroad men"; they had "played the very devil" in competing with the Central Railroad. He said that Screven's board of directors "should have known better and have done better." The Central Railroad, in Tison's estimation, could "destroy" the Atlantic and Gulf Railroad if Wadley and his directors desired that end.[57]

Savannah's aldermen also worried over Screven's actions. While most limited their opinions to private correspondence and journals, James Waring gave voice to the criticism. Waring, who owned stock in both the Central Railroad and Atlantic and Gulf Railroad, sought to expose the collusion between the Atlantic and Gulf Railroad, the Macon and Brunswick Railroad, and the injunction against the sale of the city's stock. In the summer of 1869, on behalf of the city council, he asked John Screven to provide the council with the text of the Atlantic and Gulf Railroad's agreement with the Macon and Brunswick. Screven, by this time a mayoral aspirant, stalled. Although Waring and his fellow council members rarely found themselves on the same side of any issue, in this instance they all evinced a similar concern that the Atlantic and Gulf Railroad stock transfer would become a political issue to the detriment of the city's finances. Waring strongly urged his fellow aldermen to press the issue re-garding the case immediately.[58]

In September, the council, still awaiting Screven's response, received the latest finance committee report on the status of the injunction case. The committee complained that the Atlantic and Gulf Railroad, which had petitioned for the injunction, was attempting to delay the proceed-ings, having already requested and received three postponements. As a re-sult, the next scheduled hearing would occur after the current aldermen had left office. Expressing the conviction that the incoming board would be less aggressive in its pursuit of the case, the committee warned of im-pending financial danger. If the issue were not resolved soon, the munic-ipal government would be responsible for the maturing railroad stock in November 1869 and February 1870.[59]

While members of the finance committee only hinted at their lack of confidence in a new council headed by Screven and remained vague re-garding its reasoning, Alderman Waring proved more than willing to clar-ify and expand upon the issue. He directly accused the Atlantic and Gulf Railroad's directors of having taken direct part in "embarrassing a trans-action so happy in its results"—specifically, preventing the city from ben-efiting from the sale of its stock. Echoing the finance committee, War-ing warned of impending doom for the transfer, and thus for the city, in the upcoming municipal election. The likely outcome, from Waring's per-spective, was "not only imminent danger" that the city's debt from the At-lantic and Gulf Railroad would be "fastened upon the people as a public policy by their own unwitting act" in electing Screven as mayor but also "that a natural apprehension might arise in the mind that a renewed at-tempt might be made to place the A. G. R. R. stock beyond the reach of the people by trusteeship for a term of years."[60]

Believing that Screven's nomination had been accomplished by a group of "malcontents," Anderson, like Waring, objected to their choice. Ander-son was convinced that Screven planned to use his new political position to advance the interests of his railroad over those of the city. If Screven won the election—and as long as the Democrats remained united in fear of the potential Republican threat, there was little doubt he would be—Anderson believed that Screven would not pursue the stock sale to relieve the city's debt.[61]

Following his official nomination, Screven, despite his lack of authority to do so, called a meeting of the sitting finance committee regarding the payment of the railroad bonds, due in November, right after Screven—already assuming victory—was scheduled to take office. Anderson assented to and attended the meeting but privately carped that he did not think it the duty of his councilmen to provide their services for the presumptive mayor-elect, especially since his board had provided for these bonds in the stock transfer deal with the Central Railroad and Southwestern Railroad, a deal Screven had impeded. Although he complained that Screven should be allowed to "reap the results of his own act," Anderson and his board recognized that such a deed would ultimately injure the city more than Screven personally. The city council thus agreed to ask the Central Railroad and Southwestern Railroad to take action on the bonds. Wadley initially demurred, maintaining that the injunction prevented such an action. However, in mid-October he relented and agreed to endorse a renewal of the bonds.[62]

Anderson's disapproval of Screven's nomination and his lack of confidence in his financial management tempted him to enter the contest. Businessmen, some Republicans, and even Waring, all of whom had opposed Anderson on numerous occasions, urged him to do so. Even though Anderson believed that few prominent citizens were pleased with Screven's nomination, he had to choose between two perceived outcomes: either stay out of the race and ensure Screven's victory, which could possibly lead to mismanagement of the city's finances, or challenge Screven and divide the Democratic (white) vote, which would increase the potential of a Radical Republican victory. Anderson firmly believed that because of the widespread dissatisfaction with the regular ticket, the Republicans, if they applied themselves, could "steal the election." Given the choice of Screven's potential "maladministration" of the city or control by Republicans, Anderson chose what he considered the lesser of two evils. Taking a dim view of the future, whether by Radical Republican or inept rule, a disillusioned Anderson feared Savannah was facing an administration that could bring nothing but failure and be a detriment to the city. Ultimately, as expected, Screven handily won the election. On October 18, 1869, John Screven was sworn into office as mayor of Savannah. With his successful campaign for office in 1869, Screven became a man serving two masters.[63]

CHAPTER 6

"In a Bad Fix"

FUNDING THE APPEARANCE OF
HEALTH AND WEALTH

As president of the Atlantic and Gulf Railroad and mayor of Savannah, John Screven had a doubly vested interest in the city's success. From the moment he took office, Screven demonstrated his commitment to both. His position as mayor safeguarded his presidency of the railroad, which allowed him to forge ahead with his vision of its future. Leaving harbor improvement to Edward Anderson, Screven concentrated more of his time and the city's resources on improving Savannah's physical appearance and infrastructure. Having depended on loans to fund the reconstruction of the Atlantic and Gulf Railroad, Screven used the same strategy in funding new municipal projects.

The projects Screven envisioned were neither original nor superfluous. Several had been demanded by residents for decades, and the booster press strongly supported the efforts, expressing confidence that Savannahians would willingly shoulder a greater tax burden for such improvements. Initial enthusiasm, however, gradually turned to concern as cost overruns added to the city's already significant financial burden, with investment in Screven's company constituting a significant portion of that burden.

Before implementing these new projects, Screven had to deal with servicing Savannah's already staggering debt. He assumed office in October 1869 confident that he had already laid the groundwork for this. The previous city council, at Screven's request, had negotiated an informal agreement with the Southwestern Railroad whereby the company, with the Central Railroad's blessing, had agreed to renew its November bonds. Unfortunately for the new mayor, things did not go as planned. When Screven formally made the request for renewal, the Central Railroad board declined to act, citing its desire to "avoid further complication of these matters," specifically the still-pending injunction case involving the City of Savannah and the Atlantic and Gulf Railroad.[1]

The new council discovered that the city's treasury desperately needed the funds the sale of those railroad bonds would bring. William H. Tison, the new chairman of the finance committee and an Atlantic and Gulf Railroad director, worried about the city's deplorable finances. He confided to William Washington Gordon Jr. that the city was "in a bad fix." Tison was not exaggerating. By December, the city's financial situation had grown even more dire. With only $300 in the city treasury, Savannah could not pay $1,200 interest on a loan from Duncan Sherman and Company. To avoid admitting this, the council continued to delay official authorization of payment. Tison asked Gordon, who was in New York at the time, to raise $100,000 to $200,000 for the city's notes. When Gordon suggested an arrangement using the city's railroad bonds—including the Atlantic and Gulf Railroad bonds—as collateral, Screven balked.[2]

Thwarted on the renewal of the railroad bonds, the new council worked to secure a loan to meet the city's railroad bond obligation. On being queried about the city's finances, Screven responded with a shrug of his shoulders; he remarked simply that he "could not help it." Anderson, a consistent—if private—critic of Screven and the council, pessimistically concluded that there was "a lack of head in the whole concern."[3] Anderson's observations, while undoubtedly cynical and self-serving, were nonetheless accurate. The city's increasingly embarrassing financial situation seemed to confound the new administration. Screven, unlike many other officials in the South (in Mobile and Charleston, for instance), did not have the luxury of blaming the decrepit finances on Radical Republican rule or, given his opposition to the railroad stock transfer deal, on the previous administration. Often, as Democrats regained control of local governments, they conveniently blamed inept or corrupt Republican politicians for whatever financial debacles that emerged, ignoring their collusion in such activities.[4] For instance, even though Charleston Democrats participated in the municipal governments controlled by Republicans and voted for increasing expenditures, they quite willingly blamed the city's $4 million debt on the Republican leadership.[5]

Some Savannahians continued to blame Screven for putting the interests of his railroad company over those of the city. Furthermore, while
Anderson's administration had failed to reduce the city's funded debt,
which stood at roughly $2 million, it had decreased municipal expendi-
tures from the previous year. Blame aside, the council had to deal with the
reality of the debt, and in late December it did so by passing an ordinance
to issue $500,000 in bonds. It thus embarked on the slippery slope of bor-
rowing and set the tone of Screven's three terms as mayor.[6]

In the antebellum period, Savannah's leaders had adopted an elastic view
of what promoted the city's public welfare. Like leaders elsewhere, they
believed that assistance to business and industry would ultimately benefit
the whole community. Savannah's boosters, who sought funding for projects to improve commerce, and residents, who wanted the city to accept
a more active role as public servant, used strikingly similar arguments.
Like the city's booster element, residents who pushed for greater municipal services linked their demands to the promotion of both public and
economic welfare. For instance, in entreating municipal officials to fund
mundane but desirable services, they insisted that enlarging such services
would increase property values and, as a matter of course, the amount the
city could collect in taxes, thus spreading the burden among those who
benefited.

Even boosters, who generally concentrated on projects for the city's
commercial needs, realized they had to develop new ways to compete
with other communities and to adopt modern urban standards. Increasing investor appeal necessitated fostering commerce as well as improving
and expanding pedestrian facilities. This shift in reasoning spurred demands for increased expenditures for a new city market, street paving and
maintenance, dock repair, fire and police protection, public education, water, sewer construction, and other utilities. Whether to meet constituent
demands to improve the city's physical image or to make Savannah more
commercially competitive, city leaders accepted responsibility for offering
both improved quality and a greater quantity of services. In turn, the municipal government sought ways to manage the increased financial strain.[7]

Having temporarily dealt with the city's most immediate financial concerns, Screven and his administration boldly turned to their ambitious internal improvements projects. As president of Savannah's second major

railroad, Screven recognized the importance of maintaining Savannah's competitiveness with rival ports and making it attractive to potential investors. In Savannah, private business was of public concern, and public business was essential to private enterprise. Savannah's leaders were not unusual. As cities grew and became more urbanized, citizens expected their municipal governments to provide services originally left to the individual.[8] This mentality led the new council to proceed with new capital-intensive projects even when Savannah's government could barely pay its current debts.

Continued harbor improvement, a new market building, improved water supply, and new sewer construction constituted the centerpieces of Screven's administration. In addition to the amount the city paid in interest on its loans, these projects accounted for most of the city's expenditures during Screven's tenure. Municipalities commonly resorted to loans to subsidize expensive public improvement projects, and under ideal circumstances they could expect to pay for them over time through taxation. Construction of municipal facilities like public buildings, waterworks, and sewer systems, it was reasoned, would benefit future citizens, who would rightly share in ameliorating the long-term debt burden. Furthermore, these projects would attract more people to the city and bring higher property assessments, which would in turn put more money into the public coffers to cover the future financial burden.[9]

The situation in Savannah, however, was far from ideal. In the 1870s, Savannah's population increased by less than 9 percent, unlike the three prior decades when it had increased an average of 30 percent a decade. The city annually spent from $300,000 to $600,000 more than it collected in taxes. Between 1868 and 1869 its debt increased by about $300,000. Tax receipts and license fees during the same period, in spite of increases in assessments, rose only $234,883, an increase of only 2.2 percent annually. Therefore, while Savannah's debt increased, its tax base did not. Between 1870 and 1871, the amount collected actually decreased. In essence, by the 1870s, fewer citizens carried a heavier tax and debt burden.[10]

One of council's solutions proved extremely shortsighted. Government spending on public projects may have been popular, but higher taxes were not. Increasing property taxes and tax assessments was one of the easiest ways to generate revenue. The choice to depend on property taxes was a common one. Nationally, property taxation constituted a major source of municipal revenue and the primary source of annual revenue increases, in part due to its convenience. Unlike stocks and bonds, assessors could easily track and assess real property. However, local politicians had to walk a fine line.[11] Faced with the very real prospect that residents would balk at radically higher assessments, municipal leaders often chose more politically expedient options.

Therefore, rather than increase property taxes on current residents, Savannah's city council opted to extend the city limits southward to encompass more taxable property. There was little doubt about the purpose. Since the end of the war, the area to the south of the city had experienced steady growth. The administration expected the property and business owners in the newly annexed portion of the city to make up for the shortfall.[12] Increasing Savannah's tax base also likely improved the government's negotiating power in getting loans. The council's decision reflected a typical response for companies and individuals in debt. When individuals and private corporations were faced with impending financial doom, they commonly dealt with the problem by seeking new loans to create the illusion of solvency and in an often-vain attempt to recoup their losses.[13]

Given the municipal government's difficulty in providing adequate municipal services to residents already within the city limits, opposition to the southern extension was overwhelming. In a satirical letter to the editor, "Citizen" remarked that "there should be no well-defined objection . . . to the council extending their wings over them and sending out the tax assessors."[14] Though "Citizen" admitted willingness to pay more taxes if gas and water services were extended, no one expected this to be part of the bargain. In focusing on the immediate income potential of an extension, officials ignored the long-term cost consequences, especially when property owners, as new taxpayers and voters, expected services commensurate with those taxes.[15] Looking at the extension exclusively from an income perspective, city officials seemed unconcerned that the increased limits would ultimately add to the government's overall financial burden. The previous year, Anderson's council had opposed extending the limits because the city could not provide sufficient services. Yet, facing even more adverse economic conditions, Savannah's council opted for annexation to generate income.[16]

As the extension bill wound its way through the legislature, debate continued in the local newspapers. Supporters of the plan, like attorney Henry Bryan, maintained that cities had to tax to extend improvements and that those individuals who lived within the city limits had every right to demand facilities and protection from the city. Although Bryan admitted that any citizen had the right to *ask* for municipal services, he said nothing about any right to *receive* those services. The council frequently refused petitions for various services, citing the city's poor financial condition. Opponents decried the injustice to new city inhabitants, for it was clear that officials expected annexation's benefits to flow in only one direction.[17]

Following legislative approval, the city council quickly passed the ordinance extending the limits of the city and providing for the assessment and levying of taxes. Newly annexed property owners responded by inundating the council with petitions appealing what they considered unjustifiably high property assessments. Invariably these petitions noted the lack of municipal services. Annexation antagonized the new and involuntary taxpayers, and it failed to yield any of the expected monetary benefits in a timely manner.[18]

While citizens and their elected representatives debated, the municipal government faced a nearly empty treasury and impatient creditors threatening to bring suit to recoup debts incurred prior to 1866. The council dealt with the most immediate threat first: it issued more bonds and settled the previous debt on creditors' terms.[19] The council's increasingly common practice of taking out additional short-term loans raised suspicions. Concern mounted over the council's willingness to sanction what some considered extravagant spending, especially with continuing income shortfalls. In less than a year, Screven's administration had entered into contracts in excess of $400,000. In his annual report, Screven defended the spending as necessary to maintain a decent level of services and build the city's infrastructure.[20]

However, Screven's administration was acting without the benefit of hindsight. Savannah had shouldered an increasing debt burden for several decades apparently without significant difficulty. Therefore, even as the council worked to prop up and expand the city's tax base and defend its mounting expenditures, it also made plans to embark on traditionally popular but previously unfunded and underfunded major internal improvement projects. Screven and the aldermen intended to make them a reality in spite of Savanah's precarious financial situation. Even with the taxes collected from the newly extended city limits, the added revenue would not significantly offset the costs of the contemplated projects. Financing those projects and the debt under which Savannah was already laboring required more borrowing.[21]

Screven's council began to implement the projects within its first month of taking office. Resolutions subsequently adopted in October 1869 signaled that the city was ready to initiate its new improvements program—beginning with a $350,000 loan to construct a new market building and then develop a drainage system. There was nothing new about the city's desire for a better drainage system or a new market building. What was new was the willingness of the council to take on more debt to carry them out.[22]

In the 1850s, successive mayors had consistently noted the poor condition of the old market and the need to undertake major repairs or to build a new one, but more pressing issues always intervened.[23] During the early stages of recovery in 1866, Mayor Anderson revived the idea and suggested that the city should look into building a new market house once its finances improved. The *Daily News and Herald* echoed Anderson's conviction: Savannah needed a market house to maintain and enhance the city's reputation. Beyond its importance as an indication of Savannah's recovery, Anderson noted that the old market, constructed in 1822, was in such disrepair that taxpayers would soon be forced to finance costly renovations. He warned that haphazard repairs would ultimately cost the city more than a new building.[24]

The idea of building a new market house remained a perennial demand of the local press. Newspaper editorials confidently proclaimed that Savannah's residents understood its importance to the city's image and would willingly shoulder a greater tax burden to make the new market a reality. After all, project supporters intoned, every small town had a market. Citing concerns about the old market's sanitary safety, the Board of Health also championed the idea.[25] Higher priorities—such as harbor improvement—and a weak treasury, however, precluded the project's immediate implementation. Instead, the city continued to perform only the most necessary repairs. In his annual report, Anderson lamented that city finances were in such disrepair that they just would not "warrant the expenditure involved." Hoping that a market could become a reality by some other means, Anderson suggested the entire project be "turned over to a private enterprise."[26]

Screven's administration, displaying less fiscal restraint than Anderson's, determined to borrow money to accomplish this long-desired project. When the city council received bids in the summer of 1869, it faced the conflict of vision versus reality.[27] Boosters had called for a market befitting their perception of Savannah's status. The council had instructed architects to develop plans for a much more modest structure within a budget of $60,000. Martin P. Mueller and Augustus Schwaab, who had designed the Central Railroad shops and roundhouse in the 1840s, took the fanciful notions of the press much more seriously than the council's conservative cost restrictions; all of their proposals exceeded $200,000. In addition to the basic market facility, their ostentatious plans called for a concert hall, orchestra hall, and gallery. In this clash of vision and practicality, the council ultimately chose something more practical, and ordered the architects to remove the elaborate additions from the plans. The architects pared down the design to one estimated at a more reasonable $75,000.[28]

The old market was razed in the fall of 1870, and workers laid the new cornerstone in December. From the beginning, the process of constructing the market house was fraught with difficulties. Once under construction, the new building suffered from defective material and poor workmanship; several portions had to be demolished and rebuilt. The city council had to account for delays and mediate conflicts between the contractors and the architects, who embarrassed municipal officials by carrying on their dispute in the newspapers. The public feud ultimately resulted in the removal of the architects from the project. All the while, construction dragged on.[29]

After the council fired the architects and replaced them with John Hogg, the city surveyor, work resumed at a much swifter pace. By the spring of 1872, Savannah was preparing to celebrate the opening of its new market, and the aldermen were working on regulations and increased fees to help pay for it. To offset the cost of construction, which vastly exceeded the original estimates, the council imposed daily vendor fees in addition to the usual stall rents. Shortly after the council published the ordinance listing the fees, market vendors lodged protests, which the council summarily rejected.[30] Apparently the *Savannah Morning News* had not consulted the stall renters when it had guaranteed citizen willingness to pay for a new market.

By the time this "magnificent building" that symbolized Savannah's aspirations for a bright future was completed, the project had cost the city over $160,000, more than twice the amount originally budgeted. Furthermore, the market house, in all its grandeur, did not benefit from the superior workmanship of which Screven boasted. Within two years of its completion, it was already in need of major and expensive repairs.[31]

The healthfulness of Savannah remained a perennial concern. Like other southern coastal cities, Savannah had endured cholera, smallpox, and yellow fever epidemics in the antebellum period. Aware of the deleterious effects of these scourges on Savannah's population as well as its reputation and commerce, city leaders implemented some rather innovative solutions. In 1817 the city council took a proactive approach to insulate Savannah from the surrounding disease-breeding areas by instituting a dry culture system. It passed laws prohibiting cultivation of rice within a mile of the city and appropriated $70,000 for purchasing lands and contracting with property owners to switch from rice cultivation within the city limits to some form of dry culture. In spite of planter opposition and concern about its financial cost, which was especially strong after the yellow fever epidemic of 1820, the city continued to expand the project. In the early 1850s, municipal officials provided funds to eliminate the easily flooded swampy land by purchasing Springfield Plantation in the southwestern part of the city and Hutchinson Island across the river.[32]

Residents and physicians continued to debate the success of the dry culture system. Some argued that merely drawing a ring of dry culture around Savannah was insufficient when large areas of stagnant water remained prevalent in the streets. In the 1850s, various citizen groups pushed for the establishment of an efficient urban drainage system. Even though favorable sentiment increased as Savannah suffered two outbreaks of yellow fever, city fathers accomplished little beyond some surveys and proposed master plans.

Following the 1858 outbreak, the second of the decade, city leaders felt compelled to demonstrate greater vigor. They called a public meeting to discuss issuing bonds to create a drainage system and subsequently appointed a committee to investigate the city's various options. The committee recommended filling in low areas and properly grading city streets and proposed the construction of a sewerage system to carry stagnant water and effluent away from Savannah. However, municipal officials never carried out the proposals, a deficiency the city's press regularly lamented, especially during and after periods of heavy rain. What drainage work the council undertook was haphazard and piecemeal. The resulting rudimentary system suffered from lack of planning and proper implementation as well as inferior construction. These halfhearted efforts resulted in a "system" that was improperly graded and lacked sufficient capacity.[33]

After the war, local inhabitants renewed their prewar demands. They complained of the intolerable stench and the "noxious vapors" released from "antiquated, ill-constructed sewers." Backed by Board of Health reports that the stagnant water was "breeding pestilence," citizens petitioned for a better drainage system. Ever mindful of the city council's overarching monetary interests, residents also argued that a comprehensive drainage system would increase property values, thus providing the city with more annual revenue. Louis A. Falligant, a local physician, asserted that construction of even a limited drainage system would be of "infinite advantage" to the city.[34]

In part, Savannah's willingness to carry out these capital improvements was linked to new technological advances. During the mid-nineteenth century, engineers in the United States and Europe developed increasingly sophisticated technological innovations in municipal services, especially those relating to water and drainage. The implementation of more modern sanitation technologies began about 1830, when "the miasmic theory of disease" predominated. Miasmic theory, most clearly articulated by Edwin Chadwick in 1842, held that disease spread via "putrifying wastes and sewer gas." Taking this as the most well-founded science of the day, proactive cities attempted to construct wastewater systems to take the place of privy vaults and cesspools.[35] However, it was not until the 1870s that sanitary engineering as a profession really developed. A growing body of literature produced by trained sanitary professionals began to provide the necessary resources and know-how to construct comprehensive sewer systems.[36]

Savannah's actions reflected a national trend in its efforts regarding improved sewer development. By the 1860s and 1870s, cities recognized the potential benefits of sewer construction and invested in new or expanded systems. Unfortunately, even though significant strides had been made, sanitary engineering was still in its infancy. Most sewer designs continued to focus primarily on carrying surface water, and connections between sewers and individual homes were imperfectly constructed.[37]

Responding to citizen concern and the development of better technology, Edward Anderson's postwar administration investigated the feasibility of a drainage system. In 1868, Anderson asked Jonathan Clarke, an engineer who had worked on the Central Railroad shops, to provide advice on constructing a temporary drain on Duffy Street.[38] In addition to providing the information Anderson requested, Clarke offered his opinion on the city's drainage policy—or rather its lack of one. His advice laid out the basic themes used by future drainage proponents. Savannah was wasting time and money carrying out piecemeal drainage improvements. The city would gain "very good advantages in *real* economy and utility" from "adopting at once a complete system of drainage for the whole city." Savannah would benefit from an "appreciation of prosperity" not to mention "better health," an increased population, and greater wealth. Anderson's administration agreed with Clarke's report but ultimately concluded that the municipal government's financial condition precluded the large expenditure.[39]

The election of a new city council in the fall of 1869 provided the impetus for change. Dr. James P. Screven, John Screven's father, who had defeated Anderson in the 1856 mayoral contest, had been instrumental in implementing what passed for the city's drainage "system" over the following decade. The younger Screven wanted to complete his father's project in spite of the city's financial constraints.

Having been a constant force in pushing for a new sewerage system, the *Savannah Morning News*, ever optimistic about the public's generosity, predicted that taxpayers would most certainly pay for such a worthy project aimed at increasing their health and comfort and contributing to the city's future "material prosperity." Taking the tone of financial expert, the editor assured his readers that, given the project's positive effect, there was no plausible reason why the city government could not very easily carry a debt of at least $3 million. Though the editor was overly optimistic, fanciful even, few residents could deny the need to do something. Whether they were merely concerned with the city's image, with the more practical matter of being able to cross the street in heavy rains, or with the more fearful issue of disease, they all agreed that an efficient drainage system would benefit Savannah and its residents.[40]

In the summer of 1870, the city council contracted with Augustus Schwaab to develop a drainage plan. Schwaab presented the city with several options ranging in cost. He strongly advised against adopting the "cheapest and most efficient" plan—using the Savannah River as the direct outlet above the city. Of primary concern was mixing sewage and waste matter with the waters of the Savannah River, which could then be carried to the waterworks. Having ruled out the Savannah River, Schwaab recommended the Warsaw River, now called the Wilmington River, as the best outlet. It was also the most extensive and expensive option.[41]

The council, unprepared to undertake such extensive construction, demurred on Schwaab's advice and opted for a much more limited project using existing sewers to connect with the Bilbo Canal, which ran behind the Atlantic and Gulf Railroad depot to the southeast of the city. All ef-

fluvium would drain via the main sewer line from West Broad Street east-
ward toward drains built along Broughton Street to East Broad Street,
then south to Bolton Street. From there it would be carried to the Bilbo
Canal and then out to the Savannah River far below the waterworks. Proponents stressed that this less expensive plan would "lay the foundation of
a system to be gradually enlarged" (see fig. 2).[42]

The city council awarded an $80,000 contract for drainage construction
to one of its own, Christopher C. Casey, who resigned his seat to oversee
the project.[43] By the spring of 1871, excavation was well under way. City
leaders quickly discovered the complexity of designing and implementing a comprehensive drainage system. Improving a city's infrastructure required both sufficient funding and a degree of technological expertise. The
latter often proved the more difficult to acquire. Citizens may have welcomed the introduction of modern improvements, but they also discovered the difficulty of implementing this new and imperfect technology.
This was particularly true regarding older cities with preexisting drainage
systems.[44]

The contractors employed almost exclusively African American labor for the construction of these sewers. In part, this was consistent with
prewar practices of the city hiring free blacks and renting enslaved people for work in the Scavenger Department and Street and Lane Department. Enslaved people formed an integral part of the city's infrastructural
growth. Though the *Savannah Morning News* printed article after article on the progress and problems of sewer construction, it only sporadically mentioned the labor force involved and usually did so in a typically
racist manner. It dubbed the construction crew on the Broughton Street
sewer the "African brigade" or "shovel brigade" and marveled at the "sons
of the tropics," their "merry laughter" and "old plantation songs." These
individuals who performed the backbreaking work were probably more
aware than most citizens that the optimistic targeted dates for completion would be impossible to meet.[45]

From the start, unexpected obstacles forced Savannah's engineers and
contractors into constant modification. In some areas, work crews ran into
beds of mudstone; in other areas, water poured into the trenches "as fast as
shovels removed [the dirt]." In November 1870, under the Marine Hospital, workers spent weeks in "quick sand." In addition to having to relocate some sewers, Schwaab had grossly overestimated the capacity of
the Bilbo Canal, which frequently overflowed. These accidents mired the
city in damage claims from property owners, who sought reparations for

property damage and crop destruction. Widening and deepening the canal and rebuilding a culvert through which the canal passed required additional funds. Twice during 1872, portions of the newly constructed embankments of the canal collapsed. Similarly, the new lock gate for the canal failed within a month of its completion. All the while, impatient residents complained of impassable and malodorous streets. As logistical problems caused delays and cost overruns, the *Savannah Morning News* urged patience and reminded citizens of the ultimate benefits.[46]

In spite of complaints about changes, delays, closed streets, property damage, and cost overruns, the "flattering promise" offered by the new drainage system proved very popular and "invited a demand for its expansion." People living in areas not included within the original drainage plan bombarded council with petitions to extend the system. The aldermen were initially generous in granting sewer extensions and connections. In justifying substantial expenditure increases, Screven claimed they had bowed to "well-founded public necessities."[47]

Yet, as problems, and consequently costs, mounted, the city's funds dwindled. Even though the city council had opted for a less expensive system than recommended, the ultimate cost vastly exceeded what anyone had anticipated.[48] The canal construction exhausted the funds the council had borrowed to underwrite it *and* the market building, which had also exceeded its budget. Believing that real estate taxes were already too high and that citizens would not tolerate an increase, regardless of promised benefits, the council once again resorted to loans.[49]

By the late spring of 1872, construction had progressed from the drainage outlet to the city's business district, the original destination. The council rejected requests for further expansion, citing insufficient funds. The councilmen became even more anxious about concluding the projects during the summer of 1872, when they requested that the mayor reduce all public expenditures "not absolutely essential to the public welfare." By the end of the year, the city had spent $375,000 on sewer construction.[50]

In his municipal report Screven indicated his satisfaction with the results of the city's efforts in developing an adequate drainage system. He claimed that the "noxious odors" that "pervaded the city" had entirely disappeared and boasted that the project would prove an excellent supplement to the city's "modern domestic economy" as well as enhance the value of the city's property. He also credited the new drainage system with lowering the city's mortality rate and predicted that it would now be possible for people to remain in the city even during the warm and previously unhealthy months. The new market too Screven commended as a "costly, but valuable improvement." Striking a defensive tone, Screven hailed these projects as "worthy of enlightened public enterprise." He admitted that although the projects were costly, even more so than expected, their expense would have to "be borne sooner or later." Within a few short years, Savannah would pay a much higher price for these laudable achievements.[51]

CHAPTER 7

·•·

"Making a Handle of It"

THE BURDEN OF DEBT

Progress on popular infrastructural projects like the city market and the drainage system failed to protect John Screven from critics who questioned his financial management. His fiscal decisions came under increased scrutiny as both Savannah and the Atlantic and Gulf Railroad experienced unusually serious and similar difficulties. Initially most people seemed to accept the necessity of debt increase for the purpose of progress, expansion, and prosperity. However, when both the city and, coincidentally, the Atlantic and Gulf Railroad required even more funding, Screven became a more frequent target of criticism. No one openly questioned the mayor's personal integrity, but many challenged the wisdom of his financial decisions. By the time he left office in January 1873, both the Atlantic and Gulf Railroad and Savannah were headed for even more difficult times.

The projects carried out by Screven's administration gave Savannah an image of progress. Yet, even as the city presented this favorable impression to outsiders, the municipal government continued to suffer from serious financial shortfalls. The city council attempted to deal with these shortfalls by reducing spending on low-profile services and increasing taxes, which incensed citizens.[1]

During the spring, summer, and early fall of 1871, the *Savannah Morning News* constantly bragged about the increased business activity in the city and the enterprise of "go-ahead" merchants and businessmen. The paper expressed confidence that Savannah would one day be the "metropolis of the South." In 1870, cotton exports had topped $30,000, and banking capital had climbed to $3 million; real estate values had rebounded from the wartime low of $10 million to $15 million. Savannah continued to outpace Mobile and Charleston. While private businesses were indeed active and prosperous, the city treasury, after two years under Screven's administration, was staggering under its massively increased financial burden.[2]

Both of the city's major improvement projects took longer and were more costly than anticipated. For instance, construction of the market was expected to take ninety days. Started in December 1870, it remained incomplete at the close of 1871, and costs were mounting. The drainage project proved even more complicated, time-consuming, and expensive. In the fall of 1871, as both projects crawled toward completion, the municipal government, facing a $265,000 deficit, contemplated issuing more bonds purportedly to complete these capital improvements. Even though the municipal government had the legal authority to issue bonds, the council voted to call a meeting of citizens to explain the necessity for yet another bond issue. Although aldermen clearly recognized the advantage of having the support of the public for such a financial undertaking, they were also concerned about a new bill before the General Assembly aimed at restricting the council's bond-issuing power.[3]

Some Savannah citizens, concerned about the city's mounting debts, had petitioned the legislature to vest the power to issue bonds with the people of Savannah by requiring approval by both a public meeting and a referendum. For large bond issues, the city council commonly called public meetings, though it was not required to do so. The petitioners justified their request by noting the large debt burden—approximately $3 million in bonds, floating debt, and contracts not completed, which required almost half of the city's income to service. The council, terming the state bill "objectionable," instructed the city's representatives to oppose or weaken it.[4]

At the public meeting called to discuss issuing $500,000 more in bonds, Screven addressed Savannah's financial situation and admitted that the expense of these projects was greater than anticipated. But he also touted the accomplishments of his administration in obtaining its goal of meeting the "future as well as the present exigencies of the community." Under the impression that the city needed the funds to continue the public works projects, the meeting's attendees voted in favor of issuing more bonds. However, they also adopted a resolution specifically stipulating that the "bonds shall be exclusively applied to the redemption of the existing floating debt incurred for public improvements now under contract." These included continued harbor improvement, the drainage system already under construction, additional sewer lines under consideration, and the market house. The stated purpose of the bonds may have been to cover the expenses of the most current projects "now in the course of construction and contemplation," but the city used most of the money to remove maturing bonds on much older debts.[5]

Early the next year, in March 1872, the *Savannah Morning News* happily reported that the new bonds were being sold at eighty cents on the dollar, thus proving the "stability" of the city's credit and the "confidence" in Savannah's future; soon capital investment would flow into the city. With such good news regarding the city's credit, the editor optimistically predicted that Savannah was on its way to becoming a "pay-as-you-go" kind of city.[6]

Meanwhile, the General Assembly agreed with the petitioners, who were less sanguine about council's ability to make prudent financial decisions, and amended Savannah's charter. During the 1870s, as concern mounted about municipal extravagance, state legislatures instituted various measures aimed at curbing the borrowing capacity of cities. While some states codified harsh restrictions in their constitutions, Georgia's legislators initially took a more indulgent attitude. The new law required Savannah's council to call a public meeting to authorize future loans and to submit the meeting's decision to a vote by all citizens who owned taxable property within the city limits. The law, however, was passed too late to prevent the city from issuing the $500,000 in bonds, which it did in January 1872.[7]

Efforts to restrain the city council's borrowing power aside, Screven's municipal administration faced fewer challenges than that of his railroad company, as his board of directors proved much more intractable than Savannah's councilmen and citizens. In 1869, when Screven had accepted the nomination for mayor, the Atlantic and Gulf Railroad directors acceded to the necessity of this move. The single most obvious advantage of Screven's dual role was that it allowed him to vote the city's large amount of stock at the annual Atlantic and Gulf Railroad stockholders' meeting, thereby insuring his position as president of the company.[8]

Although the Atlantic and Gulf Railroad had spearheaded the legal opposition to the Central Railroad's stock transfer deal, the Georgia Su-

preme Court, rather than Screven, had prevented the Central Railroad's
hostile takeover of the Atlantic and Gulf Railroad. Neither his position as
mayor nor his presidency of the Atlantic and Gulf Railroad had stopped
the Central Railroad's lease of the Macon and Western, which cut the
Macon and Brunswick Railroad out of the freight from Atlanta to Macon. And finally, when the Central Railroad informed the Atlantic and
Gulf Railroad and Macon and Brunswick Railroad that it planned to ter-
minate its agreement regarding freight transported via Macon, it seemed
that Screven's position as mayor gained his company very little.

When Screven considered running for reelection, his directors clearly
conveyed their opposition. For instance, Dr. William Duncan warned
Screven that another term would "seriously affect the interests of the
Road." He worried that Screven's mayoral duties prevented him from
managing the company, leaving them all to his assistant, whom Duncan
complained was not very "economical." A. T. MacIntyre, a director from
Thomasville, told a colleague that it would be "unwise" for Screven to accept the nomination unless he declined the presidency of the railroad.
Nevertheless, needing the city's stock to maintain control of the company,
Screven was determined to retain both roles. In October 1870 his name
headed all but one of the municipal tickets published, and he easily won
reelection.[9]

By early 1871, Screven's management of the Atlantic and Gulf Railroad
faced more determined opposition. R. H. Hardaway, who oversaw the
day-to-day operations of the road in Screven's stead, urged him to refocus
his priorities. He warned Screven that various stockholders from western
Georgia contemplated "making a handle of it" against Screven's leadership by supporting a challenger for the company's presidency. Hardaway
may have advised Screven to pay more attention to his presidential duties,
but he concluded his letter of warning with the following comment: "Be
sure to have the City stock ready to vote in case of emergency."[10]

Screven took Hardaway's admonition seriously. He begged Edward
Anderson not to resign as a director before the annual meeting as he
feared the opposition might be successful in efforts to "oust" him. In part,
because he believed Screven's opponents were Republicans, Anderson
agreed to delay his resignation until after the stockholders' meeting. Ultimately Screven and his entire board retained their positions. Anderson noted in his diary that, "but for the stock owned by the City, Screven
would have lost his seat." While Screven told stockholders that the prospects of the company were "altogether favorable" for the future, Anderson

privately observed that the Atlantic and Gulf Railroad's stock had plummeted to a "ridiculously low" level.[11]

The directors remained silent about their concerns at the stockholders' meeting, but they clearly viewed Screven as more of a liability than an asset to the company. Worried over the company's financial problems, the directors became more emphatic in pushing Screven to focus his energies on running the company. In May 1871, they had appointed a committee to examine the condition of the company, and the committee issued a less-than-optimistic report a month later. Due to "bad management," the road was going into debt faster than necessary. Stopping short of charging Screven with purposeful mismanagement, the committee asserted that the company was suffering from the president's lack of attention. In addressing the company's finances, it proposed a reduction of 20 percent for all wages and the elimination of various facilities across the state. The committee submitted the plan to Screven with the threat that if he ignored the report, he would have to look elsewhere for "more sanguine less timorous coadjusters than we find ourselves to be."[12]

Screven responded indirectly. He reminded the directors that he had pursued his civic chair "with a view to protecting the higher interests of the Atlantic and Gulf Railroad Company." Although Screven admitted the need to economize, he rejected the committee's retrenchment plans, believing they would lead to further "financial embarrassment" for the company.[13]

When the Democratic nominating committee once again chose Screven to head its municipal ticket, Screven, knowing his board disapproved, played coy. He told the committee that it would have to seek permission for his nomination directly from the Atlantic and Gulf Railroad board. Ultimately the board reluctantly consented, having received a vague assurance that Screven would resign at the earliest possible moment, though after the stockholder meeting. Screven accepted the mayoral nomination and in the fall of 1871 was subsequently elected for a third term.[14]

In spite of their acquiescence to Screven's renomination, his directors remained apprehensive. A. T. MacIntyre cautioned Screven that he would face trouble again at the next stockholder meeting. Hardaway had similar concerns, warning that opponents had used Screven's divided duties against him at the previous stockholder meeting and would have resulted in his defeat but for the shares controlled by the city and voted by Screven. John Stoddard, while he understood Screven's political motivations, counseled that the decision might very well be "damaging" to the railroad, which was suffering from depreciating stock values and increased indebtedness. The company needed the "undivided attention of its President" and radical changes in its management to "escape bankruptcy."[15]

More ominously, Stoddard warned Screven that the directors would "not fail to carry out" required measures to save the company from bankruptcy without increasing "our indebtedness," even if that meant a change in management from the top down. As a result of his political decision, Screven faced a revolt of his own directors. The directors had delayed taking further action on the proposed retrenchment measures, hoping that Screven, having agreed to surrender the mayoralty, would devote his energies to the management of the company. However, with Screven still firmly in the mayor's seat, the board determined to move ahead with its plans. This threat engaged Screven's full, if temporary, attention.[16]

He dealt with the most immediate problem first. Ignoring the board's concern over increasing its indebtedness, he secured a $2 million loan through Eugene Kelly, a New York banker and president of the Southern Bank of Georgia, thus narrowly avoiding the company's bankruptcy. The loan, however, failed to solve the underlying problems. Therefore, about a month before the scheduled stockholder meeting, Screven's directors issued an ultimatum. Citing "accumulating emergencies" and "overmastering circumstances," they suggested that he agree to severe retrenchment measures and resign his "civic chair."[17]

Privately Screven assured Charles Green, one of the retrenchment-minded directors and president of the Savannah Chamber of Commerce, that he planned to resign no later than March 1872 and that he would "carry out the retrenchment policy as far as practicable." The directors, however, criticized his official response as "indefinite and unsatisfactory." They demanded written assurance that the retrenchment policy would be instituted.[18] Given the potential problems that the resignation of almost half his directors would create, especially so close to the annual stockholders' meeting, Screven told them he would resign his position as mayor but not before the shareholders' meeting scheduled for mid-February and no later than March 1.[19]

Concerning the directors' demands regarding retrenchment, Screven remained vague. Believing that the measures would lead to "unfavorable results," he suggested that the board reconsider. Initially the directors remained firm on the demands and even went so far as to advise Screven to begin his search for six new directors.[20] Screven informed William Hunter, the chairman of the city council's finance committee, of the board's demands. Hunter began working with them to come up with a less drastic solution. Over the next few weeks, they worked out a compromise seemingly acceptable to all parties, and Screven received approval to develop his own retrenchment plans.[21] An additional factor may have been an unofficial offer for the lease of the entire line by an unnamed third party. At the meeting of stockholders, the controversy involving Screven and his board did not surface. The directors allowed themselves to be renominated and were reelected.[22]

As the directors awaited an official lease offer, the *Savannah Morning News* shocked its readers when it announced Mayor Screven's resignation, which he had given to Alderman Hunter nearly a month earlier. Screven's public letter to the *Morning News* cited "the urgent responsibilities of other official duties in which the city and community are deeply interested."[23] His timing could not have been worse. Screven's actions caught many by surprise, including his own board of directors. Even John Stoddard, who had been adamant that Screven resign as mayor, panicked and used a third party to urge Screven to reconsider his resignation because it was probable that the Atlantic and Gulf Railroad would be leased. In that event, the presidency of the road could become vacant, and he could possibly lose both offices and thus control over the city's stock. The city councilmen also urged Screven to reconsider, fearing that his resignation would do "fatal injury to the best interests of the City." Given the situation with both the city and the railroad, Screven acquiesced.[24]

This was either a shrewd move on Screven's part or a really foolish one. Screven's resignation, coinciding as it did with the lease offer, threw his board of directors and the city into a panic. It seemed as if he had knowingly refused to delay his resignation to call his board's bluff. Or he may have resigned, as he stated, to devote his full attention to the company so that he could prevent the lease, which he opposed. Following the board's indefinite postponement regarding the lease, Screven arranged for more funding to allow the company to pay its bills. Several directors, possibly feeling they had been outmaneuvered, sent Screven a notice that they believed he intended "no such change" in his management of the railroad, and, therefore, "further connection" with the board would be "fruitful of embarrassment to its counsels and anxiety to ourselves." With that, six of the fifteen board members resigned. Screven tried to put the best light on the event to Hardaway when he stated that it was a "relief to be rid of the miserable spirit" that had pervaded previous board meetings.[25]

The resignation of the directors, however, failed to end the controversy. Instead, it became the central focus of municipal politics. In early
June, while Screven was out of the city, James Waring petitioned the city
council to investigate what had led to the resignation of several Atlantic and Gulf Railroad directors. The aldermen tabled the petition, maintaining that, in spite of the city's considerable investment in the company,
the municipal government had nothing to do with the matter. However,
when Screven returned and learned of Waring's charges, he demanded
that the council conduct a full hearing so that he could respond to the
"discreditable" statements. A special committee of council investigated the
charges and reported that it had found no wrongdoing on Screven's part.
The council received the committee's report as information.[26]

Screven, however, remained unsatisfied with the council's decision, believing that its failure to officially adopt the report left doubt as to the
propriety of his actions. He called a meeting of his company's new board
of directors, who then issued a call for a special meeting of the stockholders to further exculpate their president. By the time the meeting
took place, Screven and his board, in Anderson's view, had "mustered up
their forces for the occasion." They had the meeting well in hand and
made sure that the attendees understood that the directors who had resigned had not done so on principle; they had acted in bad faith toward
the president. Rather than resign because Screven had failed to fulfill his
promises, they had done so because they had supported the failed lease
of the railroad.[27]

Waring, himself a stockholder in the company, faced an unfriendly audience. He alleged that the company was badly managed and warned that
if certain practices were not changed, it would wind up in bankruptcy. He
charged that Screven had paid both the interest on the company's debt
and the employee salaries in July with borrowed money. He further surprised the meeting's attendees by declaring that Screven had used the
City of Savannah's twenty-year bond issue to cover up a $500,000 loan to
the Atlantic and Gulf Railroad. When Waring demanded that Screven
provide proof to the contrary, Screven's supporters stated that the company was not required to air its private business in public, which, considering the purpose of the meeting, was rather ironic. Waring stated that he
took the silence to be an admission of guilt. From that point, the meeting
dissolved into a Waring-bashing affair. Ultimately, the attendees adopted
resolutions exonerating Screven from any wrongdoing.[28]

The display of indignation on the part of Screven and his supporters was too much even for Edward Anderson, Waring's long-time foe. Anderson remarked in his journal that prejudice against Waring overshadowed everything else. Waring, according to Anderson, was "hissed, interrupted and crowded in every way." He stated that Screven's supporters had acted toward Waring "so as to excite indignation in the minds of many who have hitherto looked upon him with unfriendliness." A letter from "Paul Pry" published in the *Morning News* a few days later condemned Waring for his actions, claiming that they were motivated by personal animosity. However, the author also sustained Waring's statistics.[29] Despite the stockholder vote of confidence in the company's management, financial problems plagued the Atlantic and Gulf Railroad Company at every turn. Only a month after the meeting, Screven applied to the state for aid, which was ultimately refused.[30]

That same year, 1872, the municipal government found itself similarly in a precarious financial condition in spite of its recent loan. The $400,000 in municipal bonds from the early 1872 issue for public improvements were either never sold or seemingly evaporated. It is possible that Screven used most of it to pay off the interest on previous loans; it is also possible that Waring's charges were correct. In midsummer, the city council discharged a number of laborers and suspended various public projects. By the fall, Screven, forced to justify shortfalls, blamed decreased tax receipts, the direct result of council's willingness to bow to citizen demand to reduce

TABLE 1. City of Savannah Tax Receipts and Expenditures, 1866–76

Year	Tax Receipts	Expenditures	Net
1866	$170,069.77	$396,644.42	−$226,574.65
1867	$238,488.34	$688,383.62	−$449,895.28
1869	$331,985.34	$749,794.99	−$417,809.65
1870	$382,216.37	$849,915.16	−$467,698.79
1870	$382,216.37	$849,915.16	−$467,698.79
1871	$383,758.92	$984,628.41	−$600,869.49
1872	$432,122.60	$1,239,066.07	−$806,943.47
1873	$350,325.75	$649,689.03	−$299,363.28
1874	$392,912.18	$720,986.51	−$328,074.33
1875	$398,367.95	$598,745.57	−$200,377.62
1876	$325,589.66	$615,809.61	−$290,219.95
TOTAL	$4,093,288.83	$9,143,888.27	−$5,050,599.44

Source: City of Savannah Mayors' Reports, 1866–76.

TABLE 2. Debt, Receipts, and Expenditures, City of Savannah, 1854–90

Year	Funded Debt	Interest Payments	Floating Debt	Money Borrowed on Mayors' Notes	Net Receipts	Total Expenditures	Notes and Outstanding Obligations
1854	$10,124,135.50	$70,232.15	not stated	$112,650.00	$235,598.54	$545,542.62	$81,650.00
1855	$1,203,624.50	$82,916.12	$24,000.00	$221,800.00	$256,256.34	$785,347.77	$222,800.00
1856	$1,675,124.50	$93,301.03	$13,000.00	$124,751.77	$257,475.76	$753,354.82	$135,500.00
1857	$1,776,112.50	$101,324.25	—	$37,500.00	$268,861.61	$817,377.37	$56,751.77
1858	$1,872,840.00	$132,621.94	$64,180.00	$277,000.00	$258,378.95	$654,961.87	$237,000.00
1859	$1,872,840.00	$96,721.86	$4,180.00	$325,000.00	$285,306.99	$709,578.84	$365,000.00
1860	$1,872,840.00	$141,220.61	$59,180.00	$320,000.00	$301,944.66	$728,997.63	$265,000.00
1861	$1,872,840.00	$133,335.56	$109,180.00	$527,000.00	$281,846.71	$804,907.25	$477,000.00
1862	$1,814,840.00	$111,051.87	—	$475,000.00	$272,822.22	$940,105.49	$580,000.00
1863	$1,814,840.00	$86,959.00	—	$80,000.00	$473,503.83	$505,802.93	$80,000.00
1864	—	—	—	—	—	—	—
1865	—	—	—	—	—	—	—
1866	$2,041,940.00	$128,777.02	—	—	$394,548.02	$367,359.16	$2,714.66
1867	$2,111,440.00	$185,499.87	—	$202,000.00	$452,078.36	$685,163.03	$146,000.00
1868	$2,048,740.00	$164,130.25	$46,321.16	$305,619.71	$491,489.42	$793,850.63	$313,000.00
1869	$2,052,380.00	$154,082.58	$47,212.50	$252,712.50	$490,623.40	$745,084.50	$247,000.00
1870	$2,318,640.00	$177,251.41	$112,000.00	$394,462.25	$549,866.51	$1,178,589.91	$329,674.75
1871	$2,817,140.00	$170,278.25	$130,383.06	$841,496.18	$567,005.36	$1,807,741.53	$823,113.12
1872	$3,300,140.00	$300,984.00	$303,366.93	$1,444,185.40	$641,485.37	$2,568,817.19	$1,329,766.12
1873	$3,700,140.00	$257,084.47	$30,500.00	$255,000.00	$562,565.67	$894,506.37	$244,802.34
1874	$3,600,140.00	$252,944.97	$111,358.00	$111,224.65	$584,712.95	$975,991.61	$255,005.00
1875	$3,572,800.00	$263,916.00	$147,826.00	$134,601.69	$563,077.31	$685,310.64	$111,358.65
1876	$3,473,800.00	$208,536.00	$226,891.00	$226,891.01	$440,841.03	$672,015.00	$147,826.69
1877	$3,472,800.00	$99,563.00	$437,281.00	$219,871.82	$467,245.77	$615,176.41	$226,891.01
1878	$3,486,400.00	$164,517.00	$292,996.00	$110,912.24	$594,902.44	$722,445.88	$219,871.82
1879	$3,399,300.00	$206,895.00	$167,706.00	$50,000.00	$492,826.12	$591,111.01	$110,912.24
1880	$3,499,100.00	$193,627.00	$99,447.00	—	$484,381.81	$486,084.06	—
1881	$3,485,000.00	$192,902.00	$74,895.00	—	$541,588.70	$512,741.77	—

1882	$3,473,000.00	$192,226.00	$131,348.00	$11,282.35	$517,638.45	$554,124.17	$18,279.95
1883	$3,457,600.00	$161,535.00	$43,367.00	—	$666,151.94	$635,751.75	$42,367.96
1884	$3,812,100.00	$191,290.00	—	—	$630,815.23	$661,539.64	—
1885	$3,737,200.00	$209,989.00	—	—	$577,019.64	$595,325.22	—
1886	$3,708,700.00	$188,146.00	—	—	$580,840.17	$618,928.16	—
1887	$3,676,400.00	$188,166.00	—	—	$590,828.42	$582,839.19	—
1888	$3,645,900.00	$178,971.00	—	—	$656,262.61	$637,340.99	—
1889	$3,615,850.00	$182,344.00	—	—	$667,060.18	$680,054.50	—
1890	$3,585,850.00	$178,366.00	—	—	$793,081.35	$699,084.21	—

Source: City of Savannah Mayors' Reports, 1854–90.

taxes on goods, wares, and merchandise, as well as the elimination of the gross sales tax. Yet, mirroring his stubborn stance against his company's retrenchment, Screven opposed raising taxes and maintained that the current improvements would benefit future citizens who had a duty to share the burden. Instead the council chose the by-now-familiar alternative.[31]

On January 1, 1873, the finance committee reported that it had underestimated the cost of the various public improvements the city had undertaken. To complete these projects and to "protect the public credit," it recommended that the council initiate legal steps to provide for the issuance of at least $500,000 more in bonds. The process had been complicated by the new legislative restrictions on the council's ability to issue bonds, which required both a public meeting and a subsequent vote.[32]

That same month, freeholders (property owners) and taxpayers met to discuss the council's bond request. The council's rapid action gave the impression that it wanted to issue bonds quickly. Given that the current council members would be leaving office within weeks, some attendees voiced suspicions about the real motives. They were even more curious to learn where funds from the last issuance had gone and why the citizens were just now being informed about the situation. William Basinger, a local attorney speaking on behalf of the council, claimed that the councilmen had simply made the mistake of not asking for more in the original issuance.[33]

Waring, who had clashed with Screven on many occasions and had a poor opinion of his ability, urged greater caution and advocated a careful study of the city's finances. Solomon Cohen, another local attorney who had served on the council several times before the war and was a current aspirant for mayoral office, agreed with Waring and put forth resolutions reflecting this attitude. Cohen ranted that Screven wanted citizens to accept the unbelievable assertion that a "small mistake" had been made that gave the city a "deficit of $400,000." Rather than borrow more money, Cohen advocated working toward the "extinction of the debt" through serious retrenchment. He proposed referring the entire matter to the next administration, which would be given the authority to investigate the causes of the deficit and develop a plan to deal with it. Henry C. Wayne, a Republican commission merchant and former commissioner for the U.S. Circuit Court, offered a resolution to establish a freeholder committee to investigate the city's finances, which was subsequently adopted. The attendees, therefore, rather than bowing to the council's desire for hasty action, opted to appoint a committee of seven freeholders to investigate and issue a report.[34]

This freeholder meeting and the subsequent investigation occurred in the midst of the city's municipal election. Thus, the condition of the city's finances and the responsibility for them finally became a significant part of the public debate. While citizens had accepted the 1872 bond measure, for many it was inconceivable that the city had spent over $350,000 in such a short time. More importantly, they expressed their uneasiness with their officials' vague explanations of exactly how the money had been spent. No doubt, Waring's charges against Screven the previous summer were given greater credence. "M" gave voice to this frustration in his letter to the *Savannah Morning News*, complaining that officials had convinced citizens to spend thousands of dollars to attract cotton to the city and, as a result, they had paid little attention to anything else. Railing against the mistake of mortgaging the future, "M" criticized the philosophy of keeping up the "appearance of wealth and prosperity when our expenses are double our income and every dollar that we own is greatly mortgaged." "M" bluntly asked, "If we cannot pay it now, how do you think we can pay it in thirty years," especially when there were no plans for ultimate repayment? Others, who wanted to see a change in the management of the city's finances, joined "M." Foreshadowing citizen reluctance to shoulder heavier burdens, "Tax-payer" asserted that the debts should not be paid through taxation, contending that bonds should be issued for the sole purpose of paying off the debts. Other *Morning News* contributors advocated various inadequate measures for retrenchment, including increasing the mayor's duties, decreasing the number of clerks and assistants, and creating a workhouse.[35]

As the municipal election approached, the city's financial condition dominated the discussion. "Sentinel" called for the election of men of "known ability and independence" who would be capable of relieving the city of "its present financial embarrassments." "Sentinel" went on to suggest a municipal ticket headed by Edward Anderson. The former mayor knew his nomination was likely. In November 1872, various Democratic and white Republican representatives initiated discussions with him regarding a possible return to the mayor's office. Republican Henry C. Wayne realized that in spite of the growing displeasure with Screven, his party could not run a successful ticket on its own. So he sought to convince Anderson to run on a fusion ticket that included Democrats and a few "respectable Republicans." Anderson, although he gave Wayne no definite answer, did not believe there were enough Republicans registered in the city to make a difference.[36]

Although the Democratic Executive Committee nominated Anderson on January 9, it delayed the announcement of its choice until a public meeting a mere two days before the election. By that time, the committee had met with Anderson and gained his preferences on nominees for aldermen—a group of men that he and his backers "felt they could manage." Waring Russell, who headed one of the more powerful local political cliques, had already assured Anderson of an easy victory because Russell claimed he had gained possession of the Radicals' registry tickets.[37]

Anderson did not think he needed the Russell family's help as he believed "everybody wants me to run," including Republicans, Democrats, and independents. Anderson's nomination, in spite of his confident assertions, did not please all citizens. Solomon Cohen ran on an opposition "People's Ticket." Cohen certainly had plenty of experience in city government. In the two decades before the Civil War, he had served five terms on the city council and one as mayor pro tem. Before that he had served as a federal district attorney for the South Georgia District. Although the fragmented Republican Party tried to field a candidate, by the day of the election they had formed an unofficial alliance with Cohen's supporters.[38]

Though Anderson believed he was universally popular, and the *Savannah Morning News* gave him its full support, the election results told a different story. At the end of the voting, those monitoring the polls asserted their belief that Cohen had received the majority of the votes. Nevertheless, the official count showed that Anderson had prevailed. Rather than a sweeping victory, however, Anderson eked out his win with a mere two-hundred-vote majority out of the eighteen hundred votes cast, possibly thanks to Russell's illegal contribution. By Anderson's reckoning, *he* was not the problem. Rather, the problem was the perceived Russell machine working on his behalf. To Anderson's way of thinking, Cohen, running on the "People's Ticket," had gained the support of the "Republicans, Irish, Negroes, Jews, and those hostile to the Russells." However, given that both Anderson and Cohen agreed that the municipal government had to curb its spending and find a way to pay down its debt, the choices that citizens made seemed to be one of personality rather than platform.

Savannah could boast of continued local conservative control, increased exports due to an improved harbor, a new drainage system to improve the health of the city, a new waterworks to supply more water, and a new market building to demonstrate the city's elevated status. Local leaders seemed to be looking to the future, and, in doing so, providing for citizen's needs. Yet each new municipal undertaking forced city leaders to tone down their grandiose aspirations and visions to accommodate economic reality. Unfortunately for Savannah, the decision to undertake expensive projects with limited budgets proved doubly detrimental. The base cost of these ventures put the city treasury deeper in debt. Additionally, carrying them out on the cheap saddled Savannah not only with a larger debt but also with defective structures on which it eventually had to expend additional funds. The choices Screven and his administration made certainly demonstrated their acceptance of the city's role as public servant. When Screven's third term ended, the city was deeper in debt than it had ever been (see tables 1 and 2).[39] The resultant staggering debt left Anderson's administration with little choice but to fight a rearguard action against default and bankruptcy.

CHAPTER 8

"To Protect the Public Credit"

ECONOMIC PANIC AND
POLITICAL CHICANERY

The same day the *Savannah Morning News* reported the election results and declared Edward Anderson the victor in the mayoral contest in January 1873, it published a letter from "Taxpayer" urging serious retrenchment measures. And indeed, retrenchment became the order of the day. Having often and bitterly complained about Screven's extravagance, Anderson and his new council acted at once to put an end to the city's "criminal waste of money." The council, in a frenzy of retrenchment, abolished offices, cut salaries, and eliminated contracts.[1]

As the new council sought ways to reduce spending, the previously appointed seven-man citizen committee, having spent six weeks debating various retrenchment measures and listening to citizen concerns about overtaxation and unfair real estate assessments, reported its findings in early March 1873. In spite of what was supposed to be a thorough investigation, the committee published a report that was more general than specific. It provided frustratingly few details regarding the municipal expenditures of the previous three years. Although a majority of the committee members claimed to have opposed issuing more bonds and further increasing the city's debt, they professed their inability to fathom any other solution to the city's financial predicament. In the end, the committee recommended that the council issue $400,000 in bonds specifically "to meet [the] outstanding indebtedness of the city which has been incurred over the past three years and to protect the public credit." For various loans due within the next few years, the committee strongly recommended that the council create a sinking fund.[2] The council received the report, concurred with the recommendation to issue bonds, and immediately began the process. As required by law, Anderson called for a vote of the taxpayers on the measure. The election, held one month later, produced a sparse turnout, and the vote was 158 to 11 in favor of issuing bonds. Following the referendum, the council produced an ordinance authorizing the mayor to do so. This last measure increased the city's bonded indebtedness to more than $1.5 million.[3]

Having taken care of the immediate shortfalls, Anderson's administration quickly lost interest in retrenchment. Boosters continued promoting ambitious schemes that promised to bring the fruits of economic prosperity to Savannah. While refraining from Screven's penchant for infrastructural improvements, they touted inland waterway routes from the west, railroad extensions, and continued harbor improvement. Despite sporadic calls for Savannah to reduce expenditures and provide for the reduction of its debt, the city council, having borrowed its way out of the immediate crisis, did little.[4]

Confidence that Savannah would eventually reap the rewards of prosperity received a major shock when events beyond the city's control demonstrated the danger of mortgaging the future. Whatever grand schemes city officials may have developed to ensure Savannah's economic success, they could not isolate the city from the radical changes in an unstable national economy. Borrowing against future success was not the decision of a few foolhardy individuals; it was common practice. Because credit was easy, cities, corporations, and individuals overextended themselves. Locally, officials based their financial decisions in part on their confidence in the city's economic future and in part on the assumption that they largely controlled that future. Using credit allowed cities to do so much more than they could through taxation, but it also made them vulnerable during severe economic fluctuations.[5] The imprudence of such notions became apparent in the fall of 1873.

In September 1873, Jay Cooke and Company, a leading investment bank that was financing the Northern Pacific Railroad, the second transcontinental line, failed. Cooke, like so many of his contemporaries, had overextended himself. The failure of his company set off a general national panic. Stock values plummeted, and the New York Stock Exchange closed for ten days. News of Cooke's failure reached Savannah on Sep-

tember 19, 1873. In spite of bank suspensions across the nation, no one yet
had an appreciation for the extent of the financial collapse or the duration
of its consequences.[6]

In a hopeful tone, the *Savannah Morning News* surmised that the
tightness would be "scarcely felt by our merchants." After all, it was to
be expected that the economy might get rocky at times. Attempting to
maintain this confidence, the newspaper optimistically predicted that
economic mayhem in the North would benefit the South since the "con-
tingencies" that caused the financial problem in the North did not "extend
here." There was "no necessity for a panic among the [southern] people."[7]
This attempt to calm fears failed. A day after the *Morning News* confidently reported that the panic had certainly passed, several local banks
experienced runs. Although the paper asserted that the runs consisted
mostly of laboring men with small sums of money, two banks paid out an
estimated $70,000. Some banks chose to suspend payments and issue cer-
tified checks while others resolved to continue doing business as long as
possible.[8]

Denial and minimization of the extent of the recession were residual
effects of the belief that local decisions could insulate the city from national economic cycles. In essence, city leaders initially refused to admit
that there were economic factors completely beyond their control. The
press continued to report on the financial calamity as if it were a faraway
occurrence whose effects could be curtailed by local action. Yet even these
optimists, who were convinced of the primacy of local influences, failed
to agree on what action would heal Savannah's economic wounds. Local
bankers, like their counterparts across the nation, beyond tightening their
currency and refusing further loans, disagreed on what actions might stem
the effects of the panic. Some wanted to suspend operations; others dis-
cussed the possibility of issuing city notes, a common practice in similar
emergency situations.[9]

The Savannah Chamber of Commerce, eager to restore confidence in
the city's financial institutions, appointed a committee to evaluate the various options, confer with the banks and railroads, and present a plan of
action. The committee's report was anything but optimistic. It rejected
a proposal for circulating municipal scrip, yet beyond that it could offer
no plan for relief. Tightening currency exacerbated the already existing
problem and made any financial transactions more difficult. In addition
to the immediate crises associated with bank runs and currency contrac-

tion, longer-term consequences soon manifested themselves, including decreased income and the increased burden of mortgage indebtedness.[10]

Despite predictions that the economy would soon rebound from the panic, the lack of currency made creditors less forgiving and investors less generous. Both trends had a direct impact on the city's finances. Following the recommendations of the freeholder committee, the council had issued $400,000 in bonds to cover the upcoming loans. By the close of the year, the city had sold only $86,500. Yet it was still responsible for previous loans coming due.[11] In November, Eugene Kelly, president of the Southern Bank of Georgia, after having given the city several extensions, sent the council a letter demanding immediate payment of $106,000 in short-term loans from Screven's administration. Unable to make the payment with available funds, the city resorted to the expedient of borrowing from other local banks and commission merchants. The city met its obligation to Kelly but could not cover its own normal monthly expenses. Using the same power to take out short-term loans, the city applied to the Central Railroad Bank, which loaned the city $8,000 to pay the police for the year.[12]

The council finally moved forward on the freeholder committee's second recommendation and established a sinking fund consisting of ground rents and rentals, which allowed it to redeem $41,000 in bonds. It also received $35,000 by selling some of its railroad stock. Local merchants aided by purchasing another $8,000; Kelly pitched in by purchasing $20,000. However, neither the sale of notes nor so-called retrenchment measures met expectations. Municipal expenses invariably ran higher than expected.[13]

Unexpected and unavoidable expenses made the situation untenable. For instance, due to a long dry spell during the summer, the city waterworks pumps, though only a few years old, failed. Faced with the possibility of future water shortages, the council contracted to have new engines installed at the waterworks for $37,000. By the end of the year, the city faced a $136,000 deficiency. This did not include a bonded debt of over $3 million, on which the city was paying $251,000 in interest, which accounted for a quarter of the city's expenses. To meet the deficit and the interest on the bonded debt, the city once again had to resort to loans from local banks. Anderson, in his annual report, expressed confidence that most of the latter amount would be offset by the taxes based on the tax ordinance due to go into effect early in 1875. As they had in 1873, the city's

financial problems became the primary issue in the 1875 mayoral campaign.[14]

Anderson's administration was not as vulnerable to attack on the grounds
of fiscal carelessness as Screven's. In two years, expenses had returned to
what they had been before Screven's tenure. However, with cost overruns
and continued dependence on loans, neither Anderson nor his administration achieved any appreciable improvement in the city's financial condition.

In 1875, the Democratic Executive Committee bypassed Anderson in
favor of Colonel Rufus Lester, who had served as president of the Georgia State Senate. He became the popular favorite, especially among the
group self-styled the Young Democracy. Lester, a native of Burke County,
had graduated from Mercer University in 1857. After opening a law practice, he ran for and won election to the state senate from the First District in 1860. A year later, he joined the Confederate army and served the
duration of the war. In 1868, he ran as a Democrat for the state senate but
lost to Aaron Bradley. Following Bradley's ouster, Lester gained the seat
and worked successfully to prevent the Republican-controlled General
Assembly from changing the makeup of the city government or redraw-
ing district or ward lines with the aim of giving Republicans an advantage
in municipal elections. With the exception of the brief period when the
legislature was reconvened under the Congressional Reconstruction Act,
Lester spent most of the postwar period in the Georgia State Senate.[15]

Though most groups agreed that Lester was the best choice for mayor,
no such consensus developed regarding aldermanic nominees. The *Savannah Morning News* dotted its pages with new tickets. Those concerned
with the possibility that Anderson planned to challenge the nomination
sent letters to the editor advocating rotation in office. Anderson, who had
given up his mayoral seat once before to avoid dividing the Democratic
vote, did not seem willing to step aside this time for anyone. From the
outset of the political maneuvering, he made it clear he would be willing
to run if he were able to choose the members of the board of aldermen.[16]

Only a few days before the election, the municipal campaign launched
into full swing with calls for two separate nominating conventions—
one in the afternoon and one in the evening. The *Morning News*, which
supported Lester's nomination, informed its readers that the afternoon
meeting had been called in the interest of Anderson. General Henry

R. Jackson, a lawyer and one-time U.S. district attorney, indeed working in Anderson's interest, organized the meeting. Despite the inconve-
nient time—likely intentional—attendance was much larger than orga-
nizers had expected, which did not bode well for an outcome favorable
to Anderson. The *Morning News*, already in Lester's camp, later reported
that the sentiment of the attendees was decidedly opposed to Anderson's nomination. Jackson, having no other choice, accepted the popular wishes of the loud and boisterous gathering. Attendees adopted a resolution nominating Lester for mayor and further resolved to attend the
meeting scheduled for that evening, which subsequently endorsed the actions of the afternoon gathering. Having received the nomination at both
meetings in addition to endorsement by a small number of white Republicans, Lester's seemingly successful campaign then suffered a major set-
back. Almost all of the nominees for aldermen refused to stand for election, with most citing business concerns. Within a day of his nomination,
Lester's aldermanic ticket was nonexistent.[17]

Confusion over aldermanic nominees kept chances open for Anderson,
who railed against Jackson's "mismanagement" of the afternoon meeting.
Even though the Democratic Executive Committee officially nominated
Lester, Anderson and his supporters refused to concede. The *Advertiser*,
the city's government's official newspaper, backed Anderson. It published
a card from "seven hundred and odd citizens and tax payers requesting the
present Board of Mayor and Aldermen to run again for office."[18]

The days prior to the election proved both exciting and divisive as both
sides expressed their views to the interested citizenry via the city's rival
newspapers. Most letters published in the *Savannah Morning News* supported Lester as the regular Democratic nominee and attacked Anderson's administration; contributors charged that Savannah was ruled by not
only a ring but also a "political dynasty which has for years fattened itself
upon the generous provender of the city." "Democrat" wondered how people could "justify their obstinate adherence" to Anderson. The most common complaints were the financial condition of the city, the increasing
and discriminatory taxes, decreasing property values, and increasing debts.
Dismissing the notion that the city's financial problems could be blamed
solely on the Panic of 1873, Lester's supporters argued that "the decadence
of Savannah" was the result of "bad management in our municipal administration." Several letters also pointed out a rather obvious fact: Lester was
running as the official Democratic candidate. From this perspective, An-

derson was a bolter, who threatened to split the white vote. From a debate of the issues, the campaign dissolved into charges, counter-charges, and mudslinging.[19]

Anderson challenged Lester indirectly by discrediting his backers, the Russell family, who had previously supported Anderson. In a letter to the editor of the *Savannah Advertiser*, Anderson called the public's attention to an incident that had occurred the previous year. When the city had begun reducing its expenditures and cutting funds to various services, Waring Russell, the city jailer, had appealed to the legislature to preserve his salary. Anderson had been outraged when he discovered that a bill terminating the council's power over the jailer's salary had been introduced into the legislature without his or his council's endorsement. By virtue of their elective offices in the General Assembly, both Rufus Lester and T. R. Mills were implicated. Mills defended his actions, claiming that he had received a letter from the city's jail committee endorsing the bill, but jail committee members denied having signed or sent such a document. In the end, the bill did not pass, but Anderson resurrected the imbroglio, hoping to influence the election of city officers, scheduled for the week prior to the municipal election. Given Russell's talent at electoral fraud, removing him from office at this time would have definitely benefited Anderson.[20]

Russell soon discovered that his position as jailer was less secure than his salary. The contest for other city officers quickly paled in comparison to the jailer contest. Russell had occupied the position of jailer since the mid-1850s, and challenging Russell shortly before the election seemed to be a shrewd move on Anderson's part. Though Anderson refused to state his intentions in the matter, privately he believed that Russell would be defeated. To his surprise, the councilmen reelected Russell as jailer by one vote. When the council returned from a private caucus to announce the outcome, Anderson told the attendees that he had voted against Russell but yielded to the wishes of the majority.[21]

Anderson, however, continued to belabor the controversy. He persuaded the *Advertiser* to publish the correspondence between the various parties on the jailer's salary bill. Conveniently, the *Advertiser* published the information the day before the election. Anderson possibly used this as a last resort. The Russell family had historically controlled much of the Election Day activities, including the previous election, which had benefited Anderson, and the one before that, which had benefited Screven. Anderson's tactic nearly resulted in bloodshed. Incensed at Frederick Sims for having published the correspondence, Lester challenged the newspaper editor to duel. Anderson had to intervene to end the dispute without force of arms.[22]

On Election Day, Anderson's supporters allegedly employed the old tactics of Reconstruction to win by any means possible. The *Savannah Morning News* noted that there was a "good deal of trickery and political chicanery in operation." It complained of instances of intimidation as Anderson supporters threatened employees with the loss of their jobs if they voted for Lester. Ultimately, in spite of the seemingly overwhelming opposition by the *Morning News*, Anderson won by a majority of 214 votes, and his entire council with him.[23] The reelected mayor, however, found his efforts to deal with the financial crisis challenged at every turn by an increasingly recalcitrant citizenry.

CHAPTER 9

Anderson's Praetorian Guard

TAXPAYER REVOLT, MUNICIPAL POLITICS,
AND THE YELLOW SCOURGE

Having secured another term, Anderson struck a tone of optimism in his annual report, saying that the city's new tax ordinance would allow Savannah to meet its financial obligations. However, he failed to consider the possibility that the city's citizens would resist paying those taxes. Savannah's taxpayers were forced to carry a financial burden that was based on the expectation of spreading the load over an increasing population. The city's taxes, always unpopular and perceived to be increasingly burdensome, faced active opposition from a variety of groups, including merchants, plumbers, draymen, lawyers, and property owners, many of whom criticized the tax code as discriminatory.[1]

Debate over rising taxes was not unusual or unique to Savannah. Finding nontax income sources to keep taxes low was generally accepted and preferred financial policy. Governments invested in various enterprises, expecting the resultant profits to obviate raising taxes on a permanent basis. Part of this decision-making involved the conviction of officials that they could control the destiny of their region or locality by using the investment capacity of local and state governments to effect commercial expansion without paying for it through direct taxation. This policy did have some success, as with the state-owned Western and Atlantic Railroad and Savannah's investment in the Central Railroad. Georgians generally had few qualms about publicly sponsored commercial expansion as long as the government did not raise their taxes indefinitely to subsidize that expansion.[2] By the mid-1870s, Savannahians consistently paid more state, county, and city taxes than ever before. Their frustration with this was manifest in revolt against the city tax system more than revolt against the state or county systems, possibly because they believed they had more sway over the city government.

The first sign of trouble with the new tax ordinance developed among draymen, individuals who carried freight on wagons through the city. It began as a dispute over the timing of the taxes, rather than the amount. The draymen, in their petition to council, asserted that their businesses were profitable for only seven months of the year; therefore, they requested that the city allow them to pay their taxes quarterly. The *Savannah Morning News*, believing this a fair request, warned that some draymen might be forced to abandon the business unless the city granted the change. The council, however, maintained a hard line and refused the petition.[3] It promptly informed the draymen that if they failed to make their payments by the following Monday, the city would attach a lien on their properties. The next Monday, the police marched out in force to inspect each vehicle that passed in front of the City Exchange (City Hall) for the proper badge indicating payment of the tax. Those without proper badges were hauled to the police barracks. Presented with such militant force, draymen who could pay the tax opted to do so. The *Morning News*, highly critical of the city's behavior, stated, "As the 'Pærtorian [*sic*] Guard' of Mayor Anderson are well known as vigorous in enforcing orders, any further dilatoriousness will meet with like summary treatment. The administration needs money and must have it." It was clear that Anderson's administration no longer had the support it once had, and that some groups were becoming openly hostile.[4]

The municipal government found it easy enough to use the police force to coerce the draymen into paying license fees. This high-profile police action certainly made an example of the draymen and possibly discouraged similar groups from following their example. Such tactics, however, were limited to those parties required to display visible badges; calling out the police would be ineffective with professionals who refused to pay similar license fees or real estate owners who refused to pay property taxes.

In late February 1875, attorneys, who were required to pay a $25 annual license fee, petitioned the council to amend the fee structure. The petitioners argued that the fee, which applied to all firms, regardless of size, inordinately harmed small firms. When the council refused this petition too, the attorneys naturally turned to the courts and petitioned for injunction. Superior Court judge Henry Tompkins ordered the mayor and aldermen to appear before him for explanations. After listening to both sides, Tompkins issued an injunction prohibiting the city from "levying, or collecting, or attempting in any way to levy or collect the tax."[5]

This successful foray inspired other groups to defy the council. Real estate owners, led by James A. LaRoche, filed an injunction against Savannah's collection of "so much of the real estate tax for 1874 as exceeds the lowest rate fixed for any species of personal property for that year" because of its discriminatory nature. LaRoche argued that in 1874, while the city taxed real estate at 2.25 percent, it taxed stocks and bonds at 1.25 percent. In 1875, the city, in spite of its explicitly stated need for income, completely eliminated taxes on stocks and bonds. Rather than challenge LaRoche in court, the council opted to compromise with the real estate owners by reducing the tax and agreeing to pay all court costs.[6] This action intimated to citizens that the aldermen doubted the legality of the tax ordinance. More groups, including other property owners, craftsmen, and merchants joined the revolt.[7]

City merchants challenged what they termed an "inquisatorial tax on gross sales," and they threatened court action if the council refused revision. The council ultimately relented. The finance committee reported that because opposition to the tax on gross sales was "so great and widespread," it had decided in favor of the petitioners.[8]

The city therefore faced several facets of the same problem: increasing debt; low population growth, which resulted in a virtually static taxpayer base; and a taxpayer revolt, with revenue expected to decrease as a result. The latter became more apparent following a report regarding the five wealthiest counties in the state. Chatham County, which encompassed Savannah, was the only county that had lately experienced a decrease in property values. One *Savannah Morning News* correspondent complained that the city was in "a deplorable dilemma." With taxpayers filing injunctions, threatening suits, and refusing to pay, Savannah's council confronted not only an increasing debt but also the inability to carry on normal public functions.[9]

The city faced a crisis that was duplicated in other cities, towns, and counties across the nation. Savannah was not a symbol of southern coastal decline but instead part of what critics soon began calling a national epidemic. Between 1866 and 1876, municipal debt had increased over 200 percent. Population had increased at a rate of only 33 percent, and taxation at 83 percent. The study that produced these numbers included eleven states; the only southern state represented was Georgia.[10]

With financial difficulties increasing, councilmen again became en-
amored with retrenchment. In May 1875 the council reduced expenses
beginning with the police force, one of the city's largest financial burdens outside of debt repayment. Given the political role of the police
force, the council did not take this decision lightly. After much debate,
it pared down the size of the force from 112 to 68 men, reduced salaries
of those remaining, and instituted a hiring freeze. The savings amounted
to $10,000. This, added to other retrenchment measures, yielded a reduc-
tion of $200,000 in city expenses from 1874. As significant as these savings
were, the amount was not equivalent to the yearly interest on the city's
loans. Additionally, expenses increased almost $100,000 from 1873. In
June, Anderson prevailed upon William Wadley, president of the Central
Railroad, to ask Moses Taylor, the controlling stockholder of the company, for a short-term loan of $25,000 for sixty days. In the fall, council
once again considered issuing more bonds.[11]

By the end of the year, the council had resolved to institute another
round of salary reductions. This time it focused on abolishing various offices and reducing pay for city employees. In addition, it considered instituting a water tax for all improved lots in reach of the water mains.[12]
Letters to the editor of the *Morning News* indicated general disapproval,
since the abolished offices were those of people elected to serve three-year
terms.[13]

The taxpayers' reluctance to pay what some considered illegal taxes in
1875 turned into a general revolt by the summer of 1876. Those who refused
to pay their taxes based their actions on issues of legality and discrimination. For instance, one group complained about the city's favorable treatment of banks. The 1875 tax ordinance had exempted banks from a tax of
1 percent on interest received from bonds, though all other corporations
were subject to it. Outrage only increased when the new tax ordinance of
1876 raised the corporate tax another quarter percent but once again exempted banks. Others objected to the city's policy toward ground rents.
Citizens who lived on city lots and, for all practical purposes, used them
as if they owned them, paid a percentage on the cost of purchase of the lot
but remained exempt from city taxes.[14]

Citizens who had sued for an injunction against the city, over an illegal tax they had paid and wanted refunded or applied to the next year's
taxes, appealed their case to the Georgia Supreme Court in late May 1876.
The court decided in favor of the municipal government by refusing to allow taxes paid in previous years to offset future taxes. The narrow ruling,

however, neither directly addressed the legality of the taxes in question nor required current citizen dissenters to pay their taxes.[15] In July, the city council attempted to compel the recalcitrant to pay their taxes by ordering the city marshal to sell all property that had taxes outstanding. When the council rejected a petition for redress, taxpayers once again turned to the courts.[16]

While council members complained about citizens not doing their duty, a letter to the editor of the *Morning News* maintained that the entire crisis was one of the council's own making. The Georgia Supreme Court had ruled the city's 1874 tax ordinance unconstitutional but had refused to allow those who paid the taxes to have their money refunded or applied. Apparently the council had not learned from the past as it proceeded to pass additional rounds of tax ordinances in 1875 and 1876. The letter writer warned, "A burnt child dreads the fire." Unlike the council, citizens would not make the same mistake twice. Those who paid what they now viewed as an illegal tax without being granted a refund simply refused to pay it again.[17]

Real estate owners also began organizing against what they saw as discriminatory taxes. Spearheaded by Louis A. Falligant, the proposed Real Estate League sought to "compel an equal distribution of the taxes on all property alike," to produce relief from property owners' "over burdened condition." The crux of the issue, as Falligant perceived it, was the "unconstitutional exemption of millions of dollars of bonds, stocks, bank capital, commission merchants' capital, and particular species of real property [ground rent], not actually used for religious or charitable purposes," while an "extra burthen is levied on the holders of real estate and merchandise to supply the deficiency caused by such partial and unconstitutional exemption." However, the interest group never came together. Some thought real estate taxation too high, others announced their willingness to pay the current taxes if the city taxed other occupations more equitably. Still others simply focused on the removal of the current administration from office.[18]

Whether acting in concert or individually, citizens refused to pay their taxes. The result for the municipal government was the same: Savannah's inability to provide basic services or to make payments on its outstanding coupons. Anderson resorted to issuing more mayors' notes and sought ways to reduce costs.[19] In late June, the city lowered lighting expenses by discontinuing gas-burning street lamps during moonlit nights. Other proposals called for reducing the number of employees in the public school system, Laurel Grove Cemetery, and the Street and Lane Department. As the *Savannah Morning News* noted, it seemed the report yielded "no very important results, so far as lessening the burthen of expense."[20]

Some questioned the focus of the reductions. In a letter to the *Morning News*, C. C. Millar questioned the spending decisions of the council. After all, he asked, if there were only $26,000 in outstanding uncollected taxes, why was the city claiming that parties owed $250,000 in taxes? In answer to this question, Millar, who had served as alderman in 1866, surmised that the problem was likely too many commissions to Washington and other jobs about which taxpayers were ignorant. The council had not only failed to reform Savannah's finances but was also contemplating an additional loan. Gugie Bourquin, a rice broker, who also called into question some of council's decisions, plainly and prophetically asserted, "We are living beyond our means; sooner or later we must fall."[21]

As debate raged regarding blame for the city's disastrous finances, rumors of a scourge worse than uncollected city taxes and unpaid debts began to circulate. The city had been inundated with rain between June 11 and 19. The next month, the extreme heat resulted in sunstroke and heat-related deaths. Despite the confident assertion that Savannah was "unquestionably the healthiest city either north or south, east or west, on this continent," by late August officials could only answer queries from neighboring cities regarding these rumors with silence, denying that Savannah had been struck by dreaded yellow fever.[22]

In mid-August, the *Augusta Chronicle* noted Savannah's anger at rival cities for slandering it by claiming the existence of yellow fever. Savannah officials scoffed that nothing more serious than "jim jams" (jitters) had appeared in the city for six months. Alexander R. Lawton, former Confederate general and attorney for the Central Railroad, wrote to his wife Sarah on August 30 and admitted that yellow fever was in Savannah. He warned, "If this is not already known to 'everybody' you can keep it to yourself." He was right to be concerned about exaggeration and panic. On September 12, 1876, one observer noted all the echoes up and down the streets because the city was so deserted.[23]

After officials belatedly admitted the truth about the epidemic, debate about city finances took a back seat to health concerns, as citizens who could flee the city did so, most traveling to Atlanta to await the first killing frost of the season. With the outbreak no longer a secret, the *Savan-*

nah Morning News reported the daily death totals, suppositions about its causes, and the activities of relief agencies and physicians.

According to later reports, the 1876 yellow fever outbreak in Savannah was the worst of the city's epidemics, with an estimated 10,000 cases and 1,066 deaths. In addition to the thousands of poor victims who lived on the outskirts of the city, the epidemic also took members of Savannah's more prestigious and well-known families, including the Andersons, the Screvens, and the Warings. The mayor noted in his annual report, "The cry of humanity went up from our gloom." Leading citizens, doctors, and average individuals answered the cry. The local Benevolent Society and the Colored Aid Society sprang into action to help those who could not leave the city. Physicians, while they did their best to treat patients, spent much of their time debating the epidemic's causes; and politicians assigned blame. At this time, no one knew the infernal mosquito carried the burden of blame.[24]

Relief agencies organized to care for the sick, supply food and medicine, and solicit outside assistance. Philadelphia and Boston quickly came to Savannah's aid with donations totaling over $20,000. Physicians and nurses arrived from New York.[25] The Savannah Benevolent Association was the most active relief organization in the city. Headed by Captain John (Jack) Wheaton, a lumber merchant, the association had an existing fund with $27,000 and eventually raised over $100,000 for distribution.[26] The efforts of Wheaton did not go unnoticed. Lawton reported that the Benevolent Association was "doing a great deal of good." Wheaton was at his desk every day directing the society's response. Lawton marveled, "I do not see how he can afford it, but it is an absolutely necessity and he is entitled to the gratitude of us all."[27]

Even as they ministered to the sick and dealt with the mounting deaths, physicians debated the causes and ultimately the blame. Dr. Louis A. Falligant, as early as August 27, was pointing to the poorly maintained Bilbo Canal as the likely culprit. Since it seemed that the outbreaks began and were most severe on the western and eastern edges of the city, both bordering canals, Falligant's assumption was a logical one.[28]

Physicians and public health officials often debated the cause of yellow fever. The theory of contagion, rejected in the early antebellum period, remained popular, especially among the lay public. Yet the observation that yellow fever occurred only in hot, humid, and dirty environments seemed to sustain those who maintained that the causes had to be local. By the

1870s, physicians began to incorporate the germ theory into their explanation of the causes of yellow fever and postulated the existence of "floating microorganisms."[29]

As the *Savannah Morning News* aired all sorts of theories, remedies, preventative measures, and even miraculous cures, the medical community and civic and benevolent societies organized a meeting to provide citizens with more reliable information. Suggestions from this meeting included burning tar and "coal kilns of pine wood." The attendees accepted Dr. James Waring's offer to look into the causes and prevention. Five days later, he made his report to council. He specified sources including spores found in green wood, molding fences, brick ponds, and large amounts of standing water. In June that year, Savannah had received an unusual amount of rain, 16.5 inches in a nine-day period. Waring also offered a plan of attack. In addition to whitewashing the city, he offered to organize a labor gang to clean and open city drains to alleviate the standing water. Council promptly appropriated $5,000 obtained from private subscription to begin the work.[30]

Some members of the Georgia Medical Society, however, disagreed with Waring's report and lobbied the city council to make him cease his activities. They claimed that plowing up the ground to open drains would exacerbate the problem— that digging in the soil would expose the putrefying matter that caused the fever. Waring, referring to this decision as "extremely imprudent and reckless," ignored the order. This controversy erupted into a war of words, as the *Morning News* printed charges and accusations along with the lists of the casualties. At one point Edward Anderson's son Edward M. Anderson, known as Eddie, challenged Waring to a duel on behalf of his father. Waring declined. Mayor Anderson later summoned Waring to the mayor's court and fined him $100 for violating the city ordinance prohibiting citizens from "turning up" the ground during certain months of the year.[31]

Waring, conversely, blamed Mayor Anderson, and he was not alone. Not long after the outbreak, John Mannerlyn, who inspected land on behalf of the city's Dry Culture Department, wrote two letters to John Screven. He stated that in 1873, upon reassuming office, Anderson had ended the policy of requiring monthly written reports from the dry culture inspectors and ordered his inspectors to report directly to him if they found any problems. Mannerlyn claimed that he had advised city officials on numerous occasions about the poor condition of the lowlands and Bilbo

Canal. Going further, he had warned one of the aldermen that "there might be trouble" and attempted to talk to the mayor, but "he was too busy to see me."[32]

Anderson had taken little interest in the city's drainage program. After he returned to the mayoralty in 1873, sewer construction declined precipitously. While Screven spent much of his annual report expounding on the virtues of the sewer system, Anderson spared only one sentence. In 1873, the city funded the construction of only one sewer, and did so only out of absolute necessity—to prevent the new market basement from flooding. The drainage-related expenses of Anderson's administration were due primarily to poor construction and inferior materials. Some drains decayed so completely that they had to be removed.[33]

The city council's declining interest and investment in maintaining and expanding the city's drainage system now left officials vulnerable to criticism. The epidemic was feared to be so catastrophic to the city's population, economy, and reputation that even in the midst of a bankruptcy crisis, city representatives worked vigorously to convince the Georgia General Assembly to provide a modern drainage system for all of Chatham County. Already in dire financial straits, leaders tied Savannah's commercial future to public confidence in its ability to prevent future epidemics. Partly as a result of the financial undertakings earlier that decade, Savannah's municipal government was in no position to finance further internal improvements on its own.[34]

The attempt to blame people or policies was in part a manifestation of the feeling of helplessness. Although Waring and Falligant were on the right track that the standing water from lack of proper drainage was a culprit, they could not marshal enough medical evidence to make the final link. As had been the pattern for other cities with these epidemics, they dealt with the reality of the situation until the first frost signaled the beginning of its demise.[35]

CHAPTER 10

---•●•---

"Present Embarrassments"

MUNICIPAL DEFAULT

In November and December 1876, as Savannahians returned to the city and focused on getting back to normal, Anderson and his aldermen fretted. In November, with the worst of the epidemic over, they turned their attention to pressing financial matters. The finance committee's report did nothing to improve the spirits of Savannah's already demoralized citizenry. In 1873, at the beginning of Anderson's latest tenure, the city was already responsible for a floating debt of $396,000, and it had made no plans for its retirement. Following the $400,000 bond issue in 1873, the council had "earnestly pursued" retrenchment, but various obstacles, including the public's recalcitrance, doomed the policy.[1]

The council won a minor victory when the Georgia Supreme Court ruled that the collection of taxes could not be prevented by injunction. However, the yellow fever epidemic interrupted enforcement and collection. The resultant shortfall prevented Savannah from making interest payments on its loans in November 1876 and again in February 1877. This put the city in an even more vulnerable position as creditors demanded payment. The finance committee pointedly blamed the city's disastrous financial situation on its citizenry: citizen refusal to pay taxes in 1875 and 1876 had forced the city to resort to loans and extreme retrenchment.[2]

Citizens quickly fired back with their own accusations. One common target was the government's credit system, derisively called the "Mercantile School of Bay Street." A letter to the *Morning News* signed "A and Z" provided the most scathing denunciation of both the "Mercantile School of Finance" and the city council's allegedly underhanded method of keeping its citizens in the dark about the city's real financial condition. The letter accused Savannah's executives of secretly borrowing money from local banks at exorbitant interest rates. This credit system, "A and Z" argued, might work for the railroads, factories, and other private enterprises, but it would not work for Savannah because the city could not "use money to make money." Rather, it "raises money, and it spends money." However, instead of facing the reality that the system could not work, "A to Z" charged, the finance committee would meet in secret whenever its members realized financial embarrassment was likely; covertly they decided to borrow with mayors' notes at criminal rates, all to maintain a "hollow show of prosperity."[3]

The city council's efforts to deny culpability by focusing attention on the taxpayers, who were also voting citizens, were politically unwise, especially in an election year. Irritated citizens called for the ouster of the current council and sought to elect a new group capable of dealing with the impending crisis. All agreed that Savannah needed "sagacious and progressive" leadership equipped to meet "emergencies of affairs." In early January, Rufus Lester, now chairman of the Democratic Executive Committee of Chatham County, called a meeting to select an official ticket composed of "good and proper men" for the upcoming municipal election.[4]

The meeting failed to accomplish this objective. In addition to debates over the choice of an aldermanic ticket, there were speeches on taxation and calls for candidates to develop platforms. The most exciting event of the evening came when Dr. Waring stood to speak. After years of being criticized and denounced, Waring was greeted with great applause from the attending crowd. During the yellow fever epidemic, Waring had been the foremost advocate of a proactive policy. He had openly criticized Anderson's administration for allowing the city's preventative measures to decline for the sake of economy. When Alderman Mathias Meyer, who was booed for his interruption, caustically reminded the crowd that Waring was not a Democrat, Waring made light of the insult. The audience grew louder, with shouts of "Better late than never!" Waring asserted that municipal affairs had been conducted in a manner "detrimental to the city." He maintained that the council had kept the people in the dark about its most important actions. The city, he proclaimed, was "now at the midnight hour." He hoped that their actions that night would help bring about a bright dawn.[5]

Following Waring's speech, Louis H. de Montmollin, a local attorney, echoed Waring's sentiment and alluded to the present as the "darkest and most trying period" in the city's history. He called for the creation of a platform on which the aldermen would be nominated and to which they would be held accountable. The platform contained five points, including demands to preserve the health of the city, establish an equitable tax system, restrict the board of aldermen in the incursion of future debt, encourage business, and directly elect city officers. This resolution and nominations were referred to a nominating committee. Two days later, the nominating committee, ignoring the platform, chose an aldermanic ticket. It was not an easy task since several nominees quickly refused.[6]

J. M. Guerard planned to enter the mayoral contest. Guerard, a former assemblyman, was an expert in Old English law, had represented James Waring on occasion, and had been among those who joined the tax revolt in 1876. George Mercer, another local attorney, derailed Guerard's plans by spreading rumors that Guerard planned to abolish the entire police force and reinstate the night watch system of earlier times. Although Guerard supporters denied the allegations, the damage was done. The committee subsequently chose Captain John F. Wheaton as the mayoral candidate and endorsed a full slate of aldermen. Wheaton, an insurance agent and lumber merchant, was well known to the citizens of Savannah for his involvement in the Chatham Artillery. Most recently, however, his high standing resulted from his efforts during the yellow fever epidemic. As head of the Savannah Benevolent Association, he was in charge of receiving and dispersing the donated money and supplies.[7]

The nominating committee then ran into an unusual obstacle: of all the nominees, only Wheaton and Waring agreed to stand for office. The committee nominated another slate of candidates and issued a reminder to those nominees of the "very grave importance of the present crisis" facing the city and the "imperative necessity" of having men who were "thoroughly identified in interest with this community" at the helm. This effort proved no more successful than the first. After several days, the committee admitted that, "after exhausting every effort," it could not present the voters with nominees acceptable to the committee. Rather than publish an official ticket, the committee published a list of suggested candidates and asserted that it would rest "with the voters of Savannah to protect the interests of their city by such other action as seems to them best."[8]

The committee's announcement led to another barrage of tickets. On the day of the election, the *Savannah Morning News* noted that there were so many tickets that there was something there to suit all tastes and views. In spite of the excitement leading up to the election, less than 800 people cast votes, with Wheaton receiving all but 131 of the votes cast for mayor. Some of the newly elected aldermen tasked with returning both health and prosperity to the city did have previous experience on council, while others were completely new to the job. None of them, however, were held over from the previous administration.[9]

At the first meeting of the new council, the members tackled the business of the city's financial predicament. The finance committee, chaired once again by William H. Tison, reported that due to "circumstances beyond its control," specifically the financial depression following the epidemic as well as the "antagonistic position" of various taxpayers, the city treasury had insufficient funds to pay for the past-due coupons. Nor, Tison predicted, would it be able to pay the coupons due the first of February. As a short-term, stopgap solution to keep the "machinery of the corporation in motion," the finance committee recommended a more flexible tax payment system: it would accept city coupons in payment of past due taxes. In this way, the city hoped to redeem some of its bonds and persuade taxpayers to come forward. However, the legality of this plan remained in question, especially after the attorney's ambiguous verbal report. Waring took a contrary position, arguing that the practice of accepting coupons in payment for taxes provided preferential treatment for a certain class of the city's creditors. The city's action was little different from the common response of individual debtors. When a debtor became aware that the creditors were closing in, the individual would often choose to pay specific creditors, usually family and friends. In this case, the city sought to collect coupons from local taxpayers.[10]

The finance committee ignored Waring's warning and approved the measure. However, within six months, Waring's concern was validated as the measure was ruled illegal and had to be repealed.[11] The city council also began reviewing various departments and programs for further reductions. The public school system was one of the first targets. The council ordered all high schools to raise tuition and put themselves on a "perfectly self-sustaining" basis.[12]

Lack of funding was not new for those who administered the city's public school system. Teachers always experienced the impact of budget cuts. When the state, county, or city failed to appropriate needed funds, teacher salaries were the first to be cut. At best, teachers could expect irregular salaries, if they received any. For instance, in 1875, due to the city's severe financial troubles, the Board of Education (BOE) reduced teacher salaries between 10 and 15 percent and eliminated all experience-based salaries. Students also felt the impact. The *Savannah Morning News* noted that while Savannah spent $9.50 per student, Boston, which was also having financial difficulties, was managing to invest $31.11 per student.[13]

In 1876, when John Stoddard assumed the presidency of the BOE, he planned a reorganization of the school system to cut expenses. He reduced the maximum student age from fifteen to eleven and eliminated separate classes for boys and girls; previously both classes and playgrounds had been segregated by gender. Additionally, he abolished single primary, intermediate, and grammar schools, with separate principals. In their place, he created three school districts, though he retained the already existing Catholic and African American schools. The board was operating eleven schools in the city and four outside the city. Finally, though the BOE retained the high schools, it initiated a three-dollar monthly tuition. Even with cost-cutting measures, the teachers ended the year having not received pay in three months.[14]

By the end of the decade, the funding situation had reached a crisis point. The city cut its school appropriation by half and considered eliminating the high schools. City leaders demanded that the funding they provided should go for "the instruction of a plain English education only." School enrollment and funding continued to drop. The number of faculty decreased, and the school year was reduced to nine months and then six months until the teachers volunteered to continue without pay for the rest of the term.[15]

Already overwhelmed by the problems at hand, councilmen were in no mood to be reminded that events were conspiring to make the city's situation even worse. Yet Waring seemed determined to force both council members and Savannah's citizens to take a realistic view of the city's situation, even if it brought universal condemnation on his head. Possibly still smarting from his treatment at the hands of the Screven-backed Atlantic and Gulf Railroad, he introduced a controversial resolution asking the city's attorney to submit a written statement regarding the "validity and binding effect" of the city's endorsement of the $300,000 in Atlantic and Gulf Railroad bonds, which were approaching maturity. Not surprisingly the council had no plans for their payment. Screven's financial management of the Atlantic and Gulf Railroad had proven no more adept than his efforts at running Savannah's municipal government. The company became yet another victim of the Panic of 1873 and subsequent depression, and its sale was imminent. Upon its sale, the city would immediately be responsible for those bonds. Council members were reluctant to add yet another crisis to the list already at hand, and they defeated Waring's resolution, calling it premature.[16]

In late February, increasingly impatient with the city council's delay in presenting the finance committee's report, Waring decided to force the issue. He introduced a preamble and a series of resolutions that did more than just spur the finance committee to action; they sent a shock wave through the city's creditors. Waring claimed that the municipal government's floating debt was fully half of the entire property value of the city and more than double its assets. Additionally, Savannah would be expected to meet almost $200,000 in bonds due in 1877, and the council had not yet provided for their payment. With an outstanding floating debt of $300,000 and an expectation of only $250,000 in receipts, Waring asserted, it was impossible for the city to meet its obligations. To add to this burden, with the bankruptcy and sale of the Atlantic and Gulf Railroad, the city would be forced to add another $300,000 to its obligations. For anyone missing the point, Waring proclaimed, "Savannah is this day bankrupt."[17]

As if Waring's charges about the condition of the city were not distressing enough, he accused his fellow council members of conspiring to hide the fact that the city was bankrupt. He charged that they had been too slow in handling the tax case making its way through the court system because as long as the case remained in the courts, it provided them the perfect excuse to hold off the creditors. He called on the city to suspend payments of all outstanding liabilities exceeding current expenses and to apply all taxes collected to cover only current expenses until the city could work out a compromise with its creditors. He proposed as a basis for compromise twenty-five cents on the dollar, a suggestion that set off a minor panic among bondholders. Obviously unprepared for such charges, the council referred Waring's resolution to the finance committee for a report.[18]

The frequently dilatory finance committee's reaction to Waring's claims was uncharacteristically quick and decisive. The hastily crafted report sought to convince bondholders that the city had no intention of following Waring's suggestion, even if, as the committee grudgingly admitted, his calculations regarding the city's finances were correct. While acknowledging certain financial embarrassments, the committee demanded that

Waring's resolutions not only be rejected but also "stamped with the most emphatic disapprobation of Council." Taking up the mantra of its predecessors, the committee asserted that responsibility for the city's financial condition was to be laid at the feet of "hostile combinations of her citizens to resist measures adopted for raising revenue" by suing over a technicality of the law. Sounding a note of pessimism, the report admitted its "grave apprehensions" about Savannah's future if its virtuous citizens did not come to the aid of the city in its efforts "to secure the only just and honorable solution of the complications of the situation." The committee apparently failed to realize that criticizing the citizenry was counterproductive to enlisting its support. Within a month, the council had adopted a less abrasive attitude toward defaulting taxpayers. It requested that recalcitrant taxpayers pay the amount of the tax that they did not contest, in order to "aid the city in its present embarrassments."[19]

Attempting to engender a more upbeat tone, the committee assured the public that if the city successfully collected the 1877 taxes and instituted the "severest economy in every branch of the public service," Savannah would be able to restore its credit. In the meantime, the council requested the "patient indulgence of creditors." The council adopted the report, with Waring casting the single dissenting vote. The querulous physician claimed that time would prove him right and that he would "stake his reputation as a prophet" that the city would be unable to collect the necessary taxes even if the courts ruled in the city's favor.[20]

When Waring attempted to respond to the finance committee's report at a subsequent meeting, Wheaton squelched the effort by ruling him out of order. The following day, Waring presented his case in the pages of the *Savannah Morning News*, which obligingly published his views in the column next to the transcript of the council meeting. Waring asserted that he had introduced his resolutions out of the conviction that only "prompt and energetic action" would "save the people of this town from ruin." He still maintained that the council would fail to raise even a quarter of the amount necessary to meet the obligations for the year. Waring then criticized the finance committee for blaming the citizens for exercising their rights to resist laws that were contrary to the state's constitution. Instead, he laid the blame on the previous administrations that knowingly made the illegal laws and did nothing to change them. Rejecting the notion that investments in public improvements (such as the recent drainage work) were to blame for the city's debt, he cited investments in railroad schemes and other worthless projects as well as the practice of issuing mayors' notes to "near a quarter of a million without the knowledge of the public."[21]

In spite of emphatic rebuttal to Waring's charges, Savannah's dire financial condition did not go unnoticed. A few days after the finance committee's response to Waring, the *Augusta Chronicle* noted the councilman's claim that the city was bankrupt and his call for compromise regarding the principal and interest of indebtedness. In South Carolina, the *Charleston News and Courier* announced that everyone would be "glad to learn" that the finance committee had rejected Waring's proposals and intimated that creditors would be very disappointed should Savannah decide upon repudiation. As these financial embarrassments received wider publicity, officials tried to reassure bondholders that Savannah would not repudiate its loans. Even as Mayor Wheaton traveled to New York and offered creditors fifty cents on the dollar, the finance committee continued to counter Waring's charges by asserting it could pay one hundred cents on the dollar. While the council might deny being bankrupt and assure bondholders of its willingness to pay, there was no denying that the city was in default.[22]

With bills coming due, the council attempted to reduce expenditures and negotiate extensions. By arranging a new agreement with the gas company, the city gained twenty additional days to pay its quarterly bill and a 20 percent discount if it paid its bills on time from that point forward. It also increased the number of nights to receive moonlight exemptions from the lighting of streetlamps. The council considered and then rejected a proposal to reduce the number of police officers and their salaries.[23] While such actions symbolized the city's efforts to convince creditors of its good faith, they failed to prevent some creditors from taking their cases to the courts to enforce payment.[24]

In any context, default creates a "financial and legal mess." When the defaulting entity was a municipality, the situation was compounded because there was no set legal remedy. News of defaults led to a chain reaction. Creditors looking out for their own interests could put informal pressure on an individual or business, which might be able to liquidate enough assets for payment. In the case of small debts, creditors rarely opted for the expensive and time-consuming legal maneuvering. But Savannah's debt was by no means insignificant.[25]

The intricacies of the legal system and its tendency to favor those who turned to the courts most quickly encouraged creditors to act without delay. Only after the first claimant received judgment against a debtor would other creditors be eligible to receive judgment. In what one historian has called the "race of diligence," when one creditor demanded payment and demonstrated that a debtor could not pay, other bondholders swooped in to collect "until failure was unavoidable." Filing by one individual often would "trigger an avalanche of suits by bondholders" who did "not want to be last in line."[26] In early April 1877, George P. Curry of Augusta became the first creditor to seek legal recourse when he initiated three actions against the city of Savannah on past-due coupons. Merchants National Bank followed Curry's actions later in April for recovery of $57,000.[27]

Turning to courts swiftly, however, did not mean the remedy or payment would be prompt. Legal delays could last for years. The wheels of justice turned very slowly, complicated by scheduling, motions, taking depositions, gathering evidence, et cetera. Litigation cost money in attorneys and court fees, and it did not guarantee success. Therefore, while creditors seemed to rush into credit litigation, in reality they viewed it as a last resort.[28]

The legal process for collection seemed clear. After a creditor filed suit, the case was heard in court. If the court judged the debt valid, the creditor received a judgment. At this point, the creditor had the right of "execution on the debtor's property." Bondholders would receive a "writ of execution empowering an officer of the court to seize" a corporation's assets.[29] At this point, the county sheriff took what equaled the creditors' claim (with certain exemptions). If the debtor did not have enough items to satisfy the debt, the courts would appoint a receiver empowered to reclaim sufficient assets to pay the creditor.[30]

However, this orderly legal process rarely proved so direct. More often the relationship between creditor and debtor was a "game of cat and mouse." When the debtor turned out to be a municipal government, where courts did not have the same power over all assets, all bets were off, and the process was further complicated by additional crafty maneuvers to avoid payment.[31] For instance, after Mobile and Memphis defaulted on their loans, city officials colluded with their respective state legislatures to revoke their city charters to avoid court judgments for payment.[32]

Debate concerning the city's finances dotted the pages of the *Savannah Morning News*. One contributor suggested that the time had come "for a general interchange of views" between the city, its bondholders, and the taxpayers who would no doubt have to "bear the burthen of debt" as real

estate was "not moveable." He implored the city council to have an open
discussion with the bondholders and adopt a plan "to relieve us from our
embarrassments." By the time the paper published this letter, city officials
were already working to that end, though citizens remained largely unaware of such action.[33]

Officials were attempting a very delicate balancing act. On the one
hand, they endeavored to calm creditor fears about the possibility of repudiation. On the other hand, they sought to provide creditors with a realistic, though bleak, analysis of the city's financial situation and its inability to continue repayment at the current interest rates. In a letter to J. B.
Manning, a New York banker, Tison attempted to squelch rumors of the
city's desire to scale and fund Savannah's debt in new bonds at seventy-
five cents on the dollar. Given the current debt, expenses, and projected
shortfalls of another $100,000 by year's end, Tison firmly stated that the
city could not afford it.[34]

TABLE 3. Resources of the City of Savannah, 1877

Railroad Stock, City Lots, and Other Property	Value
Atlantic and Gulf Railroad (12,383 shares)	$1,238,300
Western Railroad (1,307)	$130,700
Southwestern Railroad (1)	$100
SUBTOTAL	$1,369,100
Lots under lease (693)	$2,015,000
Lots not sold (35)	$20,000
Springfield Plantation	$40,000
Waterworks and site	$300,000
Part of Hutchinson Island	$10,000
City Dispensary	$8,000
Exchange Building	$100,000
New market house and fixtures	$150,000
City pound, etc.	$15,000
Fire Department lots and buildings	$76,000
Police barracks and property	$50,000
Powder magazine, keeper's house, etc.	$7,500
Tombs east of Exchange	$11,000
Streets and lands, lot, and stables	$12,000
Tract of land purchased from J. A. LaRoche	$7,000
Dredge machines, scows, and boats	$50,000
Tract of land from Georgia Infirmary on White Bluff Road	$9,000
SUBTOTAL	$2,973,500
TOTAL RESOURCES	$4,342,600

Source: Minutes of Council, May 30, 1877.

TABLE 4. Direct Liabilities of the City of Savannah, 1877

Bonds Outstanding	Value
Waterworks construction	$198,000.00
Savannah Gas Light Company	$15,000.00
Savannah River improvements	$64,000.00
Savannah, Albany and Gulf Railroad	$937,000.00
Funding coupons	$368,800.00
Redemption of bonds due 1869	$117,000.00
Redemption of bonds due 1870	$348,500.00
City improvements	$534,000.00
Harbor and other improvements	$500,000.00
To meet outstanding indebtedness	$400,000.00
SUBTOTAL	$3,473,800.00
Mayors' Notes	
Outstanding	$219,871.82
H. R. Worthington, new pump for waterworks	$25,000.00
Coupons past due and interest on past obligations	$7,500.00
SUBTOTAL	$3,798,346.82
Contingent Liabilities	
City's Atlantic and Gulf Railroad endorsement	$300,000.00
Interest on them paid and unpaid	$10,500.00
TOTAL	$4,108,846.82

Source: City of Savannah Finance Committee Report, 1877; and Gamble, *History of the City Government*, 294–95.

TABLE 5. Estimated Assets of the City of Savannah, 1877

Description	Value
Property	$584,585.00*
Taxation from income	$376,650.00
Expense	$219,450.00
Balance	$157,200.00
Matured obligations, bonds, coupons, mayors' notes	$317,046.82
About-to-mature bonds and coupons	$628,754.00

*Prior to this point, the municipal report had set the city's assets at $4,300,000.
Source: City of Savannah Finance Committee Report, 1877; and Gamble, *History of the City Government*, 294–95.

TABLE 6. Estimated Assets of the
City of Savannah, 1878

Description	Value
Income	$300,000
Expense	$180,000
Balance	$120,000
Deficit at end of 1878	$668,600

Source: City of Savannah Finance Committee
Report, 1877; and Gamble, *History of the City
Government*, 294–95.

TABLE 7. Estimated Assets of the
City of Savannah, 1879

Description	Value
Maturing bonds	$117,000.00
Atlantic and Gulf Railroad bonds and interest	$342,000.00
Deficit at end of 1879	$1,127,600.82

Source: City of Savannah Finance Committee Report, 1877;
and Gamble, *History of the City Government*, 294–95.

Though the finance committee failed to issue a detailed report, in early
May it advised the council to begin negotiations with its creditors. The
council promptly acted on the recommendation, though Waring dissented because he wanted the report to define the legal standing of the
city and the creditors.[35] By the time Savannah's leaders initiated official
negotiations, creditors were fed up with the national epidemic of cities attempting to compromise or repudiate their loans and were determined
that Savannah would not escape from its obligations.

CHAPTER 11

A "Monster and Hermaphrodite"

CREDITORS MUST HAVE THEIR MONEY

At the end of May 1877, Mayor Wheaton met with the city's bondholders in New York. Creditors hoped that Wheaton and his associates were there to convince them that they had been "unduly alarmed" by sensationalist and dire reports from Georgia and to assure them that Savannah had "no intention of repudiation." They were not pleased with what they heard. Though Savannah may have been planning to compromise its debt, its representatives assured bondholders that they expected "no such figure as twenty-five cents on the dollar" as rumors had indicated.[1]

Wheaton presented creditors with a detailed and dreary report of the city's dire financial situation: a debt of over $4 million, assets of just over $1 million, a depression in trade, bankruptcy of one of the city's railroads, the inability to collect any taxes for the previous year, and citizens poverty-stricken due in part to the recent yellow fever epidemic.

Savannah was working at a severe disadvantage. Because its population had decreased by at least four thousand since 1870, it would be impossible to tax citizens at a rate high enough to pay the interest on the debt. The most the city could expect to levy would be $350,000. Given all the factors, Wheaton predicted it would take the city twenty years "to recover from her present prostration." In a more positive vein, he reminded the creditors that the city had "not thought of repudiation." Instead, it hoped for "time and leniency concerning interest." Having shown the city's finances in the worst possible light and the city's efforts and intentions in the best light, Wheaton then laid out the city's compromise offer: Savannah's leaders wanted to issue new bonds to be held at par for thirty years with graded interest, starting with 3 percent for the first ten years, 4 percent for the next ten years, and 6 percent for the remaining years.[2]

The creditors balked. Insulted by the city's offer, especially the idea of 3 percent interest, J. B. Manning threatened to "sue the city before he would take less than 5 per cent." He warned that "too much" had been made of the city's poverty from the epidemic considering all the contributions it had received from generous donors. Eugene Kelly, who was heavily invested in both the Atlantic and Gulf Railroad and other projects in Savannah, agreed with Manning on this point, pronouncing that Savannah had gone into debt by "granting subsidies to railroads, which had been constantly increased by issuing new bonds to pay off the old ones and by borrowing." Manning advised the mayor to close all the city parks, divide them into lots, and sell them off for the benefit of its creditors.[3]

By 1877, having already experienced a spate of repudiation schemes from other states and municipalities, the piqued creditors felt justified in taking a hard line. Savannah's situation was by no means isolated or unique. In the summer of 1877, scathing editorials appeared bemoaning the "epidemic of repudiation," whereby public bodies sought to "swindle their creditors."[4] One critic warned that if public corporations were allowed to repudiate their debts, soon private corporations would find a way to do the same.[5]

Along with criticism of repudiations, which some believed had reached "frightful proportions," there were calls for legislative remedies that would "enable the courts of the United States to apply an adequate remedy to creditors, as against political communities whether they be municipalities or states."[6] In spite of burgeoning litigation, there was no single or consistently successful systematic legal remedy for defaulting and recalcitrant municipalities, for neither the creditors nor the courts had the power to levy taxes on a city's citizens. There would be no federal bankruptcy law until 1933.[7]

In part the difficulty resulted from the confusion as to where the municipal corporation existed on the political, legal, and economic spectrum. Municipalities in many ways acted as private corporations, but they existed as entities of their states, which had already demonstrated their willingness to invoke the Eleventh Amendment in defense of their own repudiation schemes. Divergent court cases reflected this difficulty in making the public-private distinction. In part, it was the heavy investment of cities and their enormous debts that undermined the de facto sovereignty of the cities by the 1880s.[8]

The creditors, having summarily rejected the city's offer, issued a counterproposal to compromise at eighty cents on the dollar for the bonds and a regular interest rate of 6 percent.[9] Wheaton warned the creditors that the council could not agree to those terms and threatened that if they "pressed too hard on the city it would be worse for both."[10]

Citizens finally received the finance committee's report after Wheaton's return from New York. The picture painted by the committee, that the "present and prospective debt of the city" was "quite double the ability of the community to sustain," was bleak.[11] In a *Savannah Morning News* summary of the report, the editor remarked that the situation was "by no means encouraging." He maintained that the city "had been brought to its present unhappy condition through a train of unfortunate circumstances which could not be foreseen, and, therefore, could not be guarded against." Savannah had acquired its debt at a time when "money was easy, business brisk, and everything looked well for the future."[12]

Like city officials, the *Savannah Morning News* worked to balance the situation with the city's objectives, all the while denying the persistent rumor that Savannah intended to repudiate its debt. City officials consistently insisted they would "make an earnest effort" to work with creditors and "submit to any burden which can be borne to satisfy the city's obligations." Nonetheless, creditors needed to understand and accept that there was a definite "point at which ability fails and burdens prove too heavy to be borne." Responding to Augusta and Macon bondholders, who asserted their confidence that the city could and would pay its debt, the *Savannah Morning News* asserted that they "overestimated [Savannah's] financial ability."[13]

Bondholders, already fed up with defaulting and recalcitrant cities, warned Savannah against repudiation and attempt to scale its debt. Those in Augusta demanded that Savannah fund its debt at no less than 7 percent and suggested that the city institute a 2 percent tax on real estate. Charleston bondholders, representing over $700,000 more bonds than those in Augusta, proved slightly more conciliatory in offering to accept 6 percent as long as the bonds would be forever exempt from taxation. It is possible that Charleston's leniency may have been related to its difficulties in servicing its own debt.[14]

A bondholder meeting held in Savannah in early June, representing

more than $1 million of the outstanding coupons, demonstrated contin-
ued intransigence on the part of the creditors to accept the city's compromise proposal. After a rancorous debate, attendees settled for the appointment of a committee to examine the city's finances.[15]

In an attempt to lift the city's spirits, the *Savannah Morning News*
printed an editorial recounting the difficulties but predicting a bright future. It observed that the people seemed to be "in the depths of despon-
dency" to the point that one would think that "the whole country was
utterly and irretrievably ruined." Accepting and perpetuating the narrative of postwar financial mistakes, the article admitted that municipal leaders had made some mistakes in management after the war, when
money "became ... regarded as a thing of no consequence" and northerners flooded the South with capital. Yet the fact that "men cannot live beyond their incomes nor on a false basis forever" was clearly demonstrated
by the Panic of 1873, "after which the cry was almost universal of 'dull
times.'" After the yellow fever epidemic, the naysayers had claimed that
the event was "the last straw to break the camel's back, and in the most
lachrymose manner pronounced that everything had 'gone to pot.'" The
Morning News editor denied that such was the case. In reality, the city
had continued to improve, houses had continued to be built, and businesses had continued to expand. Therefore, the editor asserted, "the 'hard
times' in the past and present" had been "more in the imagination than
in the reality." Readers were advised that there was "no necessity for long
faces and further complaining." Rather, they needed to "keep their spirits
up" and to look "on the bright side of the picture." As evidence, the editor noted that the cotton and rice crops, which were expected to be even
more profitable than the preceding ones, would "ensure to the city . . .
commercial prosperity.[16]

Commerce statistics seemed to support this perspective. By 1877 Savannah's share of cotton exports, the perennial bellwether of economic
health, had increased. Like other port cities, it had taken a minor hit in
1876–77, but it had been comparatively less affected than Charleston and
Mobile. Furthermore, the gap between Savannah's business and that of
the two other port cities was widening. By this point, the rail connections fostered by Savannah had initiated a shift of cotton movement away
from the Gulf ports to the South Atlantic ports. Savannah had once again
passed both Charleston and Mobile, to become the second-largest cotton
port; only New Orleans was larger.[17]

The deplorable financial situation of the municipal government, however, was not a figment of their collective imagination. Neither trusting things to work out on their own nor willing to rely on Savannah's elected officials to act in the taxpayers' interest, a group of taxpayers and bond-holders sought the aid of the courts. Represented by Henry R. Jackson, they filed a bill of injunction to prevent city authorities from paying any claims other than current expenses. Because various creditors had already demonstrated willingness to force payment though the courts, taxpay-ers believed others would follow their example. The ultimate result would be creditor competition for the earliest judgments and the further "crip-pling" of the city. The bill of injunction also requested that the court ap-point a receiver to take charge of certain municipally owned property and hold it for the court's direction. The injunction essentially sought to treat the city as an individual or private corporation, though it was neither. The proclaimed goal of this action was to "prevent the city from being forced to repudiate her obligations." If every bondholder decided to bring suit, the end would be a long time in coming, and it would force the city gov-ernment to act in a way that would ultimately be detrimental to those creditors. In other words, they were taking preemptive action in the event that Savannah lost the suits in which it was already involved. The petition, however, did not prevent Augusta's George Curry from filing six addi-tional suits.[18]

Although Jackson maintained that the injunction was absolutely nec-essary to prevent creditors from becoming vultures through the courts, one point of the injunction bill threatened to undermine all creditor claims. The suit claimed that Savannah's outstanding coupons, amount-ing to over $3 million, had been "issued without authority of law" and were therefore "invalid."[19] Cities had the authority to issue municipal bonds for public purposes, which traditionally had been defined very broadly. For over forty years, Savannahians had made the argument that railroad investment was a public enterprise; now they reversed that stance. It ap-peared that Savannah was preparing either to repudiate its debt or to bring about a compromise that would delay bondholder action and "force them into accepting such terms as the people of Savannah might, at their convenience, be graciously pleased to offer." If this move were successful, it would enable Savannah to "strip the bondholders of nearly the whole of their property." The *Savannah Morning News* attempted to defend tax-payer actions and denied that the injunction was the first step toward re-pudiation. Rather, they were trying to protect themselves from creditors who were "eager to secure the first slice of the city's property."[20]

Though such action received creditor censure, ailing cities burdened by such debt regularly made this argument, and, given the divergent court decisions whereby state courts had invalidated both state and municipal bonds issued in aid of railroads, it was a rational move that held some chance of success.[21] When a city defaulted, all creditors had to agree to an adjustment. There were no laws requiring every creditor to accept any plan, even though most creditors did so. Because minority bondholders could reject any agreement, it was virtually impossible to obtain full consent for readjustment plans.[22] In Duluth, Minnesota, for instance, while courts had ruled that the bond issues had been legal, the state had managed to avoid payment for eighteen years; as a result, some creditors eventually accepted 50 percent of what was owed to them.[23]

When Savannah's taxpayer injunction case appeared before the court, it took an unexpected turn. The original injunction had named the mayor and aldermen as defendants. After various creditor representatives made their statements, the attorney for the city council confirmed that negotiations were in process and that various suits had already been filed against the city, the goal of which was to obtain preference. With regard to the legality of the debt, however, the city's attorney demurred, stating that the courts would have to decide the question. Because the various court actions on behalf of the creditors to obtain preference would "defeat the end now sought," the mayor and aldermen, as defendants in the case, requested that the court grant the injunction.[24]

When Jackson pleaded the taxpayers' case, he explained that Savannah was no longer a municipality but a "monster and hermaphrodite." Jackson stressed the point that the city government could not be treated as a private corporation. He provided a brief summary of the municipal corporation's borrowing power, which was granted by the state legislature and had been "exercised to the great detriment and injury of the corporation." Jackson claimed that the power granted to Savannah had led to increased indebtedness and to "extravagance and ruination in the prosecution of works of public improvement." Unfortunately, while it could not be denied that the city had created the situation, it had "done nothing to afford relief." The petitioners merely wanted to give the negotiations a chance to be successful before initiating a chaotic situation whereby potentially 4,532 distinct lawsuits could be filed against the city, which would result not only in legal chaos but also in a complete devaluation of the city's real estate. In spite of Jackson's persuasive two-hour oratory, the judge denied the bill for injunction.[25]

Citizen action did not ingratiate Savannah with its creditors, especially after the mayor and aldermen sided with the taxpayers. The *New York Nation* referred to the application as "one of the most shameful exhibitions of dishonest intent ever openly published by the businessmen of a commercial and civilized city." The *Savannah Morning News* could only respond, "We do not pretend to decide whether or not such action [injunction application] was wise; but we do believe that the motive which prompted it was good."[26]

After the failure of the injunction, everyone waited for the bondholder committee to issue its report. Creditors warned the city against attempting to follow the precedents of Mobile and Memphis by trying to "scale their bond to fifty per cent" because Savannah was in much better overall economic condition than the other cities and was expected to "regain her prosperity" soon.[27]

When the bondholder committee met with the city council in a closed-door session in mid-December, the impasse that had existed in the summer remained. Bondholders offered to fund coupons up to July 2, 1878, in long bonds at 5 percent interest. Savannah would pay interest on all its bonds after July 2, 1878, and create a sinking fund commission composed of people not connected with city government. Savannah was to pay rents that it collected to the sinking fund commission, which would invest the income exclusively in city bonds. Finally, the council was to levy taxes sufficient to pay interest and current expenses. But the council refused to be moved from its proposal to implement a graduated interest payment schedule.[28]

A few days later, one of the members of the bondholder committee granted an interview to the *Augusta Chronicle*. After criticizing Savannah's plan, he added insult to injury, reminding Savannah that "Charleston had had a scalawag and negro government during ten years, and yet Charleston never talked of repudiation. Savannah's debt had been made by her own citizens, her best men, and this they did not deny."[29]

Holding Charleston up as a model to Savannah may have hit home. However, the reality was that Charleston's economic woes had been overshadowed by South Carolina's planned repudiation of the state debt. Only three months earlier, Charleston's mayor had announced that the city would be unable to meet the October interest payments on its debt due to uncollected taxes. The next month, the city council had authorized the mayor to borrow as much as possible to pay the interest on its debts.[30] Within a year came rumors that Charleston was considering following the same path as Memphis and Mobile in compromising its debt—by one account nearly as large as that of the state—and abolishing its city charter.[31]

In spite of the bondholders' rejection, the council moved forward with its proposal to compromise the debt with graded interest rates, and it passed an ordinance to that effect.[32] In an effort to rally bondholder support, the *Savannah Morning News* dutifully published an editorial commending the compromise, noting that "not one dollar of the face value would be repudiated." Rather, only the interest was to be reduced. Warming to the subject, the editor maintained that no other compromise was "so perfectly fair in every particular, or so entirely advantageous to the bondholders." Furthermore, this action would allow Savannah "to set itself on the right foot."[33] Once bondholders accepted this compromise, the city would be in a "condition to master the situation and be relieved of her financial troubles," which would, in turn, assure Savannah's future prosperity. Marshaling its forces, the *Savannah Morning News* also reprinted a *Macon Telegraph* editorial favorably disposed to the compromise, stating that the terms were "not only fair but very liberal."[34]

Augusta bondholders, on the other hand, immediately rejected the proposal. George Curry, who had been the first to initiate a suit against the city, worried that Savannah's legal counsel would argue that city property could not be sold under judgment, and he predicted that Savannah planned "to fight to the bitter end all creditors who push and will not compromise." Though Curry was confident of ultimate payment, it would come only after the cases went to the Supreme Court because the defendant had the power to "delay considerably the collection of a perfectly valid claim." Far from encouraging further negotiations, the number of suits filed against the city grew.[35]

Having failed to convince enough bondholders to accept its compromise, the city council made another attempt to resolve the matter. It finally scuttled the demand for a graded interest rate and pursued a compromise that set the interest at a uniform 5 percent, which councilmen believed would be more favorably received by the bondholders. This seemingly sudden reversal on the part of the city, which had previously rejected such a plan, may have been possible because the recent property assessment had exceeded previous projections by an estimated $2 million. The city finally agreed to convert ground rents into taxable property.[36] As predicted, bondholders welcomed this proposal. The new proposition received another boost when the *Savannah Morning News* published a letter from Robert Toombs to Alexander Lawton stating that he considered the most recent compromise proposal "fair, just and honorable" and that, as such, he planned to accept it.[37]

After overcoming the objections of several councilmen, who remained committed to the original proposal, the council received the proposition signed by bondholders encompassing this new proposal. Bondholders, under the conditions of this new compromise, would exchange their current bonds for new ones at their face value to run for thirty years and pay 5 percent quarterly interest. The council referred the proposal to the finance committee.[38]

The finance committee subsequently recommended acceptance and drafted an ordinance for that purpose. While the majority of the board wanted to pass the ordinance that same night, Waring objected, and the council was forced to table it until the next meeting. Having prevented the passage of the compromise ordinance, Waring introduced a resolution of his own. He brought to the council's notice "certain grave differences of opinion" among its members regarding the effects of the proposal on real estate owners who might "find themselves unable to carry out the sundry terms of this compromise except by forced levies of taxation, which will finally compel a ruinous sacrifice of property." Rather than summarily pass this new ordinance, Waring urged, the council ought to call a meeting of freeholders in November to consider this new proposal. In a seven-to-three vote, the council indefinitely postponed Waring's resolution. At the next meeting, the council passed the new compromise ordinance and authorized the mayor and finance committee to begin the process of obtaining bondholder consent.[39]

By early August 1878, the *Commercial and Financial Chronicle* reported that the holders of Savannah's bonds and coupons, representing about $1 million, had agreed to accept new bonds in exchange for those then outstanding.[40] Once creditors indicated their willingness to accept the compromise, the city's representatives introduced a bill in the General Assembly to authorize the municipal government to carry out its terms. The General Assembly sanctioned the compromise in mid-December. The council then authorized the mayor and the finance committee to have new 5 percent bonds engraved. By the end of the month, council had also elected the first sinking fund commissioners to supervise the amortization of Savannah's debt.[41]

In the spring and summer of 1877, as Savannah's officials negotiated its financial crisis, Georgians had begun advocating for the calling of a constitutional convention. The subsequent convention, so often associated with the reactionary policies of the indomitable Robert Toombs, also tackled the more immediate problem of municipal debt.

Alongside calls to abrogate various aspects of the state's constitution of 1868 were demands that the convention delegates deal with the problem of municipal debt. In an article published in support of calling the 1877 constitutional convention, the *Sumter Republican* listed the "bond question" as its primary concern, followed by the need to prohibit states from aiding railroads and to "restrain the municipalities and other public corporations in Georgia in the abuse of their credit." Specifically mentioning Savannah, it noted that the city was "tottering on under a bonded debt of $4 millions of dollars." It was one of many cities in similar situations.[42] Two months later, the *Macon Telegraph* reiterated the need for a convention for the "regulation of municipal indebtedness and taxation."[43]

One proponent maintained that the convention should "restrict the money borrowing power of the Legislature, and of the municipal government of every town and city in the State."[44] There was little doubt that one of the most important and pressing issues would be the "regulation of municipal indebtedness and taxation," which had been a "great embarrassment." Though the state had readily enough repudiated portions of its own debt and successfully challenged the federal courts, there was great support for doing something to "check municipal extravagance" and thus "save the bondholders from repudiation" and the citizens from "excessive taxation." Those advocating for a constitutional convention and those setting the agenda for it saw a great need to "protect the towns and counties from the incompetency, extravagance or corruption of local government." Otherwise, the threat was repudiation.[45]

The convention ultimately "put its strong hand on this evil" and set to "throttling the monster of unrestricted municipal and county indebtedness." One commentator noted that this was "alone worth all that the Convention cost."[46] The convention addressed the issue of municipal debt in two ways. First, it limited municipal indebtedness to 7 percent of the assessed value of all taxable property. Second, it instituted more stringent requirements for debt repayment. While municipalities kept the power to incur indebtedness, they had to provide for a tax that would cover both the principal and interest of the debt within thirty years. Municipalities, which had opted to borrow rather than raise taxes, would no longer have that option.[47]

The relief with which the city greeted the debt resolution quickly evapo-
rated. Councilmen had willfully ignored Waring's warning regarding the
Atlantic and Gulf Railroad bonds, but his prediction had proved correct.
In 1859 the mayor and aldermen of Savannah had endorsed $300,000 in
bonds, to run for twenty years, for the Savannah and Albany Railroad.
Until January 1877, the Savannah and Albany, subsequently the Savannah,
Albany and Gulf and then the Atlantic and Gulf Railroad, had managed
to cover the interest coupons on those bonds. Since then, the Atlantic and
Gulf Railroad had defaulted, and the company had passed into receiver-
ship. When the bonds matured on January 1, 1879, the railroad's creditors
pressed the city for payment.[48] Not surprisingly, councilmen disagreed
over the proper response. Echoing some of the claims recently presented,
the finance committee reported that it had "grave doubts as to the legality
of the city endorsements of said bonds." The committee further warned
that, depending on the court's ruling, if council paid any of the creditors
and the court ruled that the city was not liable, the property of individual aldermen might be liable for misappropriation of the city's money.[49]

When asked for a legal opinion, William D. Harden, the corporation
attorney, stated that he did not believe that the city was "legally liable" for
payment. He further maintained that the city, because it had not paid its
"legal indebtedness," probably did not have the right to make such a payment. Atlantic and Gulf Railroad bondholders turned to the courts and
brought suit against the city. Not all councilmen accepted this argument.
Alderman Henry Blun offered a resolution that council was "ready to en-
tertain propositions" from bondholders who were seeking adjustments on
liability for more than $300,000. Daniel G. Purse, the chairman of the fi-
nance committee, opposed Blun's resolution. He argued that such an action was "virtually acknowledging the liability of the city for this endorsement." If the courts ruled in the city's favor, Purse cautioned the aldermen,
they would be "liable for its misappropriation of the city's money." Blun,
unmoved by Purse's argument, maintained that the endorsement appeared to have been given by the city "in good faith." Blun failed to convince enough of his fellow councilmen, and they voted to table his resolution indefinitely. This disagreement was not unusual. As James Burhans
noted in 1889, "Probably no question in American jurisprudence has been
more persistently and thoroughly litigated than the validity of municipal
bonds issued in aid of railroads."[50]

Having only recently settled matters with their own creditors, the city
faced another embarrassing financial situation. Divided over the endorse-

ment's validity, the aldermen left the decision to Mayor Wheaton, who formed a separate committee to determine the most effective means of protecting the city's interests.[51]

Ultimately, the city, most likely for purposes of delay, opted to let the courts decide the issue of responsibility in the suit filed by Eugene Kelly and A. M. Martin, who held coupon bonds of the Savannah, Albany and Gulf Railroad Company, which bore the endorsed guarantee of the City of Savannah. In a U.S. circuit court, William S. Chisholm, the city council's attorney, argued that Savannah's guarantee had been made without legal authority and was therefore void. The municipal government had no authority to endorse the bonds, and it had never directly issued the bonds; furthermore, the bonds were not issued for works of internal improvement, "for which purpose alone the city was ever authorized to issue any bonds." Chisholm also argued on a more technical basis that, when the Savannah, Albany and Gulf Railroad consolidated with the Atlantic and Gulf Railroad, Kelly had accepted the Atlantic and Gulf Railroad as his debtor in place of the Savannah, Albany and Gulf Railroad. The introduction of this new party therefore relieved the city from its liability.[52] Savannah's effort at repudiating its railroad-related indebtedness was not without precedent. In 1872 and again in 1875, the Georgia General Assembly engaged in two rounds of railroad bond repudiation.[53]

Judge William B. Woods of the Fifth Judicial Circuit rejected all of the city's arguments. The questions were whether Savannah had the power to guarantee these bonds and whether there was "a good and valid consideration for the guaranty." The bonds were issued only after the city held a public meeting at which there were no protests regarding council's recommendation to issue the bonds. Unable to pay the costs demanded by the court immediately, the city deposited new city bonds into the hands of a trustee for sale in the event that the city's appeal to the Supreme Court failed. Encouraged by the result of the lower court's decision against the city, other bondholders opted to file suit.[54]

In the spring of 1883, the U.S. Supreme Court finally settled the case by upholding the ruling of the circuit court. It directed the city to establish a sinking fund and issue new bonds as part of another compromise with bondholders, who agreed to accept new bonds payable in thirty years at 5 percent interest.[55] The city thus became responsible for $390,000 in bonds, which required $19,500 in annual interest. After initial reluctance, most bondholders accepted the compromise. By the close of 1884, the city had exchanged all but $9,500 of those bonds. By 1885, that number had been reduced to $2,500.[56]

By the early 1880s, Savannah had reached a compromise on its debt, and it appeared that it had learned from the consequences of the decisions of the previous decade. What an analysis of the city's receipts and expenditures indicates is that the city did not make any drastic changes in its taxes. Receipts averaged between $500,000 and $600,000, comparable to the receipts of the 1870s. The expenditures, however, demonstrate that the city had decided to eschew the types of large projects and improvements subsidies that had drowned the city in debt. From a high of $2,586,817 in expenditures in 1872, the city lowered its average annual spending to between $500,000 and $600,000 in the next decade.[57]

The compromises also lowered the amount of interest for which the city was responsible each year. At no time during the next ten years did Savannah face the $250,000 to $300,000 payments under which it had once struggled. And finally, the most striking difference in the 1880s was the total amount of mayors' notes issued. During the 1870s, Anderson, Screven, and Wheaton issued mayors' notes amounting to $3,788,642. During the 1880s, only $11,282 of mayors' notes were issued.[58] Rather than pinning its hopes on achieving greatness through large-scale public works in order to enhance the city's image and prestige, Savannah focused on sustaining what it already had.

Savannah ended the decade on a much more optimistic note. With cotton receipts once again up, one could witness the "long procession of cotton loaded drays" carrying their burdens along the waterfront.[59] By 1880, Savannah, with a fourth straight year of export increases, was outpacing every major Atlantic Coast rival except Norfolk. The following year, Savannah exported nearly double the amount of cotton it had in 1861 on the eve of the war. Merchants invested in two new cotton presses— United Hydraulic and Tyler. Naval and lumber sales also did well. Prospects for naval stores were especially bright, and Savannah hoped to establish itself as the "grand centre of the naval store trade in the South." Savannah Paper Mill Company was producing three tons of paper daily, making it the largest in the South. The Ocean Steamship Company (osc), originally organized by the directors of the Central Railroad, was planning the construction of a new iron ship with a capacity of six thousand bales. By the mid-1880s, osc was the largest and wealthiest local steamship line on the coast between Baltimore and New Orleans. And the

Central Railroad once again began paying dividends, which it had suspended after the 1873 panic.[60] None of these things would have been possible had the city government failed to pursue the path of aggressive risk
taking.

By 1880, the city was looking forward to the next decade and predicting good things to come. Savannah was in "a state of prosperity." "Hardy
congratulations" went around as the commerce of the port exceeded all
expectations. Merchants were less indebted, the price of lumber had rebounded, truck farmers were doing well, and naval stores commerce had
increased. The *Savannah Morning News* confidently predicted that there
was nothing "to prevent Savannah from progressing steadily and surely
onward in commercial importance."[61]

——— •◆• ———

Lessons Learned,
Ambitions Reevaluated

Cities like Savannah had pursued aggressive policies of municipal entrepreneurship in their quest to maintain, protect, or extend their status vis-à-vis other cities. Not every venture succeeded. The Savannah and Ogeechee Canal certainly failed to meet Savannah's expectations. Other projects, however, proved enormously successful. The investment in the Central Railroad not only protected Savannah from Charleston but also enabled it to emerge from its elder sibling's shadow. That company's financial success tempted Savannah into investing, sometimes with more bravado than financial good sense, in similar enterprises. While the Southwestern Railroad, thanks to its connection with the Central, also emerged as a solid line, others—like the Atlantic and Gulf, were less fortunate.

On the eve of the Civil War, the various railroads in Georgia had expanded into the interior and continued to serve their own interests as well as the cities from which they originated. This symbiotic relationship initially continued after the war. The expansion of transportation produced more tightly integrated regional and national economies, which decreased the influence cities once had over locally started transportation facilities. Improved transportation also allowed for more efficient communication with the interior. Merchants in small towns connected by railroads began usurping the roles played by coastal cotton factors, undermining their influence and wealth. Similar trends can be seen with cotton compressors and crediting.[1] This fundamentally limited the power of port cities to determine their own destinies.

Railroad companies, like cities, sought to expand their reach and protect themselves from competition. Ultimately, expansion made competition inevitable. Such was the case when Savannah's two major roads
found themselves fighting for the same territory in southwestern Georgia. Rather than benefiting Savannah, the Central Railroad and the Atlantic and Gulf Railroad attempted to use their power to influence Savannah's financial policies, which ultimately undermined Savannah's ability
to relieve itself of debts worth over $1 million. Furthermore, these types of
clashes over territory accelerated efforts to eliminate competition through
exclusive contracts, lease agreements, and freight-sharing arrangements.
These new alignments did not always produce the relationship that had
once been so symbiotic.

Significant changes in the lives of Savannahians occurred after the
Civil War, but their outlook regarding their city's purpose or potential
did not necessarily change. Savannah's leaders accommodated themselves
to the new order of constant change while trying to maintain the methods that seemed to have served them so well in the decades before the
war. Even as they strove to realize the goals of the past, they faced increasing obstacles to further growth and advancement related to unique
southern conditions: traditional one-party politics, natural disasters, financial disasters—both national and local; dependence on an extractive
economy; competition from other seaport cities for a piece of an increasingly smaller pie; and hostility from the state's interior.

Municipal leaders pursued economic recovery and revitalization even
as they sought to maintain political stability. This meant maintaining local control over their government and the labor force. These objectives
ran counter to those of the federal government and freedpeople. Yet conservative leaders in Savannah fervently believed that economic prosperity would return to the city with the end of political uncertainty. Between
1865 and 1873, Savannah's leaders continued to engage in municipal entrepreneurship. They devoted their energy and the city's treasury to repel-
ling Republican bids for political power, protecting the precarious public
credit, subsidizing the restoration of river operations, and underwriting
the improvement of the city's infrastructure.

The federal government's interest in reconstructing the South waned,
and southern conservatives regained home rule. Throughout the South,
as municipalities from Mobile to Memphis began faltering under the
weight of municipal debt, they readily portrayed themselves as victims of

Radical Reconstruction. Such claims made threats of repudiation or mer-
cenary compromises politically acceptable. Democrats in Savannah, however, never surrendered control of the city. In this sense, Savannah's narrative did not mirror that of other southern cities. John Screven, a Democrat
and native son, had escalated municipal spending beyond what the treasury could sustain.

When Edward Anderson succeeded Screven as mayor in 1873, he discovered a financial crippled city, and the situation was exacerbated by the
Panic of 1873 and the subsequent depression. Anderson, who had been a
frequent, if private, critic of Screven's management ability, attempted to
clean up what he considered his predecessor's mess. Over the next three
years, Anderson fought a rearguard campaign to keep the city solvent. He
recognized that his administration would have to take drastic measures to
alleviate the city's financial situation. However, increased taxes, decreased
municipal services, Anderson's increasingly abrasive attitude, and his willingness to use the police force to enforce tax collection disaffected the citizenry, who revolted. The end of the revolt coincided with a yellow fever
epidemic, which further strained the city's precarious financial position.
Decades of optimistic yet at times reckless risk-taking finally caught up
with the city. It would be left to Anderson's successor to rectify the problems. By the time the nation was emerging from the depression triggered
by the 1873 panic, the City of Savannah was still in the midst of negotiating with its creditors over the huge debt it had already acquired.

Yet, as the city's treasury lay prostrate, creditors prepared their legal of-
fensives, and observers maligned such abuses of municipal credit, the reality for Savannah business was somewhat brighter. As several creditors
had pointed out at the height of the default crisis, Savannah was in a better financial condition than other cities. Though one would not use the
term "booming," Savannah's commercial condition was healthier, in part
because its rail lines continued to transport cotton to the coast city for export. Savannah's situation was better than that of its old rivals, in part because of the very rail connections the city fostered both directly and indirectly. For the city itself, the hard times of the 1870s eventually faded,
replaced by the more prosperous 1880s. Savannah's municipal treasury experienced slow but steady improvement during the last two decades of the
century. By 1883, Savannah had settled its debt crisis and, like its southern
counterparts, begun focusing again on updating and expanding its municipal services. This time, though, in part due to lessons learned and in part

due to constitutional restrictions, leaders accepted the need for more stability and predictability in annual budgets. They were more careful and realistic about matching projects to expected revenue.

The slow population growth that characterized the 1870s (just under 9 percent for the decade) did not continue into the 1880s, during which the population increased by 40 percent. And between 1890 and 1920, the population continued to grow at an average of nearly 25 percent per decade. What this meant for the city was a larger tax base from which to draw revenue. The increase in population reflected the improved economy, with more businesses opening and paying license fees and more property being purchased and improved. For instance, the value of taxable property increased from 1899 to 1904 by over $5 million. In one year, 1915–16, tax revenue from real estate alone increased by 25 percent. The new income from these taxes and the more responsible handling of finances allowed Savannah to pay down the debt that had nearly crippled it in the 1870s. By 1906, the city reached the point at which it was "within the constitutional limitation as to the bonded indebtedness of Georgia municipalities." In other words, Savannah "once more" had "the borrowing power within its hands." With improved credit, money that the city borrowed could be had at lower interest rates. The city's debt again went up during the second decade of the twentieth century, but so did its ability to service it.

In 1885, Timothy Harley, an English-born Baptist minister who toured the South, said of Savannah: "There are far vaster and wealthier cities, with much more commerce and culture than this city, but for the architectural simplicity and natural beauty, for an indescribable charm about its streets and buildings, its parks and squares, its trees and flowers, its general climate and congenial inhabitants, there is but one Savannah. Without a rival, without an equal, it stands unique."[2] Harley succinctly described both what Savannah had achieved and failed to achieve by the waning decades of the nineteenth century. Asserting that Savannah might yet be the next "New York or Liverpool of the Southern States," Harley was obviously impressed by the city and its potential. His optimism was similar to that which had so long permeated the hearts and minds of Savannah's citizens. For over five decades—long before so-called New South boosters tapped into the nation's imagination of what the South could be—Savannah's municipal government had aggressively pursued projects aimed at promoting the city's economic growth. More importantly, Savannah's efforts were little different from any urban area, as it sought ways to survive and thrive in the nation's ever-changing economic circumstances. Yet, by 1885, despite the municipality's mighty endeavors and the rhetoric of newspaper editors and other boosters, Savannah had yet to realize such lofty goals. Savannah's experience during those two turbulent decades following the war forced it to accept, albeit grudgingly, more limited goals. In participating in the larger national trend of boosterism long before its railroad helped establish cities like Atlanta, Savannah had already played its hand. Its leaders came to recognize that its self-concept ought not to be based on exaggerated claims of preeminence by New South boosters. The reality was more promising. Savannah's aggressive municipal entrepreneurship had provided the foundation for healthy commercial activity in a city whose economy allowed its "diligent citizens" to "cultivate the tree in winter, and in the summer sit down and enjoy the fruit."[3]

NOTES

———•◆•———

INTRODUCTION

1. Scrapbook, 1862–1896, in Sarah Alexander Cunningham Collection, MS 194, Georgia Historical Society, Savannah, Georgia.

2. Deaths attributed to yellow fever totaled 940. *Savannah Morning News*, July–November, 1876; Gamble, *History of the City Government of Savannah*, 288 (hereafter cited as Gamble, *History*); Georgia, State Board of Health, *Report of the Board of Health*; Le Hardy, *Yellow Fever*; James Johnston Waring, *Epidemic at Savannah, 1876*; Usinger, "Yellow Fever from the Viewpoint of Savannah."

3. Robert E. Wright, *One Nation under Debt*, 273–77; Miner, *Most Magnificent Machine*, 74; Amdursky and Gillette, *Municipal Debt Finance Law*, 14–18.

4. Holcombe and Lacombe, "Factors Underlying the Growth of Local Government in the 19th Century United States," 359, 372; Lance E. Davis and Legler, "Government in the American Economy," 523.

5. Amdursky and Gillette, *Municipal Debt Finance Law*, 18; Orth, *Judicial Power of the United States*, 113–14.

6. Dillon, *Commentaries on the Law of Municipal Corporations*, 181. Hillhouse estimates that from 1860 to 1880 there was a "fourfold increase" in municipal indebtedness. Hillhouse, *Municipal Bonds*, 39.

7. Dillon, *Commentaries on the Law of Municipal Corporations*, 181.

8. Holcombe and Lacombe, "Factors Underlying the Growth of Local Government in the 19th Century United States," 359. Bonds became the instrument of choice to finance railroads and other internal improvements. Cities either directly purchased bonds, guaranteed bonds, or subscribed to the capital stock of the corporation. Amdursky and Gillette, *Municipal Debt Finance Law*, 18.

9. Williams and Nehemkis, "Municipal Improvements as Affected by Constitutional Debt Limitations," 178.

10. Other examples include Rahway, New Jersey; Hudson County, New Jersey; Watertown, Massachusetts; Knox County, Indiana; Dubuque, Keokuk, and McGregor, Iowa; Winnebago and Johnson Counties, Iowa; Red River Parish, Louisiana; New Orleans and Shreveport, Louisiana; Winnetka, Quincy, and Cairo, Illinois; Macoupin County, Illinois; St. Joseph and Cape Girardeau, Missouri; Leavenworth, Lawrence, and Topeka, Kansas; Nebraska City, Nebraska; and Little Rock and Helena, Arkansas. "Enforcing Payment of Municipal Securities after Judgment," 159–60; Hillhouse, *Municipal Bonds*, 39–42, 88–95; Hume, "Are We a Nation of Rascals?" 131;

Orth, *Judicial Power of the United States*, 113–15; *New York Times*, August 11, 1873, June 8, 1877, December 24, 1878, and January 16, 1879.

11. Hillhouse, *Municipal Bonds*, 33–34, 42–43; Webb, *Railroad Construction, Theory and Practice*, 522; Thomason, *Mobile*; Ross, "Resisting the New South," 59–76; Wrenn, *Crisis in Commission Government in Memphis*; Sbragia, *Debt Wish*, 19–79; Monkonnen, "Politics of Municipal Indebtedness and Default, 1850–1936."

12. Sbragia, *Debt Wish*, 91.

13. Burhans, *Law of Municipal Bonds*, 3–4, 58; Frug, "City as a Legal Concept," 1101; Bensel, *Political Economy of American Industrialization, 1877–1900*, 65.

14. Hillhouse, *Municipal Bonds*, 43.

15. Neuteboom, *On the Rationality of Borrowers' Behaviour*, 14–16; Adams, *Risk*, 3.

16. Carl Abbott, *Boosters and Businessmen*, 199.

17. Robert E. Wright, *One Nation under Debt*, 25. Regarding "municipal entrepreneurship," historians have used a variety of terms to describe urban boosters. Brownell prefers "commercial-civic elites." Brownell, "Commercial Civic Elite and City Planning in Atlanta, Memphis, and New Orleans in the 1920s." Abbott refers to "collective entrepreneurship," which he defines as actions or ideas "expressed through city governments, corporations, and voluntary business associations" and requiring "consensus on common goals." Abbott, *Boosters and Businessmen*, 8–9. Rubin uses the term "municipal mercantilism." Rubin, "Canal or Railroad?," 14. In doing so, Rubin cites Cairns, "Response of New Orleans to the Diversion of Trade from the Mississippi River 1845–60," 144–45.

18. Fraser, *Savannah in the Old South*; Haunton, "Savannah in the 1850s"; DeCredico, *Patriots for Profit*; Abbott, *Boosters and Businessmen*, 5; Robert E. Wright, *One Nation under Debt*, 247–48.

19. Abbott, *Boosters and Businessmen*, 5.

20. Taylor, *Transportation Revolution, 1815–1860*, 86–88.

21. Goodrich, "Internal Improvements Reconsidered," 296. See also Goodrich, "Virginia System of Mixed Enterprise," 355–87.

22. Hartz, *Economic Policy and Democratic Thought*, 104.

23. Brown, *Municipal Bonds*. For example, between 1840 and 1850, Georgia's General Assembly devoted one-third of the state budget to railroad construction. Heath, *Constructive Liberalism*, 286–90; Brownell, "Commercial Civic Elite and City Planning in Atlanta, Memphis, and New Orleans in the 1920s," 339–68; Burhans, *Law of Municipal Bonds*, 19.

24. Balleisen, *Navigating Failure*, 31.

25. Construction on the canal began in 1817 and was completed in 1825. Quoted in Sellers, *Market Revolution*, 42. For additional information in the Erie Canal, see Bernstein, *Wedding of the Waters*; Koeppel, *Bond of Union*; McGreevy, *Stairway to Empire*; Howe, *What Hath God Wrought*, 222; Abbott, *Boosters and Businessmen*, 15.

26. Julius Rubin, "Canal or Railroad?"

27. Sellers, *Market Revolution*, 42–43. See also Downey, *Planting a Capitalist South*; Larson, *Internal Improvement*; Shaw, *Canals for a Nation*.

28. Sellers, *Market Revolution*, 44; Jackson and Schultz, *Cities in American History*, 5; Howe, *What Hath God Wrought*, 562–69.

29. Sellers, *Market Revolution*, 149; Downey, *Planting a Capitalist South*, chapters 2–3; Shore, *Southern Capitalists*, 101, 170.

30. Additional railroad investment included the Augusta and Waynesboro Railroad, Macon and Western Railroad, Milledgeville and Eatonton Railroad, Opelika Railroad, Muscogee Railroad, Savannah and Augusta Railroad, and the Monroe Railroad. Other infrastructural investments included gas and waterworks and river dredging operations. Regarding dry culture: Savannah officials, hoping to insulate the city from yellow fever, purchased lands and contracted with property owners to switch away from rice cultivation within the city limits. Annual Reports of the Mayor of Savannah, Georgia, 1855–1917, City of Savannah Research Library and Municipal Archives, Savannah (hereafter cited as Mayor's Reports); City of Savannah Minutes of Council, 1820–1860, Office of the Clerk of Council, Savannah; Minutes of the Central of Georgia Railway Company, 1840–1860, Central of Georgia Railway records, MS 1362, Georgia Historical Society, Savannah (hereafter cited as Central Railroad Minutes); Gamble, *History*, 188–200; Fraser, *Savannah in the Old South*, 244; Haunton, "Savannah in the 1850s," 156; "Commerce of Savannah," *DeBow's Review* 29 (November 1860): 669–70; Nimmo, *Annual Report Internal Commerce of the United States*, 81.

31. Municipal leaders referred to short-term loans as "mayors' notes." City of Savannah Minutes of Council, 1866–77; City of Savannah Finance Committee Papers, City of Savannah Research Library and Municipal Archives; *Savannah Morning News*, January 22, 1873.

32. This interpretation is associated with Don Harrison Doyle's excellent *New Men, New Cities, New South: Atlanta, Nashville, Charleston, Mobile, 1860–1910*, especially chapters 1–2. Goldfield, *Cotton Fields and Skyscrapers*; Brownell, "If You've Seen One, You Haven't Seen Them All"; Brownell, "Idea of the City in Southern History"; Folsom, *Urban Capitalists*; Chesson, *Richmond after the War*; Thomlinson, *Urban Structure*; Curry, "Urbanization and Urbanism in the Old South," 43–60; Blouin, *Boston Region, 1810–1850*; Rubin, "Canal or Railroad"; Belcher, *Economic Rivalry Between St. Louis and Chicago, 1850–1880*.

33. Woodward, *Origins of the New South, 1877–1913*. Southern historians took their cues from Woodward and generally followed his model. Examples include Grantham, *Democratic South*; Thomas Harry Williams, *Romance and Realism in Southern Politics*; Brandfon, *Cotton Kingdom of the New South*; Billington, *American South*; Kirwan, *Revolt of the Rednecks*; Going, *Bourbon Democracy in Alabama, 1874–1890*; Hair, *Bourbonism and Agrarian Protest*; Ezell, *South Since 1865*. In 1971 Sheldon Hackney asserted that there had been "no major challenge to *Origins of the New South*." Hackney, "'Origins of the New South' in Retrospect," 197. Beginning in the late 1970s, Woodward's thesis began to come under sustained attack. In 1978, James Tice Moore challenged Woodward's argument that a new group of men assumed the mantels of power after the Civil War. A forerunner of numerous planter persistence studies, Moore asserted

that a significant number of prewar political leaders regained political prominence in the postwar period. Further, he maintained that willingness to borrow for internal improvements so characteristic of postwar southern Democratic governments was merely an expanded version of prewar activity. Moore, "Redeemers Reconsidered," 357–78. Persistence provided the theme for additional challenges. Examples include Wiener, *Social Origins of the New South;* Billings, *Planters and the Making of a "New South";* Rabinowitz, *First New South, 1865–1920* and "Continuity and Change"; Temin, "Post-Bellum Recovery of the South and the Cost of the Civil War"; Bartley, "In Search of the New South"; and Mandle, *Roots of Black Poverty.* Other studies that weigh in to some degree on these debates include Gary Bolding, "Change, Continuity, and Commercial Identity of a Southern City"; Fraser and Moore, *From the Old South to the New;* Platt, *City Building in the New South;* Russell, *Atlanta, 1847–1890;* Cobb, "Beyond Planters and Industrialists"; Lewis, "Emergence of Birmingham as a Case Study of Continuity between the Antebellum Planter Class and Industrialization in the New South," 62–79; Gavin Wright, *Old South, New South;* Woodman, "Political Economy of the New South"; Ross, "Resisting the New South"; and Boles and Johnson, *Origins of the New South Fifty Years Later.* For detailed historiographical essays, see Reidy, "Economic Consequences of the Civil War and Reconstruction"; and Berry, "South: From Old to New."

34. For a discussion of this debate and representative works, see Edwards, "Southern History as U.S. History."

35. Davis and Legler, "The Government in the American Economy," 523–25. The period from the 1830s to the 1870s is often characterized as a time of "transition from the commercial to the industrial city." Yet, as Carl Abbott notes, this leaves "the complexities of change . . . largely unexplored." Abbott, *Boosters and Businessmen,* 32–33. Just as significant, it writes southern coastal cities out of the larger narrative. Cities like Savannah remained largely commercial. Thus compared to rapidly industrializing cities, they appeared to decline.

36. Abbott, *Boosters and Businessmen,* 4.

37. The Central Railroad connected to the Western and Atlantic via the Macon and Western in part to compete with the Augusta-based Georgia Railroad, which shipped goods to Charleston. Heath, *Constructive Liberalism,* 272; McGuire, "Railroads of Georgia, 1860–1880," 179–82.

38. "Commerce at Charleston," *DeBow's Review* 31 (October–November 1861): 460; "Commerce of Savannah," *DeBow's Review* 295 (November 1860): 669–70.

39. Klein, "Strategy of Southern Railroads," 1,061–65; Klein, *Great Richmond Terminal,* 1–29, 235–58; Klein, *History of the Louisville and Nashville Railroad,* 123–94, 263–87; Woodman, *King Cotton and His Retainers,* 12–30, 141–47, 205, 279; Woodman, "Political Economy of the New South," 795–99; Woodman, "Itinerant Cotton Merchants of the Antebellum South"; Woodman, "Decline of Cotton Factorage after the Civil War."

CHAPTER 1. "FAR FROM THIS 'RUIN'"

1. Historians estimate that no more than a dozen debtors arrived at the Trustees' expense. Saye, *New Viewpoints in Georgia History*, 3–50; Ready, "Georgia Concept"; Saye, "Genesis of Georgia Reviewed."

2. Miller, "Failure of the Colony of Georgia under the Trustees"; Wood, "Thomas Stephens and the Introduction of Black Slavery in Georgia."

3. For additional information on the Revolution in Georgia, see Coleman, *American Revolution in Georgia*; Pressly, *On the Rim of the Caribbean*.

4. Abbot, "Structure of Politics in Georgia," 47–65; Pressly, "Nationalizing the Lowcountry," chap. 11 in *On the Rim of the Caribbean*.

5. Pope, *Tour through the Southern and Western Territories of the United States of North-America*, 81.

6. George Washington, *Diary of George Washington, from 1789 to 1791*, 188.

7. Gibson, *Population of the 100 Largest Cities and Other Urban Places in the United States*.

8. Debow, *Seventh Census of the United States*, table 34; Charles C. Jones Jr., *History of Savannah, Ga.* (hereafter Jones, *History of Savannah*), 407.

9. Bonner, *History of Georgia Agriculture, 1732–1860*, 49; Jones, *History of Savannah*, 467.

10. Lee and Agnew additionally record 6,226 whites and 237 slaves and 415 kitchens. Lee and Agnew, *Historical Record of the City of Savannah*, 73, 137.

11. Soltow and Aubrey, "Housing and Social Standing in Georgia, 1798," 454–56.

12. John Davis, *Travels of Four Years and a Half in the United States of America*, 94, 100. In 1818 Savannah had some of the highest recorded temperatures in the nation. *National Weekly Recorder*, October 8, 1819.

13. La Rochefoucauld-Liancourt, *Travels through the United States of North America*, 610.

14. Gamble, *History*, 57, 64.

15. Gamble, *History*, 42, 79, 80, 82; Strong, "Glimpses of Savannah, 1780–1825," 32–34; Fraser, *Savannah in the Old South*, 166; Cates, "Medical History of Georgia in the First Hundred Years, 1733–1833," 61–62, 79, 101–2, 108.

16. Gibson, *Population of the 100 Largest Cities and Other Urban Places in the United States*; Gillespie, *Free Labor in an Unfree World*, 12; Gillespie, "Artisans and Mechanics in the Political Economy of Georgia 1790–1860," 7–19, 39.

17. Lee and Agnew, *Historical Record of the City of Savannah*, 137; Sholes, *Chronological History of Savannah*, 67; *Georgia Gazette*, March 19, 1801. In 1800 Savannah exported 3,444,420 pounds of cotton, and Charleston exported 6,425,163 pounds.

18. Gillespie, *Free Labor in an Unfree World*, 13.

19. Ryan and Golson, *Andrew Low and the Sign of the Buck*, 42.

20. Wallace Calvin Smith, "Georgia Gentlemen, the Habershams of Eighteenth-Century Savannah," 367–68; *Columbian Museum*, February 16, June 25, and September 2, 1802.

21. While Charleston managed to retain its position as the fifth-largest city in the United States in 1810 with 24,711, Savannah dropped to twenty-eighth with 5,215. New Orleans made its first national census appearance with 17,242. Population of the 46 Urban Places: 1810, table 4"; MacKay, MacKay, and Hartridge, *Letters of Robert MacKay to His Wife*, 92; Ryan and Golson, *Andrew Low and the Sign of the Buck*, 49.

22. Ryan and Golson, *Andrew Low and the Sign of the Buck*, 48.

23. Pressly, "Northern Roots of Savannah's Antebellum Elite, 1780s–1850s," 157–64; Morse, *American Geography*, 450.

24. Mohl, "Scotsman Visits Georgia in 1811," 251, 261.

25. Lambert, *Travels through Canada, and the United States of North America, in the Years 1806, 1807, and 1808*, 267–68.

26. *Niles' Weekly Register*, February 17, 1816, 430; July 29, 1815, 369–70; April 19, 1817, 128.

27. In 1814, the Georgia General Assembly granted Howard a monopoly on propelling vessels with steam on Georgia's waterways. Georgia General Assembly, *Acts of the General Assembly of the State of Georgia*, 1814, 28–30 (hereafter cited as *Georgia Acts*); Lamar, *Compilation of the Laws of the State of Georgia*; Charles C. Jones and Dutcher, *Memorial History of Augusta, Georgia*, 469–72; Goff, "Steamboat Period in Georgia," 239–42.

28. Lerski, *William Jay, Itinerant English Architect, 1792–1837*, 149.

29. Imports totaled $2,976,257. Gamble, *History*, 128–33; Eisterhold, "Savannah," 526–27, 538–39; Jones, *History of Savannah*, 407; Sholes, *Chronological History of Savannah*, 69.

30. Jones, *History of Savannah*, 469.

31. Lerski, *William Jay*, 46; Talbott and Telfair Museum of Art, *Classical Savannah*, 53, 65, 67; Toledano, *National Trust Guide to Savannah*, 16, 30, 80–81.

32. *Daily Savannah Republican*, May 7, 1818; Lamar, *Compilation of the Laws of the State of Georgia*, 524–25.

33. *Philadelphia Register and National Record*, April 3, 1819.

34. Thomas Gamble, "Savannah Enterprise Makes Memorable Voyage Possible," *Savannah Morning News*, March 31, 1919; Lawton, "Address by Alexander R. Lawton"; *National Recorder*, August 18, 1819.

35. *Savannah Daily Republican*, September 9, 1818, August 28, 1819, December 2, 1819; *National Recorder*, October 2, 1819, reprint from *Chester Chronicle* in London.

36. Lee and Agnew, *Historical Record of the City of Savannah*, 76. For a detailed account of the life of the SS *Savannah*, see Braynard, *S.S. Savannah, the Elegant Steam Ship*; Lawton, "Address by Alexander R. Lawton."

37. After the conclusion of the Napoleonic Wars, cotton exports became a major driver of America's economy, comprising 39 percent of American exports. By 1816, cotton accounted for over half of all agricultural exports. Charles C. Jones, *History of Savannah*, 407; Howe, *What Hath God Wrought*, 131; Rothbard, *Panic of 1819*, 9.

38. Rothbard, *Panic of 1819*, 10–11.

39. Rothbard, *Panic of 1819*, 20; Richard E. Ellis, "Market Revolution and the Transformation of American Politics, 1801–1837," 163; Howe, *What Hath God Wrought*, 142.

40. Richard E. Ellis, "Market Revolution and the Transformation of American Politics, 1801–1837," 163; Howe, *What Hath God Wrought*, 142–43; Rothbard, *Panic of 1819*, 17–19, 86.

41. Lerski, *William Jay*, 88; Jones, *History of Savannah*, 470.

42. Coulter, "Great Savannah Fire of 1820," 1–2; Gamble, *History*, 115; Collection on William Harris Crawford, MS 186, Georgia Historical Society, Savannah; *Savannah Georgian*, January 17, 1820.

43. Lane, *Rambler in Georgia*, 52.

44. Estimates range from seven hundred to fifteen hundred. Joseph Ioor Waring, "Yellow Fever Epidemic of Savannah in 1820," 400–402; Gamble, *History*, 114; Fraser, *Savannah in the Old South*, 201; Finlay, "Panic in Savannah."

45. By comparison, Charleston's population increased 39 percent during the first decade of the nineteenth century. Still, Charleston, with a population of 24,780, had slipped to sixth-largest city in the United States, while Savannah had moved up to eighteenth. Savannah's population in the first decades of the nineteenth century: 5,166 (1800); 5,215 (1810); 7,523 (1820); 7,776 (1830); 11,214 (1840); 15,312 (1850). Debow, *Seventh Census of the United States*, 192, with specific information derived from vol. 4, pt. 4, "Cities, Towns, and Counties"; Gibson, "Population of the 100 Largest Cities and Other Urban Places in the United States"; Melish, *Travels through the United States of America, in the Years 1806 and 1807, and 1809, 1810, and 1811*, 148.

46. Phillips, *History of Transportation of the Eastern Cotton Belt to 1860*, 76; Bonner, *History of Georgia Agriculture, 1732–1860*, 56; Gavin Wright, *Political Economy of the Cotton South*, 19–22, maps 20–21; Ford, *Origins of Southern Radicalism*, 14–15, 18, 38–39; Freehling, *Road to Disunion, vol. 1*, 255–56; Gordon, *Passage to Union: How the Railroads Transformed American Life, 1829–1929*, 15–16. Abbott refers to "boundaries between two contiguous hinterlands" as "zones of equilibrium." Abbott, *Boosters and Businessmen*, 78.

47. In 1814 the General Assembly granted Samuel Howard a monopoly on steam navigation in Georgia's waters. In 1817, that same body incorporated the Steam Boat Company of Georgia, formed by Howard and his associates, and granted it a twenty-year monopoly to conduct steam navigation in Georgia's waters. Phillips, *History of Transportation of the Eastern Cotton Belt to 1860*, 76; Lamar, *Compilation of the Laws of the State of Georgia*, 510–11.

48. Downey, *Planting a Capitalist South*, 68–69. The company also had a monopoly on the Altamaha River.

49. *Savannah Republican*, January 12, 1841.

50. Cox, *Gibbons v. Ogden, Law, and Society in the Early Republic*; MacKay and Hartridge, *Letters of Robert MacKay to His Wife, Written from Ports in America and England, 1795–1816*, 263; Hopkins, "Thomas Gibbons, Esquire"; Savannah Unit, Georgia Writers' Project, Works Projects Administration in Georgia, "Whitehall Plantation, Part II," 45–46; Thomas Gibbons Business Papers, Baker Library Historical Collections, Harvard Business School, Cambridge, Massachusetts.

51. Downey, *Planting a Capitalist South*, 73–74.

52. Pitkin, *Statistical View of the Commerce of the United States of America*, 57–82.

53. *Savannah Georgian*, December 11, 1823, April 23, 24, 1824.

54. *Savannah Georgian*, April 29, 1824, June 20, 1838.

55. *Savannah Georgian*, June 20, 1838; Wetherington, *New South Comes to Wiregrass Georgia, 1860–1910*, 1–28, 303.

56. *Savannah Georgian*, April 29, 1824.

57. Freyer, *Producers versus Capitalists*, 112–13. Hartz refers to this as the "ideology of regional self-interest" or "mass of conflicting sectional ambitions." Hartz, *Economic Policy and Democratic Thought*, 9–14.

58. Larson, "Bind the Republic Together," 366, 374. See also Goodrich, "Gallatin Plan after One Hundred and Fifty Years," 440.

59. Larson, "Bind the Republic Together," 367. They emphasized "the principle of indivisibility and the interdependency of the economic community." Community self-interest was repackaged as "public spirit." Hartz, *Economic Policy*, 14, 136.

60. *Savannah Georgian*, November 23, 1822, June 16, 1825, September 20, 27, 1825. For information on the regional canal schemes, see Shaw, *Canals for a Nation*; Armroyd, *Connected View of the Whole Internal Navigation of the United States*, 138, 148–49.

61. *Savannah Georgian*, May 12, 1824.

62. *Savannah Georgian*, November 3, 1825. For additional information on the Erie Canal, see Filante, "Note on the Economic Viability of the Erie Canal, 1825–1860," 95; Bernstein, *Wedding of the Waters*; Koeppel, *Bond of Union*; McGreevy, *Stairway to Empire*.

63. Julius Rubin, "Canal or Railroad?" 6.

64. *Savannah Georgian*, February 1, 1826, May 28, 1826.

65. *Savannah Daily Republican*, June 20, 1823; *Savannah Georgian*, February 24, 1825.

66. *Savannah Republican*, December 3, 15, 24, 1824.

67. *Savannah Republican*, October 8, 1825, December 2, 1825.

68. *Savannah Georgian*, May 14, 1825.

69. *Savannah Georgian*, December 1, 1825.

70. *Savannah Georgian*, December 23, 27, 30, 1825. The bank had been on the verge of collapse, and the notes were significantly discounted. For more information on the problems and scandals related to the Darien Bank, see Heath, *Constructive Liberalism*, 183–87, 222–23

71. *Savannah Georgian*, February 15, 1826; *Savannah Republican*, January 21, 24, 1826, February 1, 1826.

72. Alexander Telfair was the older brother of Mary Telfair, who is notable for bequeathing her home, art collections, and a substantial endowment to establish the Telfair Academy of Arts and Sciences. "Mary Telfair." Other directors: Joseph Cummings, Thomas Young, William C. Daniell, R. F. Williams, Benjamin Burroughs, and John D. Mongin. *Savannah Republican*, March 3, 1826. The SOAC was officially granted a charter in December 1826. *Georgia Acts*, 1826.

73. *Savannah Republican*, March 11, 1826.

74. *Savannah Georgian*, February 3, 1827.

75. For advertisements for labor, see *Savannah Georgian*, April–June, 1826, specifically *Savannah Georgian*, June 12, 1826; *Savannah Republican*, December 22, 1826; *Savannah Georgian*, January 1, 1827.

76. *Savannah Republican*, December 22, 1826; *Savannah Georgian*, January 1, January 24, 1827. For more information on the practice of slave hiring, see Wade, *Slavery in the Cities*; David Brion Davis, *Inhuman Bondage*; Martin, *Divided Mastery*; Dorsey, *Hirelings*; Zaborney, *Slaves for Hire*.

77. *Savannah Georgian*, December 21, 1826; *Savannah Republican*, December 22, 1826, September 1, 1827.

78. *Savannah Georgian*, December 19, 21, 1826; *Savannah Republican*, December 22, 1826.

79. *Savannah Georgian*, December 19, 21, 1826; *Savannah Republican*, December 22, 1826. The Hibernian Society of Savannah, founded in 1812, sought to offer assistance to Irish immigrants arriving in Savannah.

80. *Savannah Republican*, September 1, 1827; *Daily Savannah Republican*, March 31, 1830.

81. *Savannah Georgian*, January 7, 1828, February 29, 1828; *Savannah Republican*, November 27, 1828.

82. Hartz, *Economic Policy*, 142.

83. *Savannah Republican*, December 23, 1828.

84. *Savannah Republican*, December 17, 22, 1828; *Georgia Acts*, 1828, 72–73; Hacker, *Course of American Economic Growth and Development*, 107.

85. *Georgia Acts*, 1829, 210–11 ("Joint Committee on Agriculture and Internal Improvement, to which was referred so much of the Governor's message as relates to the Savannah, Ogeechee, and Altamaha Canal"); *Savannah Georgian*, December 4, 22, 1829, March 22, 31, 1830; *Savannah Daily Republican*, January 6, March 27, November 10, 1829. The committee report was made by James Habersham, a close personal friend of Alexander Telfair, the president of the SOAC.

86. *Savannah Georgian*, March 22, 1830. Another bill was introduced into the U.S. House of Representatives in May 1830. *Savannah Georgian*, May 13, 1830; *Savannah Daily Republican*, March 31, 1830.

87. *Savannah Daily Republican*, December 17, 23, 1830, March 30, 1831.

88. Wallis, Sylla, Grinath, and National Bureau of Economic Research, *Sovereign Debt and Repudiation*, 268–69.

89. Sylla and Wallis, "Anatomy of Sovereign Debt Crises," 268; Balleisen, *Navigating Failure*, 33; Amdursky, *Municipal Debt Finance Law*, 16; Orth, *Judicial Power of the United States*, 3. While states and cities sought to emulate New York's success with the Erie Canal, Sylla and Wallis ("Anatomy of Sovereign Debt Crises," 27) maintain that they failed to follow New York's funding model in earmarking taxes to service their debts. Jocelyn Wills describes this for St. Paul, Minnesota, in *Boosters, Hustlers, and Speculators*, 69.

90. Waibel, *Sovereign Defaults before International Courts and Tribunals*, 69.

91. Amdursky, *Municipal Debt Finance Law*, 17.

CHAPTER 2. "BUT WHAT A PRETTY THING A RAIL ROAD IS!"

1. "An Old Engineer," letter to the editor of the *Augusta Constitutionalist*, September 13, 1833, reprinted in *Savannah Georgian*, September 17, 1833.

2. For details on the Charleston and Hamburg Railroad, see Downey, *Planting a Capitalist South*, especially chapter 4.

3. The Central Railroad and Canal Company became the Central Railroad and Banking Company in 1835. The company will be hereafter referred to as the Central Railroad. The company was granted the exclusive right to construct and maintain a line from Savannah to Macon for thirty-six years (with the option of legislative renewal) and was granted a monopoly on the area within twenty miles of its line. *Savannah Republican*, June 28, 1833; Prince, *Digest of the Laws of the State of Georgia*, 300–303; Phillips, *History of Transportation of the Eastern Cotton Belt to 1860*, 253–63; Taylor and Neu, *American Railroad Network, 1861–1890*, 41–46; Weaver, "Spatial Strategies in Railroad Planning in Georgia and the Carolinas, 1830–1860"; Heath, *Constructive Liberalism*, 254, 258; Lee and Agnew, *Historical Record of the City of Savannah*, 136.

4. Gordon Family Papers, MS 318, Georgia Historical Society, Savannah; Knight, *Standard History of Georgia and Georgians*, vol. 5, 2772; Northen, *Men of Mark in Georgia*, 30–31; Bickel, "Life of William W. Gordon," 8.

5. *Savannah Georgian*, December 5, 1834.

6. For detailed discussion of southern views of northern progress, see Wells, *Origins of the Southern Middle Class, 1800–1861*.

7. *Southern Banner* [Athens], July 6, 1833.

8. *Savannah Georgian*, December 5, 1834, January 3, 1835.

9. Wells, *Origins of the Southern Middle Class*, 55–65.

10. *Savannah Georgian*, December 5, 1834. The proposition that railroads helped unify the nation obscures the reality that they were constructed largely on the basis of local and sectional rivalry. Gordon, *Passage to Union:*, 15–16.

11. Sherwood, *Gazetteer of the State of Georgia*, 50.

12. The letter was published in *Southern Banner, Augusta Chronicle, Savannah Georgian*, and *Columbus Enquirer* on August 10, 1833, and in the Milledgeville *Federal Union*, August 22, 1833.

13. *Savannah Georgian*, July 25, 1833; *Augusta Courier*, August 14, 1833, reprinted in *Savannah Georgian*, August 20, 1833.

14. *Augusta Chronicle*, August 17, 1833.

15. *Macon Messenger*, reprinted in *Savannah Georgian*, September 3, 1833.

16. *Southern Banner*, August 24, 1833.

17. *Savannah Republican*, September 23, 1833.

18. *Southern Banner*, September 7, 1833.

19. *Augusta Chronicle*, August 10, 1833; *Macon Telegraph*, reprinted in *Savannah Georgian*, September 5, 1833.

20. *Savannah Georgian*, December 5, 1834.

21. *Savannah Georgian*, November 4, 1833.

22. For detailed discussion of the nullification crisis, see Freehling, *Prelude to Civil War*, and Ellis, *Union at Risk*. H. Craig Miner has called for studies that place the railroad within the proper social, economic, and political context. Miner, *Most Magnificent Machine*, viii–ix.

23. Howe, *What Hath God Wrought*, 396; Majewski, *Modernizing a Slave Economy*, 45.

24. Coulter, "Nullification Movement in Georgia," 20. For a national perspective on the nullification crisis, see Howe, *What Hath God Wrought*, 395–410. For the specific political and economic drivers in South Carolina, see Ford, *Origins of Southern Radicalism*, 99–144.

25. Mayor's Report, 1834–35, published in *Savannah Georgian*, July 16, 1835.

26. *Savannah Georgian*, November 17, December 15, 1834, January 3, 12, 1835; Mayor's Report, 1834–35, published in *Savannah Georgian*, July 16, 1835.

27. *Savannah Republican*, May 14, 1835; *Savannah Georgian*, May 28, 1835.

28. Minutes of Council, June 25, 1835; *Savannah Georgian*, September 1, 1835.

29. Freyer, *Producers versus Capitalists*, 82; Wills, *Boosters, Hustlers, and Speculators*, 4; Cleveland, *Railroad Promotion and Capitalization in the United States*, 167–76. Half of the installments made by the stockholders were to be invested in the railroad construction; the other half were to be used for banking purposes. While the railroad was expected to yield only 4 percent interest, banks were expected to yield more than twice that (10–12 percent). Gerstner, "Letters from the United States of North America," 363. Green, *Finance and Economic Development in the Old South*, 33–34, notes that these "improvement banks" were rarely successful and "quite insecure," at least in Louisiana. Bray Hammond makes a similar argument. He notes that states created these banks "under the delusion that banks by a sort of fiat could create capital for the needy enterprise." Instead these banks were "thoroughly unsound," with most of them collapsing following the Panic of 1837, though this was not the case with Georgia's Central Railroad. Hammond, "Long and Short Term Credit in Early American Banking," 86.

30. *Savannah Georgian*, February 9, 1836.

31. The Central Railroad began construction in October 1836.

32. *New Jersey Emporium and True American*, April 28, 1837; Larson, *Market Revolution in America*, 92–97; Howe, *What Hath God Wrought*, 503. The traditional date for the start of the Panic of 1837 has been May 10, 1837. However, Jessica Lepler pushes the date back to March 4 of that year. Between those two dates, people began experiencing "acute financial uncertainty," and they "panicked." Lepler, *Many Panics of 1837*, 2.

33. This second crisis fell more heavily on southern and western banks. Howe, *What Hath God Wrought*, 505–7; Wallis, "What Caused the Crisis of 1839?" 3, 10–11; McGrane, *Panic of 1837*, 122.

34. Ward, "New Look at Antebellum Southern Railroad Development," 414; Thornton, *Politics and Power in a Slave Society*, 268; Sacher, *Perfect War of Politics*, 86; Wallis, "What Caused the Crisis of 1839?," 30.

35. Phillips, *History of Transportation in the Eastern Cotton Belt to 1860*, 262; Dixon, "Central Railroad of Georgia, 1833–1892," 76.

36. Third Report, 1839, in Central Rail Road and Banking Company of Georgia, *Report of the Presidents, Engineers-in-Chief and Superintendents of the Central Rail-Road and Banking Company of Georgia*, 48–49 (hereafter cited as *Central Rail Road Report*).

37. *Savannah Republican*, December 10, 1840, March 4, 15, 1842. The company's chief engineer disapproved of the company's policy of paying contractors in bonds because they could not be compelled to work faster. Third Report, May 1839, *Central Rail Road Report*, 68.

38. *Savannah Republican*, March 28, 1842.

39. Dixon, "Central Railroad of Georgia, 1833–1892," 71.

40. Shoemaker, "Strangers and Citizens," 244.

41. First Report, 1838, *Central Rail Road Report*, 14.

42. Shoemaker, "Strangers and Citizens," 252; O'Connell, *Catholicity in the Carolinas and Georgia*, 515–516. This story is also briefly mentioned in Gleeson, *Irish in the South, 1815–1877*, 53; Walter J. Fraser, *Savannah in the Old South*, 232; Jennison, *Cultivating Race*, 252.

43. Third Report, May 1839, *Central Rail Road Report*, 34.

44. Dixon, "Central Railroad of Georgia, 1833–1892," 64–65; Third Report, May 1839, *Central Rail Road Report*, 35; Fourth Report, November 1, 1839, *Central Rail Road Report*, 44. By the end of 1840, the same was true. *Macon Weekly Telegraph*, December 8, 1840.

45. Jennison, *Cultivating Race*, 253; Cotterill, "Southern Railroads and Western Trade, 1840–1850," 436; Shoemaker, "Strangers and Citizens," 252; Phillips, *History of Transportation in the Eastern Cotton Belt to 1860*, 261.

46. Fourth Report, November 1, 1839, *Central Rail Road Report*, 44.

47. Third Report, May 1839, *Central Rail Road Report*, 44.

48. Fifteenth Report, December 4, 1849, *Central Rail Road Report*, 200; Twenty-fifth Report, December 1859, *Central Rail Road Report*, 55; Jennison, *Cultivating Race*, 253.

49. Phillips, *History of Transportation in the Eastern Cotton Belt to 1860*, 253–63; Taylor and Neu, *American Railroad Network, 1861–1890*, 41–46; Weaver, "Spatial Strategies in Railroad Planning in Georgia and the Carolinas, 1830–1860," 9–23; Heath, *Constructive Liberalism*, 254, 258; Lee and Agnew, *Historical Record of the City of Savannah*, 136.

50. Lee and Agnew, *Historical Record of the City of Savannah*, 136. In 1851 Savannah sold $30,000 of its Central Railroad bonds at par. With this, the city was able to redeem city bonds. *Savannah Republican*, January 10, 1851. In 1857, the council authorized the mayor to sell enough of the Central's stock to cover the cost of outstanding bonds issued by the company. It was at this point that the municipal government was able to liquidate "the entire indebtedness of the city on account of the Central Railroad." Savannah was able to retain two hundred shares that were paying annual dividends at 10 percent. The mayor predicted that the city would be able to follow the same policy in liquidating its Southwestern Railroad bonds. Mayor's Report, 1857.

51. Nimmo, *Report on the Internal Commerce of the United States*, 81.

52. Gibson, *Population of the 100 Largest Cities and Other Urban Places in the United States.*

53. In the dry culture system, the city paid property owners to forego rice cultivation and to drain lowlands and marshes to prevent yellow fever. Railroad projects included the Muscogie Railroad; Savannah, Albany and Gulf Railroad (Atlantic and Gulf); Western Railroad; Southwestern Railroad; Augusta and Waynesboro Railroad; and Montgomery and West Point Railroad. Mayor's Reports, 1850–60. Although courts generally accepted municipal railroad investment as constitutional, there were dissenters in 1853. Judge C. J. Black dissented with the majority court ruling in the *Sharpless* case, asserting that it was outside the purview of the municipality to "promote the wealth and commerce of a city or district." Cecil, "On Municipal Subscriptions to the Stock of Railroad Companies," 2. Savannah was not alone. There was a national uptick in municipal borrowing in the 1850s. Robert E. Wright, *One Nation under Debt*, 277.

54. For details on additional city investment in railroads, see *New York Daily Times*, March 25, 1853, and Mayor's Report, 1857.

55. By the summer of 1853, citizens had subscribed $400,000. Almost all investors resided in Chatham, Bryan, and Liberty Counties. The Savannah, Albany, and Gulf Railroad was incorporated in February 1856. Construction continued after the outbreak of fighting in 1861. Western Georgia feared that Savannah was intent on destroying the Brunswick Railroad so as to maintain the monopoly by the Southwestern Railroad. *Daily Morning News*, July 28, 1852; *Albany Patriot*, November 9, 1849, May 7, 1852; August 6, 1852, December 24, 1852, June 19, 1853; *Daily News and Herald*, February 27, 1856, February 28, 1867.

56. The original plan of development called for the construction of a line running from Savannah or "some point on the Central Railroad near Savannah, if the companies could agree to terms," to Albany, located on the Flint River, with the option to extend the line to the Chattahoochee River, so long as the company's actions did not violate those delineated in the Southwestern Railroad's charter. The company was required to commence operations within six years. *Georgia Acts*, 1847, 190–92; *Savannah Georgian*, November 22, 1847; *Albany Patriot*, May 14, 1852.

57. *Savannah Daily Republican*, August 13, 1852; *Daily Morning News*, August 24, 1852.

58. When Dr. Screven died in 1859, he owned two rice plantations, a cotton plantation on Wilmington Island, 266 slaves, two rice mills, city property (including Savannah Steam Rice Mill), and much stock in banks and railroads. His assets totaled $688,545. Screven, "Georgia Bryans and Screvens 1685–1861," 343–46; Harden, *History of Savannah and South Georgia*, 589–94; Rowland, Moore, and Rogers, *History of Beaufort County, South Carolina*, 314–23; Smith, *Slavery and Rice Culture in Low Country Georgia, 1750–1860*, 221–22; Georgia Writers' Project and Federal Writers' Project, *Savannah River Plantations*, 136.

59. The house was located on southwest corner of Congress and Abercorn (across the street from Lucas Theatre) on Reynolds Square. It was a Georgian style house

built for Governor John Houstoun in 1785. Screven, "Georgia Bryans and Screvens," 346; Harden, *History of Savannah and South Georgia*, 594–95.

60. Screven, "Georgia Bryans and Screvens," 346; Harden, *History of Savannah and South Georgia*, 594–95; Smith, *Slavery and Rice Culture in Low Country Georgia*, 221. Details regarding Screven's early involvement in the Savannah and Albany Railroad can be found in the *Daily Morning News*, November 13, 1851, August 13, 24, November 11, 1852, and March 3, 1853; *Savannah Daily Republican*, August 13, 1852.

61. *Daily Morning News*, October 22, 1852; *Albany Patriot*, June 19, 1853.

62. The meeting was held on November 10, 1852. The two competing resolutions were introduced by Richard R. Cuyler and James P. Screven. It was estimated that $3 million would pay for an air-line railroad from Savannah to the Chattahoochee and prepare for an expansion to Pensacola. They agreed that Savannah should subscribe $1 million provided others came up with the other $2 million. *Savannah Daily Republican*, November 11, 1852.

63. Because of the competing resolutions regarding how much and on what terms the city should subscribe, subsequent meetings were held to discuss the proposed subscriptions ranging from $300,000 to $1 million. Cuyler's competing resolutions dealt with reserving Savannah's right to pursue its own route should the funds not come through from western Georgia, specifically Albany, the original objective of the railroad. The company also was to reserve the right to alter the route. *Savannah Daily Republican*, November 12–13, 1852; *Albany Patriot*, August 20, 1852; *New York Daily Times*, October 26, 1852; *Albany Patriot*, October 29, 1852; *American Railway Times*, September 16, 1852.

64. *Albany Patriot*, October 29, 1852, reprint from *Savannah Georgian*; *Albany Patriot*, November 12, 19, 1852, and June 10, 1853; *Southern Recorder*, April 12, 1853; *Albany Patriot*, May 5, 1853.

65. *Albany Patriot*, May 20, September 16, 1853. In 1854, the General Assembly authorized a change in the name to the Savannah, Albany, and Gulf Railroad, indicating its expanded scope. *Georgia Acts*, 1853–54, 454–55; *Georgia Acts*, 1855, 181; *Albany Patriot*, February 1 and 10, 1854. The depot was located on the eastern edge of the city, across town from the Central Railroad.

66. Incorporation of the Atlantic and Gulf Railroad was approved February 27, 1856. *Georgia Acts*, 1855–56, 158–61, and 1857, 67–68; Mayor's Reports, 1857, 1859, 1860; *Federal Union*, December 18, 1855; *Albany Patriot*, February 21, 1856, April 10, October 9, April 2, 1857, May 14, 1857, May 21 and 28, 1857; *Georgia Telegraph*, February 19, 26, 1856; *Columbus Tri-Weekly Enquirer*, February 19, 23, 1856, November 11, 1856; *Southern Recorder*, February 25, 1856; Wilson, *Digest of All the Ordinances of the City of Savannah*, 14–18. For a summary, see Phillips, *History of Transportation in the Eastern Cotton Belt to 1860*, 357–59.

67. *Albany Patriot*, November 11, 1858, June 2, 1859; *Augusta Chronicle*, December 2, 1858; *Columbus Daily Enquirer*, December 4, 1858; *Macon Weekly Telegraph*, December 7, 1858. There was an effort to prevent the governor from making more payments to the Atlantic and Gulf Railroad until the company chose an alternate route in line

with the original charter requirements. *Daily Morning News*, November 20, 22, 1858, December 6, 1858.

68. The Savannah, Albany, and Gulf Railroad's first and only president to that point, James P. Screven, had resigned in February 1859 due to poor health, and the directors immediately reelected him. The elder Screven's illness created a great deal of delay and uncertainty. He died later in the year, and his son John Screven took his place. At a meeting of the stockholders, with an ill Screven in absentia, a financial report was provided (though the press did not provide details). John Screven offered a resolution, unanimously adopted, that the stockholders "recommend" that the city council "guarantee the bonds of this company," as recently requested by the board of directors. The mayor, who was present, concurred in this but preferred to submit it to a citizen meeting. *Augusta Chronicle*, February 18, May 18, July 28, 1859; *Albany Patriot*, November 3, 1859; *Daily Morning News*, May 11, 12, 1859; Minutes of Council, September 17, 1858, March 1, 1860.

69. *Report of the State Commissioners Representing the Stock Held by the State in the Atlantic and Gulf Rail Road Company.*

70. The city owed $1,872,840, most of it the result of the last investment in the Savannah, Albany and Gulf Railroad; annual interest on the railroad alone was $131,098. Mayor's Reports, 1856–60; City of Savannah Cash Ledgers, City of Savannah Research Library and Municipal Archives; Haunton, "Savannah in the 1850s," 235; Gamble, *History*, 288, 225, 293.

71. Tax totals exclude fines, licenses, and rents, which accounted for approximately $40,000. Gamble, *History*, 290–96, 308–9; Haunton, "Savannah in the 1850s," 235–36; Mayor's Reports 1856–60.

72. According to the 1866 Mayor's Report, the city carried a funded debt of over $2 million, on which it was required to pay $125,000 in annual interest.

73. Chudacoff, *Evolution of American Urban Society*, 38; Sbragia, *Debt Wish*, 28–32; Monkkonen, *America Becomes Urban*, 152; Monkonnen, "Politics of Municipal Indebtedness and Default, 1850–1936," 134.

74. Hillhouse, *Municipal Bonds*, 255.

CHAPTER 3. "THE WORST WHIPPED AND SUBJUGATED YOU EVER SAW"

1. The population increased to 11,214 in 1840 and to 15,312 in 1850. United States Census Office, *Ninth Census of the United States*, 20; Herbert Weaver, "Foreigners in Antebellum Savannah," 1.

2. Males were more heavily represented among the immigrant population than females, at more than 56 percent. Weaver, "Foreigners in Antebellum Savannah," 1–2; Shoemaker, "Strangers and Citizens," 31; *Ninth Census*, 306, 386–91.

3. "Gilmerville" is a variant spelling. In Oglethorpe Ward, there were seventy-three liquor shops, and to the east of Habersham there were one hundred such establishments. Bellows, "Tempering the Wind," 160–62; Rousey, "From Whence They Came

to Savannah," 305–36. For more information on the intersection of race and labor, see Gillespie, *Free Labor in an Unfree World.*

4. Shoemaker, "Strangers and Citizens," 255, 261–66, Weaver, "Foreigners in Antebellum Savannah," 1–3; Haunton, "Savannah in the 1850s," 50–56.

5. Byrne, "Burden and Heat of the Day," 204–5. One-third of free blacks lived in Oglethorpe Ward. Gillispie, *Free Labor in an Unfree World*, 165; Whittington B. Johnson, "Free Blacks in Antebellum Savannah," 418–31; United States, Census Office, *Ninth Census of the United States, Population*, 21. See also Harris and Berry, *Slavery and Freedom in Savannah.*

6. United States, Census Office, *Ninth Census of the United States, Population*, 21, 100.

7. Weaver, "Foreigners in Antebellum Savannah," 8, 12; Shoemaker, "Strangers and Citizens," 343; Jacqueline Jones, *Saving Savannah*, 40–41. For the origins of Irish political participation in American cities, see Golway, *Machine Made.*

8. Weaver, "Foreigners in Antebellum Savannah," 9, 18; Shryock, *Georgia and the Union in 1850*, 89; Montgomery, *Cracker Parties.*

9. Montgomery, *Cracker Parties*, 123–27; Derek Smith, *Civil War Savannah*, 10.

10. Freehling, *The Road to Disunion*, vol. 2, 406–14; Jacqueline Jones, *Saving Savannah*, 122–23.

11. Montgomery, *Cracker Parties*, 123–27; Fraser, *Savannah in the Old South*, 319.

12. Montgomery, *Cracker Parties*, 123–27; Fraser, *Savannah in the Old South*, 319; Smith, *Civil War Savannah*, 21; Lawrence, *Present for Mr. Lincoln*, 8–11, 16–19. The Georgia militia, commanded by Alexander R. Lawton, in a parade-like atmosphere, steamed down the river and seized the dilapidated fort from a sergeant and a caretaker. Jones, *Saving Savannah*, 126. Two recent and excellent works covering this period are Jacqueline Jones, *Saving Savannah*; and Durham, *Guardian of Savannah.*

13. Kearns, "Secession Diplomacy"; Welborn and Richard, "Union Blockade and Coastal Occupation," 52; Melton, *Best Station of Them All*, 91; Smith, *Civil War Savannah*, 97–100; Jacqueline Jones, *Saving Savannah*, 152.

14. Smith, *Civil War Savannah*, 85; DeCredico, *Patriots for Profit*, 39; Kearns, "Secession Diplomacy," Jacqueline Jones, *Saving Savannah*, 144–52; Fornell, "Civil War Comes to Savannah."

15. Jacqueline Jones, *Saving Savannah*, 133, 193.

16. Jonathan Wilder to Joseph J. Wilder, January 5, 1865, King and Wilder Family Papers, MS 465, Georgia Historical Society, Savannah; Jacqueline Jones, *History of Savannah*, 377. For a detailed account of the Union army's exploits on the coast, see Durham, *Guardian of Savannah.* For full accounts of Sherman's march to the sea, see Bailey, *War and Ruin*; Trudeau, *Southern Storm.*

17. General P. G. T. Beauregard had ordered Hardee to hold the city as long as practicable but not to unnecessarily endanger his command. United States, War Department, *War of the Rebellion*, vol. 53, 38, 940; Charles Green Papers, Hargrett Rare Book and Manuscript Library, University of Georgia, Athens; Pepper, *Personal Recollections of Sherman's Campaign in Georgia and the Carolinas*, 280, 282; Nichols, *Story of the Great*

March, 96; Padgett, "With Sherman through Georgia and the Carolinas," 62; Jacqueline Jones, *Saving Savannah*, 205–6.

18. Sherman, *General Sherman's Official Account of His Great March through Georgia and the Carolinas*, 80; Lawrence, *Present for Mr. Lincoln*, 210.

19. Jonathan Wilder to Joseph Wilder, January 5, 1865, King and Wilder Family Papers, MS 465, Georgia Historical Society, Savannah; Byrne, "'Uncle Billy' Sherman Comes to Town," 92, 97; *New York Times*, December 20, 1864; Nichols, *Story of the Great March*, 96; United States, War Department, *War of the Rebellion*, 793.

20. Boston and New York and their chambers of commerce played prominent roles in the attempt to send aid to Savannah; both hoped to reestablish economic ties with Savannah. *New York Times*, January 6, 1865; Henry D. Hyde to Richard D. Arnold, March 8, 1865, Richard D. Arnold Papers, 1849–1876, no. 1261, Southern Historical Collection, Wilson Library, University of North Carolina, Chapel Hill; Dyer, "Northern Relief for Savannah during Sherman's Occupation," 457–72.

21. *New York Times*, January 6, 1865.

22. Handwritten transcript in Aaron Wilbur Papers, Duke University, Durham, North Carolina; Hitchcock, *Marching with Sherman*, 196–203.

23. Jonathan Wilder to Joseph Wilder, January 18, 1865, King and Wilder Family Papers, MS 465, Georgia Historical Society, Savannah; Pepper, *Personal Recollections of Sherman's Campaign*, 290; Nichols, *Story of the Great March*, 102; Howard, *Autobiography of Oliver Otis Howard*, 18; Byrne, "'Uncle Billy' Sherman Comes to Town," 92.

24. Nichols, *Story of the Great March*, 102; Byrne, "'Uncle Billy' Sherman Comes to Town," 93.

25. Byrne, "'Uncle Billy' Sherman Comes to Town," 95; Coffin, *Four Years of Fighting*, 429–35.

26. Swint, *Dear Ones at Home*, 190; Padgett, "With Sherman through Georgia and the Carolinas," 64; "History of Beach Institute," Joseph Frederick Waring II papers, MS 1275, Georgia Historical Society, Savannah; Jacqueline Jones, *Saving Savannah*, 216–18, 227–28.

27. Foner, *Free Soil, Free Labor, Free Men*.

28. There is no accurate count for the number of refugees who arrived in Savannah following its surrender; estimates range from six thousand to seventeen thousand. Foner, *Reconstruction*, 52, 130–47; Westwood, "Sherman Marched—and Proclaimed 'Land for the Landless'," 35; Botume, *First amongst the Contrabands*, 169–71.

29. "Colloquy with Colored Ministers," 88–91; Byrne, "'Uncle Billy' Sherman Comes to Town," 109; Sherman, *Memoirs of General W. T. Sherman*, 245–48; Howard, *Autobiography of Oliver Otis Howard*, 189, 190–91; Blight, *Race and Reunion*, 23–26. Stanton's visit was probably more a response to the poor reputation Sherman's army had acquired in its dealings with African American refugees.

30. The formal name of the Freedmen's Bureau was the Bureau of Refugees, Freedmen, and Abandoned Lands. Howard, *Autobiography of Oliver Otis Howard*, 191–92; *New York Times*, January 29, 1865; *Savannah Daily Herald*, February 3, 1865. For Union efforts in coastal South Carolina, see Rose, *Rehearsal for Reconstruction*.

31. Howard, *Autobiography of Oliver Otis Howard*, 192; Woodman, "Class, Race, Politics, and the Modernization of the Postbellum South," 3.

CHAPTER 4. "ARTERY OF WEALTH AND PROSPERITY"

1. Diary of George Anderson Mercer, June 11, 1865, no. 503, Southern Historical Collection, Wilson Library, University of North Carolina, Chapel Hill.

2. *Daily News and Herald*, March 20, May 9, 1868.

3. *Savannah Morning News*, March 20, May 9, 1868; Foner, *Reconstruction*; Perman, *Road to Redemption*.

4. *Daily News and Herald*, November 4–December 9, 1865.

5. Anderson, *Florida Territory in 1844*, 1, 12; Bulloch, *History and Genealogy of the Habersham Family*, 1, 205–8; Desai, "Biographical Sketch of Edward Clifford Anderson, Sr.," 5.

6. Anderson, *Florida Territory in 1844*, 5–10; Desai, "Biographical Sketch of Edward Clifford Anderson, Sr.," 2–3, 7–9. Jonathan Daniel Wells discusses the trend towards such endeavors for urban southerners in *Origins of the Southern Middle Class, 1800–1861*.

7. *News and Herald*, November 4–December 9, 1865; Edward Clifford Anderson Papers, no. 3602, Southern Historical Collection, Wilson Library, University of North Carolina, Chapel Hill; Haunton, "Savannah in the 1850s," 236; Desai, "Biographical Sketch of Edward Clifford Anderson, Sr.," 18; *Daily Morning News*, January 3, 1855, and April 3, 1856.

8. Neblett, "Major Edward C. Anderson and the C. S. S. Fingal," 132–58; Edward Clifford Anderson Papers, no. 3602, Southern Historical Collection, Wilson Library, University of North Carolina, Chapel Hill; Haunton, "Savannah in the 1850s," 236; Fraser, *Savannah in the Old South*, 307.

9. *Savannah Republican*, October 5, 1865.

10. Mayor's Reports, 1861–67. No reports are available for 1864–65.

11. The amount of the bond was not to exceed $400,000 and was to run for twenty years. *Daily News and Herald*, January 10, 1866; Minutes of Council, August 23, 1865, January 24, 1866; City of Savannah Ordinance Papers, City of Savannah Research Library and Municipal Archives. The city realized $299,600 from the bond issue. Mayor's Reports, 1866–67.

12. These loans were due within one year, sometimes six months; the goal was to pay them once the city raised the funds through taxes or bonds. Unfortunately, cities often overestimated the annual tax revenue as well as the prospects for future prosperity; as a result, banks often "rolled over" the notes, and interest compounded. Brown, *Municipal Bonds*, 2–3; Carlson, "Banking in Georgia, 1865–1929," 28–37; Mintz et al., *Fundamentals of Municipal Finance*, 9–10.

13. The city was paying $142,935 in interest on a funded debt of over $2 million. The total expenses of the city for the year were $396,644. Mayor's Reports, 1866–1867.

14. City Treasurer Reports, in Mayor's Reports, 1866–78; Griffin, "Savannah's City Income Tax," 173–76.

15. The United States inherited the tradition of ground rents from England. They are essentially long leases; another term would be "perpetual annuities." Allinson, *Ground Rents in Philadelphia, 1860–1921*, 6–7; Gouge, *Curse of Paper-Money and Banking*, 29; Wright, *Origins of Commercial Banking in America, 1750–1800*, 168–80. A more detailed discussion of Savannah's policy regarding ground rent can be found in a letter from Louis A. Falligant to the City of Savannah, December 27, 1871, City of Savannah Finance Committee Papers, City of Savannah Research Library and Municipal Archives. Debates about ground rents are located in a series of *Savannah Morning News* articles, March 17–24, 1871.

16. Percent increase is in dollars. "Cotton Statistics: Port of Savannah," Mayor's Report, 1877; Diary of George Anderson Mercer, November 3, 1865, no. 503, Southern Historical Collection, Wilson Library, University of North Carolina, Chapel Hill; Reid, *After the War*, 135–36.

17. In the 1850s, the federal government proved to be very generous in appropriating money to the city for wreck removal and harbor dredging. "Report of Commissioners on the Improvement of the Savannah River, February 11, 1853," *Savannah Georgian*, April 30, 1853; Carter, "History of Past Work"; Haunton, "Savannah in the 1850s," 81–82. Beginning in 1862, the U.S. Navy had also sunk ships into the river to close it off to blockade runners. Cribs constitute a common form of river obstruction. Designed variously to be temporary or permanent, the frames were constructed of timber and filled with rock and later concrete. Granger, *History of the Savannah District, 1829–1968*, 81–82.

18. The Macon and Brunswick Railroad was the product of this plan. Mayor's Report, 1866; *Savannah Morning News*, February 2, 8, 1867; Wertenbaker, *Norfolk*.

19. Haunton, "Savannah in the 1850s," 81–82; "Report of Commissioners on the Improvement of the Savannah River, February 11, 1853," *Georgian*, April 30, 1853; Granger, *History of the Savannah District*, 81. Sporadically, in the 1820s, the federal government had funded removal of obstructions and improvement of the harbor. For the roles of James P. Screven and Mayor William McDaniel, see Rowland, Moore, and Rogers, "Alone on the River," 121–50, and Rowland, Moore, and Rogers, *History of Beaufort County, South Carolina*, 316–23. Congress passed the first river and harbor bill in 1822. However, it failed to specifically apply to harbor or waterway improvement. Parkman, *History of the Waterways of the Atlantic Coast of the United States*, 43–44, 47.

20. "Commerce at Charleston," *DeBow's Review* 31 (October–November 1861): 460; "Commerce of Savannah," *DeBow's Review* 29 (November 1860): 669–70.

21. The focus was on lighthouses, buoys, and beacons. Between 1830 and 1876, Congress proved reluctant to appropriate money to river and harbor improvement unless it was tied to fortification appropriation bills. The Rivers and Harbors Act of 1852 included funding for dredging and channel improvement of Savannah. In 1852 Democrats won the congressional elections and curbed further improvements; Savannah was one of three eastern projects approved. When these funds were exhausted, the work stopped. Johnson, "River and Harbor Bills," 50–80; Carnes, "Georgia Deepwater Ports and their Role in the Economy of the State," 29–31; Richard E. Ellis, *Union at Risk*, 19–25; Haunton, "Savannah in the 1850s," 184–87; Carter, "History of Past Work."

22. The work was partially completed by the U.S. Army's Quartermaster Corps and partially by the U.S. Navy under the supervision of Admiral John A. Dahlgren's men. This work took four weeks and cost approximately $30,000. *New York Times*, January 5, 1865; Granger, *History of the Savannah District*, 82; George Winston Smith, "Cotton from Savannah in 1865," 496–97. The channel ranged from 13.5 feet to 17.5 feet of water at mean high tide. Carter, "History of Past Work." The depth was 8 feet at mean low. Letter from the Secretary of War, in U.S. Congress, House, 41st Cong., 2nd sess., Executive Document 153, 1870, 41–42.

23. Sherman, *Memoirs of General W. T. Sherman*, 219; United States, War Department, *War of the Rebellion*, 792; Mayor's Report, 1866; *Savannah Morning News*, September 15, 1871, March 5, 1872; Gamble Scrapbooks, book 2, vol. 8, Thomas Gamble Collection, Kaye Kole Genealogy and Local History Room, Live Oak Public Library, Savannah; Stewart, *What Nature Suffers to Groe*, 229–30.

24. The Treasury Department granted permission for the city to make a contract provided that the contract met with the department's approval. The initial goal was to increase the river's depth from 13.5 feet to 18 feet. Letter from the Secretary of the Treasury, in U.S. Congress, House, 40th Cong., 2nd sess., Executive Document 123, 1868, 40–42.

25. In 1861, the Brunswick and Albany Railroad Company superseded the Brunswick and Florida Railroad Company, incorporated in 1835. It was sold in October 1873 to Jacob de Neufville and reorganized under the same name. Thomas, *Digest of the Railroad Laws of Georgia*, 163–65. Welles, a native of Pennsylvania, began his career in railroading in 1847 with the construction of the Great Western Railroad in Canada. In 1853, he participated in the building of part of the New York and Erie Railroad along with mileage on the New York Central and Hudson River Railroad. He was a director of the Brunswick and Florida Railroad prior to the Civil War. All of the directors of this company were from New York except Levi Knight, president. By 1861, H. S. Welles & Company had built most of the Brunswick and Albany Railroad. "Brunswick and Florida Railroad Company," 330; *New York Times*, August 29, 1895; Southern Railroads Report of the Select Committee on Southern Railroads, House of Representatives, 40th Cong., 2nd sess., Report 3, page 49.

26. City of Savannah Harbor and Wharf Committee Papers, December 5, 1865, City of Savannah Research Library and Municipal Archives; Mayor's Report, 1866.

27. In September 1865, the city began negotiating with William Webster of Boston to remove the obstructions, allowing as his compensation the material he raised. In its official protest of Welles's contract, the city complained that the value of the materials in the cribs was not sufficient to reimburse the expense of removing them. Without the incentive of cash payment, the city could not make a favorable contract; thus, the cribs would continue to obstruct the river and its commerce. Mayor's Report, 1866; City of Savannah Harbor and Wharf Committee Papers, December 6, 1865, City of Savannah Research Library and Municipal Archives.

28. Letter from the Secretary of the Treasury, in U.S. Congress, House, 40th Cong., 2nd sess., Executive Document 123, 1868, 40–42; Mayor's Reports, 1866–67; *Daily News and Herald*, May 30, July 2, 1866.

29. *Savannah Morning News*, July 1866–December 1867; Edward C. Anderson Diary (hereafter Anderson Diary), July 1866–December 1867, Edward Clifford Anderson Papers, no. 3602, Southern Historical Collection, University of North Carolina, Chapel Hill; Letter from the Secretary of the Treasury, in U.S. Congress, House 40th Cong., 2nd sess., Executive Document 123, 40–42; Mayor's Report, 1867.

30. The decision to do so was not without controversy. Some aldermen feared that dredging would compound the river's problems. *Daily News and Herald*, October 25, 1866; City of Savannah Harbor and Wharf Committee Papers, 1865–66; Minutes of Council, October 22, 1866; Mayor's Report, 1866.

31. There were some optimists like the Commissioners of Pilotage, who asserted that, given the importance of commerce to the entire state, the Georgia General Assembly might reimburse the city for the expenses of river improvement. City of Savannah Harbor and Wharf Committee Papers, March 6, 1867.

32. Mayor's Report, 1866.

33. Originally Anderson had estimated that the dredge would cost no more than $18,000; the city also had to purchase a tug steamer and dumping flats. The purchase initially seemed a sensible move, as the port's prospects continued to improve. The city leased Hutchinson Island for the construction of a dry dock and provided the use of the dredging machine in preparation. City of Savannah Harbor and Wharf Committee Papers, March 6, 22, April 27, 1867, October 4, December 23, 1868, January–February 1869, and other undated correspondence; Mayor's Reports, 1866–69; *Daily News and Herald*, July 21, October 4, 25, November 14, 1866, February 15, March 22, June 3, 6, 11, September 22, October 7, 24, November 5, 1867; Minutes of Council, October 22, 1866, January 1, 20, February 6, August 4, 1869; Gamble, *History*, 268–70; United States, Army, Corps of Engineers, *Annual Report of the Chief of Engineers to the Secretary of War for the Year 1872*, 6, 260; Somers, *Southern States since the War, 1870–71*, 72–75.

34. *Savannah Morning News*, April 26, 1869; City of Savannah Harbor and Wharf Committee Papers, October 4, December 23, 1868, January–February 1869, and other undated correspondence; Minutes of Council, January 1, 20, February 6, August 4, 1869; United States, Army, Corps of Engineers, *Annual Report of the Chief of Engineers to the Secretary of War for the Year 1872*, 656–57, 661 ; Mayor's Report, 1869; *Nimmo, Report on the Internal Commerce of the United States*, 81.

35. Letter from the Clerk of the War Department, in U.S. Congress, Senate, 43rd Cong., 1st sess., Executive Document 5, 1873, 17–18; Letter from the Secretary of the Treasury, in U.S. Congress, House, 40th Cong. 2nd sess., Executive Document 123, 1868, 40–42; Mayor's Reports, 1867–69, *Daily News and Herald*, October 1867–August 1868; *Savannah Morning News,* October 1868–April 1869; Diary of George Anderson Mercer, June 1868, no. 503, Southern Historical Collection, Wilson Library, University of North Carolina, Chapel Hill.

36. *Savannah Morning News*, February 24, 1869; Letter from the Clerk of the War Department, in U.S. Congress, Senate, 43rd Cong., 1st sess., Executive Document 5, 1873, 11.

37. Welles later filed a petition for reimbursement and in 1874 received $193,000.

Granger, *History of the Savannah District*, 82; *Savannah Morning News*, February 27, 1874.

38. Letter from the Clerk of the War Department, in U.S. Congress, Senate, 43rd Cong., 1st sess., Executive Document 5, 1873, 11.

39. Two particularly problematic locations were the Wrecks, located at the lower end of Fig Island, and the Garden Banks, located at the foot of East Broad Street, about two hundred feet from the wharf. City of Savannah Harbor and Wharf Committee Papers, March 6, 1867; *Daily News and Herald*, June 11, 1867, September 9, 1868; Mayor's Report, 1868; Communication from John Stoddard to City Council, 1869, City of Savannah Harbor and Wharf Committee Papers, scattered and undated correspondence, 1869, November 18, 1872; Mayor's Report, 1870.

40. This $125,000 does not include bimonthly Commissioners of Pilotage expenditures, which averaged $3,000. Minutes of Council, January 5, 1870; Granger, *History of the Savannah District*, 82; *New York Times*, January 3, 1871.

41. In early 1869 a bill was introduced into Congress asking for such an appropriation. The city's hopes soared in February when the *Savannah Morning News* reported that $150,000 was proposed for the Savannah River. By March that figure had dwindled to $30,000. *Cong. Globe*, 40th Cong., 3rd Sess. (1869), 281, 580; *Cong. Globe*, 41st Cong., 2nd Sess. (1870), 1120; *Savannah Morning News*, January 26, February 1, February 14, March 31, 1869; Mayor's Report, 1869.

42. Minutes of Council, January 5, 1870; Anderson Diary, January 5–February 11, June 16, June 24, 1870, Edward Clifford Anderson Papers; *Savannah Morning News*, January 7, June 22, 1870; Mayor's Report, 1870; *Savannah Morning News*, June 22, 1870; Anderson Diary, June 16, June 24, 1870, Edward Clifford Anderson Papers; City of Savannah Harbor and Wharf Committee Papers, March 4, 1870.

43. On January 25, 1869, Joseph W. Clift, Republican congressman from the First Congressional District, introduced a bill asking the House for river appropriation, which was referred to Committee on Commerce. *Cong. Globe*, 40th Cong., 3rd Sess. (1869), 281, 580; *Savannah Morning News*, January 26, 1869; Anderson Diary, April 11, 1870, Edward Clifford Anderson Papers. Thomas P. Robb, a native of Bath, Maine, moved to Chicago and then Sacramento before the war. In 1867, he was appointed postmaster in Savannah; in 1869 he received the position of collector of the port in Savannah. Under suspicion of embezzlement, he resigned in 1872. Rogers, *Scalawag in Georgia*, 88, 97–98; Jacqueline Jones, *Dreadful Deceit*, 172, 176, 180; Grant, *Papers of Ulysses S. Grant*, vol. 23, 26–32.

44. The city council also grew impatient with the lack of success of its political representatives, even though they were of the right political persuasion. It decided that the city's interest would be better served in sending its own agents to Washington—someone familiar with the history of the river improvements and immediately interested in Savannah's commercial success. Therefore, in early January 1872, the council voted to send Anderson and William W. Paine, who had served in Congress the previous year, to Washington to lobby Congress. The council instructed Anderson and Paine that their primary objective was to seek reimbursement for the money Savannah had already spent. Although Anderson thought the city should focus on obtain-

ing funding to continue improvements, he consented to go on the council's terms. In conjunction with the arrival of Anderson and Paine in Washington, Georgia's elected representatives introduced bills into Congress requesting a $220,000 remuneration and an additional $300,000 to complete the work. The council voted on this expedition in secret session; Anderson opposed the idea of a secret session and believed that it should have been a public meeting. Minutes of Council, December 7, 1871; William Wiseham Paine Papers, MS 603, Georgia Historical Society, Savannah; Anderson Diary, December 27, 1871, January 5, 1872, Edward Clifford Anderson Papers; *Savannah Morning News*, January 22, 1872; *Cong. Globe*, 42nd Cong., 2nd Sess. (1872), 196, 605; *Savannah Republican*, January 22, 1872.

45. *Savannah Morning News*, January 22, February 9, February 12, March 4, 5, April 2, 22, 1872; *Laws of the United States Relating to the Improvement of Rivers and Harbors from August 11, 1790 to March 4, 1913*, vol. 17, 370.

46. *Savannah Morning News*, July 9, 10, 1872; Mayor's Report, 1871; J. S. Kennard to John Stoddard, November 18, 1872, and Commissioners of Pilotage to John Screven, December 18, 1872, City of Savannah Harbor and Wharf Committee Papers.

47. *Savannah Morning News*, July 30, 1872; J. S. Kennard to Council, July 31, August 14, and November 18, 1872, City of Savannah Harbor and Wharf Committee Papers; *Savannah Morning News*, September 23, October 5, 1872; Granger, *History of the Savannah District*, 65. Quincy A. Gillmore, an 1849 graduate of the U.S. Military Academy, gained prominence in his use of rifled canon to reduce Fort Pulaski in 1862. It was the fall of this fort that prompted the city to block the harbor. Reid, *Ohio in the War*.

48. Minutes of Council, March 13, 1873; *Savannah Morning News*, August 29, October 5, 12, 1872.

49. City of Savannah Harbor and Wharf Committee Papers, November 11, 1872; Mayor's Report, 1874.

50. Minutes of Council, March 13, 1873; Gamble, *History*, 432.

51. Part of the cost was offset by a $300,000 bond issue to fund the public debt and the Savannah River improvements, on which the city paid $20,972 interest annually. This figure does not account for the expense of numerous trips to Washington. Anderson Diary, February 3, April 5–15, 1874, Edward Clifford Anderson Papers; Mayor's Reports, 1866–73.

52. Minutes of Council, February 5, 1874; Anderson Diary, February 3, April 5–15, 1874, Edward Clifford Anderson Papers.

53. Sloan was a native of Henry County, Georgia. After the Civil War, he moved to Savannah and served as deputy collector of customs and district attorney. In 1874, Morgan Rawls of Effingham defeated Sloan for the congressional seat. Sloan challenged the election with the passive support of Savannah Democrats, who believed that he would more vigorously pursue their interest than Rawls. Sloan subsequently unseated Rawls. *Biographical Directory of the United States Congress*; *New York Times*, February 25, 1875; Shadgett, *Republican Party in Georgia, from Reconstruction to 1900*, 94; Seip, *South Returns to Congress*; Currie-McDaniel, *Carpetbagger of Conscience*, 128–29; Minutes of Council, May 8, 1874; *Savannah Morning News*, April 30, May 12, June

27, August 20, 1874; Gamble, *History*, 432, 435; United States, Army, Corps of Engineers, *Laws of the United States Relating to the Improvement of Rivers and Harbors from August 11, 1790, to March 4, 1913*, 222; Barber and Gann, *History of the Savannah District, U.S. Army Corps of Engineers*, 38, 82.

54. Bonds were to be repaid within sixty to ninety days. As financial difficulties increased, Savannah increasingly depended on long-term bonds to cover short-term loans. City of Savannah Cash Ledgers, City of Savannah Research Library and Municipal Archives; Mayor's Reports, 1867–70; Minutes of Council, Report of the Financial Condition of the City, May 31, 1877; Gamble, *History*, 340–41.

55. *Daily News and Herald*, November 15, 18, 1867; Cozzens, *General John Pope*, 283.

56. Fitzgerald, *Urban Emancipation*; Doyle, *New Men, New Cities, New South*.

57. For instance, in 1872, interest amounted to $300,000, while the city collected only approximately $600,000 in receipts. Gamble, *History*, 340–41; Mayor's Reports, 1867–69.

CHAPTER 5. "KNOCKING IT INTO 'SMITHEREENS'"

1. Dan Carter, *When the War Was Over*, 64; Foner, *Reconstruction*; Cimbala, *Great Task Remaining before Us: Reconstruction as America's Continuing Civil War*; Cimbala, "The Freedmen's Bureau, the Freedmen, and Sherman's Grant in Reconstruction Georgia, 1865–1867," 597–632; Cimbala, *Under the Guardianship of a Nation*; Downs, *Declarations of Dependence*.

2. *Daily News and Herald*, July 11, August 5, 14, 1867; *Savannah Morning News*, November 4–5, 1868, December 24, 1868–January 15, 1868; Drago, *Black Politicians and Reconstruction in Georgia*, 31, 51–55, 78–80; Bell, "Ogeechee Troubles," 375–97; Jacqueline Jones, *Saving Savannah*, 323–25; Reidy, "Aaron A. Bradley," 281–308, quotation from 282.

3. *Savannah Morning News*, April 3–4, 1869, October 15, 1869. For discussion on persistence of mixed residency patterns for African Americans and whites in southern cities, see Goldfield, *Region, Race and Cities*, 60; Blassingame, "Before the Ghetto," 464–65.

4. *Report of the State Commissioners Representing the Stock Held by the State in the Atlantic and Gulf Rail Road Company*, 5–13; *Augusta Chronicle*, July 28, 1859; Harden, *History of Savannah and South Georgia*, 596–98; Southern Historical Association, *Memoirs of Georgia*, 413–14; Jones, *History of Savannah*, 625.

5. The debate over nominations concerned the issue of whether councilmen should be nominated by district or at large. Party leaders compromised by combining the two. *Savannah Morning News*, August 23–31, 1869.

6. *Savannah Morning News*, November 4–5, 1868.

7. John Stoddard to John Screven, September 13, 1869, Arnold and Screven Family Papers, no. 3419, Southern Historical Collection, Wilson Library, University of North Carolina, Chapel Hill; Anderson Diary, October 25, 1869, Edward Clifford Anderson Papers.

8. Savannah had a tradition of mayors who served as railroad presidents, including William Washington Gordon and James P. Screven.

9. Anderson never explained his decision not to run. Anderson Diary, July–September 1869, Edward Clifford Anderson Papers.

10. William Richard Waring papers, MS 838, Georgia Historical Society, Savannah.

11. *Savannah Georgian*, May 5, 1828.

12. *Savannah Republican*, August 30, 1820, May 6, 1825; *Savannah Georgian*, August 2, 1821.

13. *Savannah Georgian*, May 5, 1828; *Savannah Daily Georgian*, May 25, 1837.

14. Minutes of Council, August 12, 1831; *Savannah Daily Georgian*, October 4, 1836.

15. Alston family papers, 1846–1902 (1002.00), South Carolina Historical Society, Charleston.

16. Jones, *History of Savannah*, 444; Wilson, *Historic and Picturesque Savannah*, 294–95; Indenture, folder 36, Joseph Frederick Waring II papers, MS 1275, Georgia Historical Society, Savannah.

17. Folder 36, Joseph Frederick Waring II papers, MS 1275, Georgia Historical Society, Savannah.

18. *Augusta Chronicle*, October 13, 1866; "Brief Sketch of the Life of Dr. James J. Waring," in Joseph Frederick Waring II papers, MS 1275, Georgia Historical Society, Savannah.

19. *Daily News and Herald*, July 11, 1867; miscellaneous newspaper clippings in Joseph Frederick Waring Letters and Diary, MS 837, Georgia Historical Society, Savannah.

20. *Savannah Morning News*, October 7, 1869; Anderson Diary, October 25, 1869, Edward Clifford Anderson Papers.

21. John Screven to Georgia Screven, July 29, 1865, Arnold and Screven Family Papers; A. Porter Alexander to A. L. Alexander, August 2, 1865, Alexander and Hillhouse Family Papers, no. 11, Southern Historical Collection, Wilson Library, University of North Carolina, Chapel Hill.

22. John Screven to Georgia Screven, October 5, 1865, Arnold and Screven Family Papers. The Atlantic and Gulf Railroad issued $500,000, with the "1st mortgage on the division from Savannah to No. 7." Atlantic and Gulf Railroad Annual Report, published in *Daily News and Herald*, February 13, 1868. More information on the various mortgages on road sections can be found in the U.S. District court decision to sell the Atlantic and Gulf Railroad, published in *Savannah Morning News*, June 24, 1879; and Fish, *Restoration of Southern Railroads*, 7–11, 14, 21.

23. The roads connected briefly during the Civil War. In 1853, as the Savannah press was embroiled in a war of words with the *Albany Patriot*, there was some hint that the Central Railroad was somewhat concerned about future territorial competition. *Albany Patriot*, April 22, 1853, and April 28, 1854.

24. The Southwestern Railroad was chartered in 1845. Running west from Macon and acting as a Central feeder, it became a profitable line. From the outset, the Central invested in the construction of the Southwestern's line into western Georgia. In 1849, the City of Savannah invested $150,000 for the company's purchase of iron rails.

Although the legislature authorized the Central to lease the Southwestern in 1852, the Central delayed action until June 1869. Details of the Central Railroad's financial investment in the Southwestern are located in Report of the President and Directors of the Central Railroad and Banking Company, published in *Savanah Republican*, December 5, 1850. For details of the legislation and the lease, see *Savannah Morning News*, June 28, 1869, and *Central of Georgia Railway Company v. Wright, Comptroller General of Georgia, Federal Reporter*, vol. 206, 107–16. Details of the city's investment in the Southwestern Railroad can be found in *Savannah Daily Republican*, January 22–23, 1849; Minutes of Council, January 18, 1849, and March 1, 1870; Mayor's Report for 1849 published in the *Savannah Daily Republican*, November 22, 1849.

25. The steamship company was Barnett Steamboat Line. *Columbus Daily Sun*, December 13, 1867, March 8, 17, 1868; Peeples, "Georgia Railroads," 79, 83; *Daily News and Herald*, January 16, 1868; reprint of *Albany News* in *Daily News and Herald*, January 6, 21, February 13, 1868.

26. *Daily News and Herald*, February 13, April 2, 1868.

27. At one point the shipping rate dipped to sixty cents per bale of cotton. *Eufaula News*, January 19, 1868, reprinted in *Daily News and Herald*, January 21, 1868.

28. Wadley's appointment to the Confederacy came in 1862, but due to his controversial opinions, the Confederate Senate rejected his appointment. Cumming, *Life and Labors of William M. Wadley*; Dorothy Houseal Stewart, "Survival of the Fittest," 39–65; DeCredico, *Patriots for Profit*, 75, 86, 90; Central Railroad Minutes, May 23, 1865; Central Railroad Annual Report to Stockholders, 1869.

29. Central Railroad Minutes, March 3, 1868.

30. The compromise set the cotton shipping rate by the Atlantic and Gulf Railroad, from Bainbridge to Savannah, at thirty-five cents per hundred miles. The Central and Southwestern roads were to adopt the same rates from Eufaula and Columbus. The compromise also ended discrimination by steamship lines against the Atlantic and Gulf Railroad. Central Railroad Minutes, January 28, 1868; *Columbus Daily Sun*, January 23, 1868; Peeples, "Georgia Railroads," 82, 84–85; *Savannah Morning News*, February 11, 1869.

31. Central Railroad Minutes, March 10, 1868; Peeples, "Georgia Railroads," 82–83; Central Railroad contracted with Atlantic Coast Mail Steamship Company, William R. Garrison Company, and Murray, Ferris and Company. The Muscogee Railroad cut its rate of carrying cotton to Savannah to seventy-five cents per hundred pounds. *Daily News and Herald*, January 21, February 13, February 17, 1868; *Columbus Daily Sun*, March 10, 1868.

32. Technically, the Southwestern controlled the Muscogee Railroad. Central Railroad Minutes, April 28, May 21, April 28, June 29, July 7, 19, 1868; *Columbus Daily Sun*, June 13, August 22, 1868; *Daily News and Herald*, July 21, August 24, 1868; *Savannah Morning News*, November 6, 1868.

33. *Columbus Daily Sun*, July 26, 1868. The railroad was being touted as one partially financed by elite northern capitalists, and Macon saw it as the city's ticket to being the next "great distribution point," for whose business Charleston, Savannah, and Brunswick would compete. *Macon Weekly Telegraph*, July 10, 1868.

34. *Columbus Daily Sun,* July 7, 1868; *Macon Telegraph,* February 12, 1869; Central Railroad Minutes, July 7, 1868.

35. Less than a month later, the Central Railroad approved a request by the Macon and Western for endorsement of an additional $100,000. In June, Wadley announced that the Central Railroad could purchase $200,000 of the second mortgage that the Central Railroad had just guaranteed at ninety cents on the dollar if the Central Railroad would release the Macon and Western from the interest due on their debt of $100,000 and agree to pay the balance of $92,000 on the Macon and Western due in August. The board authorized the purchase. In July, the Central Railroad agreed to endorse an additional $8,000. Central Railroad Minutes, April 28, May 9, June 2, July 28, 1868; *Columbus Daily Sun,* July 30, 1868.

36. *Columbus Daily Sun,* December 22, 1868, January 2, 1869; *Bainbridge Argus,* January 9, 1869. For detailed discussion on antebellum Upcountry anti–Central Railroad sentiment, see Dixon, "The Central Railroad of Georgia, 1833–1892," 6–11.

37. The bonds were dated from July 1, 1867, payable at thirty years and bearing 7 percent interest. Report of John Screven, president of the Atlantic and Gulf Railroad, published in *Daily News and Herald,* February 13, 1867.

38. Report of John Screven, president of the Atlantic and Gulf Railroad, published in *Daily News and Herald,* February 13, 1867. In late January, the Central Railroad began working to reduce salaries to make them "consistent with the interest of the road." In February, the Central Railroad loaned the Muscogee $27,000 to pay an upcoming loan. Central Railroad Minutes, January 28, February 18, October 20, 1868; William Tison to William (Willy) Washington Gordon, July 19, 1869, Gordon Family Papers, no. 2235, Southern Historical Collection, University of North Carolina, Chapel Hill; William Washington Gordon Jr. was the son of the Central Railroad's first president, William Washington Gordon.

39. The Central Railroad representative suggested that the companies fix the rates on the two lines to give advantage to the Atlantic and Gulf Railroad over all points to and from southern and southwestern Georgia except in the immediate vicinity of the Southwestern Railroad's termini and directly on its line. Because this proposal required the Atlantic and Gulf Railroad to surrender the area around Bainbridge and Albany, the Atlantic and Gulf Railroad committee refused the proposition. Rather, it proposed that the Central Railroad permit the Atlantic and Gulf Railroad to carry a set number of bales from certain points at lower rates and to have other lines in the area agree not to receive any cotton which would interfere with the Atlantic and Gulf Railroad line. The Central Railroad committee dismissed the plan, claiming a lack of control over all of those points. *Savannah Morning News,* October 26, 1868; *Central Georgian,* November 4, 1868; Central Railroad Minutes, October 20, November 24, December 22, 1868; *Columbus Daily Sun,* December 27, 1868; Minutes of Council, December 23, 1869.

40. *Columbus Daily Sun,* December 27, 1868; Central Railroad Minutes, December 22, 1868; Minutes of Council, December 23, 1869.

41. The official offer was to buy 12,383 shares of Atlantic and Gulf Railroad totaling $944,000, 307 shares in the Montgomery and West Point Railroad, 424 shares of

the Augusta and Savannah Railroad totaling $174,500, and 1 share of the Southwestern Railroad, worth $117,000. Mayor's Report, 1869; Minutes of Council, December 23, 1868; Central Railroad Minutes, December 18, 1868.

42. Central Railroad Minutes, December 29, 1868; Atlantic and Gulf Railroad Report, published in *Savannah Morning News*, February 11, 1869.

43. The Macon and Brunswick Railroad Company was incorporated in 1856. *Southern Recorder*, April 1, 1856. The state granted aid to the railroad in 1866. *Macon Telegraph*, December 10, 1866; *Columbus Daily Sun,* November 13, 1869; *Macon Telegraph*, January 21, 1869; Dixon, "Georgia Railroad Growth and Consolidation, 1860–1917," 36.

44. The dispatch of the president of the Macon and Brunswick Railroad stated that the contract had been signed, sealed, and delivered. Screven noted that as a matter of "self-protection against the antagonism of the Central and Southwestern Railroad companies," the Atlantic and Gulf Railroad had formed an alliance with the Macon and Brunswick. Annual Report of Atlantic and Gulf Railroad, published in *Savannah Morning News*, February 11, 1869; *Thomasville Times*, reprinted in *Savannah Morning News*, January 9, 1869; *Columbus Daily Sun,* July 4, December 22, 1868.

45. Extract from Central Railroad Minutes, published in Minutes of Council, December 23, 1869; *Savannah Morning News*, January 9, 18, February 1, 1869.

46. *Columbus Daily Sun*, January 2, 1869; *Macon Telegraph*, January 23, 1869; *Savannah Morning News*, February 1, 1869.

47. Hahn, *The Roots of Southern Populism*; Woodward, *Tom Watson*; Pollack, *Populist Mind*; McCabe, *History of the Grange Movement*; McMath, *Populist Vanguard*; Hicks, *Populist Revolt*; Hild, *Greenbackers, Knights of Labor, and Populists*; Schwartz, *Radical Protest and Social Structure*.

48. *Savannah Morning News*, January 9, 18, February 1, 1869.

49. *Albany News*, January 15, 1869.

50. *Columbus Daily Sun*, January 21, 1869.

51. *Macon Weekly Telegraph*, February 26, 1869, reprint from the *Columbus Sun*.

52. *Columbus Daily Sun*, January 5, 1869; *Macon Telegraph*, January 22, 1869; *Milledgeville Union*, reprinted in *Savannah Morning News*, October 15, 1869.

53. Judge Cole ruled that the company's charter did not grant it the authority to purchase such stock. Due to the injunction, neither the Central Railroad nor the Southwestern Railroad could vote the 12,383 shares. M. Cuyler to William Washington Gordon Jr., January 12, 1869, Gordon Family Papers, no. 2235, Southern Historical Collection, University of North Carolina, Chapel Hill; *Savannah Morning News*, January 5, February 11, March 1, November 8, 1869; *Macon Telegraph*, January 8, 1869; Mayor's Report, 1869; Gamble, *History*, 224–25.

54. W. J. Harden, the city's attorney, claimed that the complainants' case was shaky at best in spite of Judge Cole's ruling. Minutes of Council, January 20, 1869.

55. Annual income decreased by over $16,000. *Savannah Morning News*, January 28, 1869; annual report of Atlantic and Gulf Railroad, published in *Savannah Morning News*, February 11, 1869.

56. Annual report of the president of the Atlantic and Gulf Railroad, published in

Savannah Morning News, February 11, 12, 1869. For more information on Lamar, see Coddington, "Activities and Attitudes of a Confederate Business Man," 3–36.

57. *Macon Telegraph*, February 12, 1869; annual report of the president of the Atlantic and Gulf Railroad, published in *Savannah Morning News*, February 11, 12, 1869; William Tison to William Washington Gordon Jr., July 19, 1869, Gordon Family Papers, no. 2235, Southern Historical Collection, University of North Carolina, Chapel Hill.

58. Minutes of Council, June 9, 23, July 21, 1869.

59. Report of Finance Committee in Minutes of Council, September 15, 1869. As the city council had feared, the scheduled hearing for October 1869 was again postponed. Mayor's Report, 1869.

60. Minutes of Council, September 15, 1869.

61. Anderson Diary, August 21–30, September 2–18, 1869, Edward Clifford Anderson Papers; Minutes of Council, January 20, 1869; *Savannah Morning News*, January 1869–October, 1869; *Bainbridge Argus*, January–March 1869; *Columbus Daily Sun*, January 1868–June 1869; *Macon Telegraph*, January 1869–August 1869.

62. Anderson Diary, September 25, 1869, Edward Clifford Anderson Papers; Minutes of Council, September 29, October 27, 1869; Central Railroad Minutes, October 5, 1869; T. M. Cunningham to the City of Savannah, October 19, 1869, in Mayor's Report, 1869.

63. In early September, the *Savannah Morning News* began reporting on Republican organization in the city. Charles Hopkins, a native of McIntosh County, and Walter M. Walsh, a local physician, were potential candidates. Anderson Diary, August 17, September 3, 4, 14, 17, 19, 24, October 3, 9, 12, 18, 1869, Edward Clifford Anderson Papers; *Savannah Morning News*, September 24, 27, October 7, 1869.

CHAPTER 6. "IN A BAD FIX"

1. In early November, Judge Carlton Cole upheld the injunction against the stock transfer. The City of Savannah, Central Railroad, and Southwestern Railroad appealed the decision. Minutes of Council, September 29, 1869; Central Railroad Minutes, November 23, 1869.

2. Communication between William Washington Gordon Jr. and W. H. Tison, October 22, 25, 27, 1869, Gordon Family Papers, Georgia Historical Society, Savanna.

3. In late October 1869, the new city council passed an ordinance to renew the $117,000 bonds issued for stock in the Southwestern Railroad. Bypassing the council, Screven gave the city's reserve bonds to Henry Bryan for sale, a legally questionable act at best. Anderson Diary, October 20, 22, 1869, Edward Clifford Anderson Papers, no. 3602, Southern Historical Collection, University of North Carolina, Chapel Hill; *Savannah Morning News*, October 6, 28, November 8, 1869; Minutes of Council, October 17, 20, 1869; Mayor's Report, 1870; *Macon Weekly Telegraph*, February 15, 1870. This action would have been forced on the council regardless because in February 1870, the Georgia Supreme Court ruled in favor of the Atlantic and Gulf Railroad. While the Central Railroad's charter had authorized the building of a line from

Macon to Savannah, the Supreme Court contended that the company did not have the authority to control a railroad running from Savannah to Bainbridge. Furthermore, because the banking powers of the Central had expired on December 14, 1868, it had no right to acquire stock in other railroad companies. *Central Railroad of Georgia v. Stephen Collins*, 40 *Georgia Reports* 583 (1869); Minutes of Council, March 1, 1870.

4. Fitzgerald, *Urban Emancipation*; Doyle, *New Men, New Cities, New South*; Ewert, "New South Era in Mobile, 1875–1900."

5. South Carolina, Department of Agriculture, and Hammond, *South Carolina*, 672–73.

6. Funded or bonded debt is a debt acquired from selling interest-bearing bonds that mature after one year, usually a long-term loan. Steiss, *Local Government Finance*, 108–11. In his 1869 report (his last before Screven entered office), Anderson set the debt at $2,051,880. Mayor's Report, 1869. Rumors circulated that Eugene Kelly, a New York banker and railroad magnate with several Savannah investments, had offered to purchase the city's Southwestern Railroad bonds but that Screven had refused to sell. Kelly did in fact purchase a note of $35,000, which was negotiated by Anderson's council. In January 1870, Henry Bryan traveled to New York to negotiate another loan for the city. *Savannah Morning News*, November 8, 1869; Anderson Diary, December 3, 8, 1869, March 3, 1870, Edward Clifford Anderson Papers, no. 3602, Southern Historical Collection, University of North Carolina, Chapel Hill; Minutes of Council, December 3, 1869; Mayor's Reports, 1867–69; City of Savannah Ordinances, January 5, 1870, City of Savannah Research Library and Municipal Archives.

7. Melosi, *Effluent America*, 144. See also Cutler and Miller, *Water, Water, Everywhere*.

8. Heilbrun, *Urban Economics and Public Policy*, 324.

9. Stabile, *Origins of American Public Finance*, 5; John E. Anderson, *Public Finance*, 608; Hyman, *Public Finance*, 461.

10. Taxation totals are exclusive of fines, license fees, and rents, which ranged from $50,000 to $70,000 annually. The city's population increased by 8.7 percent during the 1870s. Gamble, *History*, 288, 507; Financial Committee Report, Minutes of Council, May 30, 1877; Mayor's Reports, 1866–79; Lehmann, "Federal Municipal Bankruptcy Act," 241. For similar examples throughout the South and the nation, see Brownell and Goldfield, *City in Southern History*; Hillhouse, *Municipal Bonds*; Larsen, *Urban South*; Monkonnen, "Politics of Municipal Indebtedness and Default, 1850–1936," 125–59; Monkkonen, *America Becomes Urban*; Platt, *City Building in the New South*; Sbragia, *Debt Wish*; Steiss, *Local Government Finance*; Wallenstein, *From Slave South to New South*.

11. Corporate taxes made up the second-largest category of municipal taxes. Holcombe and Lacombe, "Factors Underlying the Growth of Local Government in the 19th Century United States," 367; Higgens-Evenson, *Price of Progress*, 14; Aronson, Hilley, and Maxwell, *Financing State and Local Governments*, 120; Sylla and Wallis, "Anatomy of Sovereign Debt Crises," 273.

12. L. B. Sweat to William Harris Garland, March 21, 1872, in the William Harris

Garland Papers, no. 2982, Southern Historical Collection, Wilson Library, University of North Carolina at Chapel Hill; *Daily News and Herald,* August 2, November 22, 1867, January 22, 1868, *Savannah Morning News,* July 9, 1868, February 20, June 4, 1869, March 4, June 27, 1870.

13. Balleisen, *Navigating Failure,* 75, 84.

14. *Daily News and Herald,* May 5, 1868; *Savannah Morning News,* June 7, 1870.

15. Minutes of Council, May 26, June 8, September 1, 1870; Mayor's Office Papers, May 1, June 2, 1870.

16. Minutes of Council, August 5, 1868, May 26, June 8, July 7, 1870; City of Savannah Finance Committee Papers, July 6, 1870, City of Savannah Research Library and Municipal Archives; *Savannah Morning News,* June 7, July 21, 1870.

17. The city could not even afford to keep park lights lit. Minutes of Council, June 8, 1870; *Savannah Morning News,* June 27, August 19, September 23, 1870.

18. Minutes of Council, August 31, 1870; City of Savannah Finance Committee Papers, March 28, 29, May 10, 1871.

19. *Savannah Morning News,* July 21, 1870; Minutes of Council, August 5, 1868.

20. Citizens contradictorily demanded more services and complained about increased expenditures. A few of the aldermen confessed that they believed Screven's council was wasting public money. After investigating the matter, Anderson noted in his diary that he had "had a long talk with the mayor about the board's extravagance." Anderson Diary, June 6, July 20, 22, August 2, September 28, 1870, Edward Clifford Anderson Papers, no. 3602, Southern Historical Collection, University of North Carolina, Chapel Hill; Mayor's Report, 1870.

21. *Savannah Morning News,* November 25, 1869.

22. Minutes of Council, November 10, 24, 1869.

23. The city's first market, built in 1763 on Ellis Square, was destroyed in the large 1820 fire, after which a market was set up at South Broad Street and Oglethorpe. Two years later, Ellis Square again became home to the city market after reconstruction of the building there. This structure remained intact until it was destroyed in 1872 for the new market. Watkins and Watkins, *Digest of the Laws of the State of Georgia,* 87–88; Wood, *Women's Work, Men's Work,* 213.

24. The market brought between $15,000 and $20,000 to the city treasury annually. Municipal Reports, 1857, 1858, 1866–70; *Savannah Morning News,* August 23, 1869; Tarr and Konvitz, "Patterns in the Development of the Urban Infrastructure," 198.

25. *Daily News and Herald,* May 20, 29, July 24, November 13, 1867, July 20, 1868; *Savannah Morning News,* November 12, 1868.

26. Mayor's Reports, 1857, 1858, 1866–70; *Savannah Morning News,* August 23, 1869.

27. Minutes of Council, November 24, 1869.

28. The city awarded contracts on October 1. Citizens would later request that the council authorize a second story while the building was still under construction because it would cost less than adding it later. The market committee, mindful of mounting expenses, refused the petition. City of Savannah Market Committee Papers, July 31, 1870, City of Savannah Research Library and Municipal Archives; Min-

utes of Council, July 20, 28, August 17, September 5, 14, 17, 28, 1870; *Savannah Morning News*, July 8, 29, October 25, 1870; Mayor's Report, 1870.

29. The dispute arose over a difficulty in supplying the stone to finish the superstructure. The *Savannah Morning News* felt obliged to remark on all the rats the demolition unearthed. *Savannah Morning News*, August 3, September 22, 28, October 25, December 22, 28, 1871; Minutes of Council, July 28, August 17, September 5, 14, 17, 28, 1870, October 3, 12, 13 1870, January 4, July 19, December 6, 11, 1871; City of Savannah Market Committee Papers, February 25, March 13, 1871, City of Savannah Research Library and Municipal Archives; City of Savannah Ordinances, October 30, 1870; Mayor's Report, 1871.

30. *Savannah Morning News*, April 4, May 14, 29, 31, June 11, 1872.

31. Mayor's Reports 1869–73; Minutes of Council, August 14, 1872; *Savannah Morning News*, August 19, 1872, July 29, 1874.

32. The Georgia Medical Society, from its founding in 1804, advocated the dry culture solution. Le Hardy, "Sanitary Progress in Savannah, Georgia," 30–36. In response, the council convened the Board of Health intermittently—usually when the city was threatened by various epidemic outbreaks. The board carried out various duties, including "inspecting lot enclosures and yards, reporting filth in the streets and along the wharves, inspecting vacant buildings and privies, and reporting any violations to the City Council." Wilson, *Digest of All the Ordinances of the City of Savannah*, 14–19; Gamble, *History*, 142–46, 205–7; Minutes of Council, June 16, 1850; Haunton, "Savannah in the 1850s," 296–97. For more information on how cities dealt with sanitation issues, see Melosi, *Garbage in the Cities*.

33. John Screven provided a basic history of the city's previous drainage efforts in the 1870 Mayor's Report. See also Gamble, *History*, 205–6, 235–36.

34. Diary of George Anderson Mercer, December 12, 1867, #503, Southern Historical Collection, Wilson Library, University of North Carolina, Chapel Hill; Minutes of Council, January 7, February 17, 1869; City of Savannah Sewer Committee Papers, July 14, 1867, City of Savannah Research Library and Municipal Archives.

35. Melosi, *Effluent America*, 224–25.

36. Duffy refers to the period 1870–90 as "the sanitary revolution," the era when many large and medium-size towns expanded their sewer and water systems or built new ones. Duffy, *Sanitarians*, 139, 147; Melosi, *Sanitary City*; Melosi, *Pollution and Reform in American Cities, 1870–1930*.

37. Cutler and Miller, *Water, Water Everywhere*, 157–58.

38. Duffy Street, just south of Forsyth Park, runs east to west between West Broad Street (now Martin Luther King Jr. Blvd) and East Broad Street.

39. Jonathan Clarke to Mayor Edward C. Anderson, May 27, 1868, and July 14, 1867, City of Savannah Sewer Committee Papers; Minutes of Council, February 19, 1866; Mayor's Report, 1867; *Daily News and Herald*, July 12, 1867.

40. *Savannah Morning News*, July 14, 1870.

41. Schwaab provided four plans. He favored establishing an outlet at the Vernon River, but he admitted it would be quite costly and face difficult right-of-way issues. The Warsaw River is now called the Wilmington River, part of the Intracoastal Wa-

terway. Minutes of Council, November 24, 1869, April 13, June 3, 27, 1870; Report to Sewer Committee, July 30, 1870.

42. Report of Augustus Schwaab presented to Council, July 30, 1870, City of Savannah Sewer Committee Papers; Mayor's Report, 1870; *Savannah Morning News*, April 6, December 22, 1871.

43. Christopher C. Casey, a native of New York, established himself as a contractor and became involved in Savannah's public life in the 1850s. In 1858, he was appointed to the Board of Health for Percival Ward. In 1865, he became the chairman of the fire committee and was elected chief fireman. He served as alderman during the Civil War and was one of three individuals who surrendered the city to John Geary in 1864. After the war, he served as a poll challenger in 1871 and on the Democratic Executive Committee for the Third District. He became a member of the Savannah Jockey Club and the Republican Blues. *Daily Morning News*, April 3, 1858; *Savannah Republican*, October 20, 1863, January 9, 1865; *Savannah Morning News*, December 18, 1871, April 27, December 6, 11, 1872; *Atlanta Constitution*, July 23, 1888. This was one of several contracts awarded. At the time, Casey was a member of council; upon receiving the award, he resigned his seat to devote his efforts to drain construction, though he eventually resumed this position. *Savannah Morning News*, October 24, 1872. Casey's contract would be increased to $99,000 by the conclusion of the work. City of Savannah Mayor's Office Papers, December 6. 1870; City of Savannah Sewer Committee Papers, July 30, 1870; Minutes of Council, September 5, October 3, 13, 28, 1870.

44. *Savannah Morning News*, April 6, December 22, 1871; Duffy, *Sanitarians*, 139.

45. Mayor's Reports, 1855–60; *Savannah Morning News*, January 31, February 6, March 20, April 3, 9, 1872.

46. Minutes of Council, September 13, 1871, January 4, 31, August 14, 1872; Mayor's Reports, 1869, 1871; *Savannah Morning News*, April 6, 16, 26, May 4, December 22, 1871, January 15, February 14, March 16, August 5, 10, 1872.

47. Minutes of Council, April 27, 1870, January 18, February 15, 1871; Mayor's Report, 1871; *Savannah Morning News*, July 1, 8, 1870, March 6, 1871.

48. City of Savannah Finance Committee Papers, October 20, 1871; Minutes of Council, February 14, March 13, 1872; *Savannah Morning News*, December 22, 1871.

49. Minutes of Council, October 22, 26, December 27, 1871; *Savannah Morning News*, December 22, 1871, January 15, 1873; Mayor's Report, 1872.

50. This expenditure included $50,000 on improvements to the Bilbo Canal. Gamble, *History*, 290; Minutes of Council, January 18, February 15, March 29, November 8, 18, December 11, 1871, February 14, March 13, 27, July 3, August 14, September 11, 1872; *Savannah Morning News*, March 7, May 4, 1872.

51. While Screven did not detail exactly how the drainage system would lead to prosperity, he certainly hoped that it would aid the Atlantic and Gulf Railroad, which had been granted the privilege of building its track to the Bilbo Canal. Other than cotton, lumber was one of the primary products that the Atlantic and Gulf Railroad brought to the coast. The Bilbo Canal would be able to carry this lumber to the river, as the Atlantic and Gulf Railroad had no tracks to that location. Mayor's Report, 1872, published in *Savannah Morning News*, January 15, 1873.

CHAPTER 7. "MAKING A HANDLE OF IT"

1. City of Savannah Finance Committee Petitions, February 28, March 28, 29 1871, Savannah Municipal Research Library and Municipal Archives; Minutes of Council, February 1, April 12, 1871; *Savannah Morning News,* July 27, 1871.

2. *Savannah Morning News,* March 2, 27, April 4, May 13, June 6, 14, July 19, 23, August 17, August 25, September 19, 1871. By comparison, Charleston exported cotton worth $27 million but by one estimate had less than $1 million in banking capital. Somers, *Southern States Since the War, 1870–71,* 44, 75, 79; United States, Congress, Joint Select Committee on the Condition of Affairs in the Late Insurrectionary States, *Report of the Joint Select Committee Appointed to Inquire into the Condition of Affairs of the Late Insurrectionary States,* 148; Nimmo, *Report on the Internal Commerce of the United States,* 81.

3. City of Savannah Finance Committee Petitions, October 24, 1871; Minutes of Council, October 25, 26, December 27, 1871; Mayor's Report, 1872; *Savannah Morning News,* December 22, 1871, January 15, 1872.

4. Floating debt is a short-term debt that is renewed or refinanced often. City of Savannah Finance Committee Petitions, November 20, 1871; Minutes of Council, November 25, 1871, January 15, 25, 1872.

5. Rebarer, *Rebarer's Digest,* 24–25; Minutes of Council, December 27, 1871; *Savannah Morning News,* December 22, 1871.

6. The city realized $324,730 of the issue. *Savannah Morning News,* March 4, 25, 1872; Gamble, *History,* 289.

7. Sbragia, *Debt Wish,* 82; *Georgia Acts,* 1872, 258–59.

8. The Atlantic and Gulf Railroad received one advantage of which the public was not aware: it did not pay taxes while Screven was mayor. Minutes of Council, February 2, 1871; Central Railroad Minutes, November 14, 1871; City of Savannah Tax Digests, 1867–75, City of Savannah Research Library and Municipal Archives.

9. MacIntyre's name is alternately spelled "McIntyre" in the records. William Duncan to John Screven, July 30, 1870 and A. T. MacIntyre to T. M. Cunningham, September 9, 1870, Arnold and Screven Family Papers; Knight, *Standard History of Georgia and Georgians,* vol. 6, 3157. Screven's contemplation of another year in office may have been prompted by rumors that Governor Rufus Bullock planned to replace him with fellow Republican Foster Blodgett as president of the Atlantic and Gulf Railroad. However, Blodgett never challenged Screven for control of the Atlantic and Gulf Railroad. *Savannah Morning News,* November 4, 1870.

10. R. H. Hardaway to John Screven, January 5, 1871, Arnold and Screven Family Papers; Henry S. Haines to John Screven, April 3, 1871, Henry Stevens Haines Books, no. 3283, Southern Historical Collection, University of North Carolina, Chapel Hill.

11. Anderson resigned a few weeks later. Anderson Diary, January 23, February 6, 8, June 10, 1871, Edward Clifford Anderson Papers, no. 3602, Southern Historical Collection, University of North Carolina, Chapel Hill; Edward Anderson to John Screven, February 20, 1871, Arnold and Screven Family Papers.

12. Atlantic and Gulf Railroad Directors (Charles Green, John Stoddard, John L.

Villalonga, A. M. Sloan, Hiram Roberts, W. H. Wiltberger) to John Screven, January 18, 1872 and February 3, 1872, Arnold and Screven Family Papers. Correspondence regarding the board's specific retrenchment demands, along with a summary of Screven's response, was published in *Savannah Morning News*, June 20, 1872. Hiram Roberts's account of the investigation was published in *Savannah Daily Republican*, July 4, 1872.

13. Atlantic and Gulf Railroad Directors to John Screven, January 18, 1872 and February 3, 1872, Arnold and Screven Family Papers.

14. Another reason Screven may have wanted to retain his position as mayor was to get from the city council a subscription for the Huntsville and Eufaula Railroad as a feeder line for the Atlantic and Gulf Railroad. J. H. Johnston to John Screven, February 2, 1872, and John Screven to Morris K. Jesup, February 17, 1872, Arnold and Screven Family Papers; *Savannah Morning News*, September 27, October 10, 1871.

15. John Stoddard to John Screven, October 7, 1871, Arnold and Screven Family Papers; Knight, *Standard History of Georgia and Georgians*, vol. 6, 3157.

16. A. T. MacIntyre to John Screven, October 2, 1871, R. H. Hardaway to John Screven, October 7, 1871, John Stoddard to John Screven, October 7, 1871, Arnold and Screven Family Papers.

17. Original indenture was entered into on January 1, 1872. The indenture was a second mortgage on the entire line. Charles Green, et al. to John Screven, January 18, 1872 in Arnold and Screven Family Papers.

18. Charles Green to John Screven, January 27, 1872, Arnold and Screven Family Papers.

19. John Screven to Directors, January 29, 1872, and Directors to John Screven, January 30, 1872, Arnold and Screven Family Papers.

20. John Screven to Directors, January 29, 1872, and Directors to John Screven, January 30, 1872, Arnold and Screven Family Papers.

21. When Screven informed Hunter of his directors' demands and submitted his letter of resignation, Hunter began working with John Stoddard and Charles Green to come up with a less drastic solution. Hunter met with the two men and warned them that more complications than advantages would arise from any resignations. The written account fails to specify those complications. At a subsequent meeting of all the directors who had threatened to resign, Hunter, along with Green and Stoddard, convinced the other directors to withdraw their demand for Screven's resignation. A few days later, Charles Green followed up with a less strident ultimatum that consisted of some modified retrenchment measures. Furthermore, Green told Screven he could agree to the retrenchment measures proposed by the board or present an alternate plan that the board might find acceptable. Although he had already informed Hunter that he still planned to resign and ordered him to submit his resignation to council, Screven responded favorably to the compromise and all looked well for the upcoming meeting. Charles Green to John Screven, February 2, 1872, and John Screven to Charles Green, February 3, 1872, Arnold and Screven Family Papers; Letter of William Hunter, March 25, 1872, provided to the Atlantic and Gulf Railroad stockholder meeting and published in *Savannah Morning News*, July 4, 1872.

22. Proceedings of the Atlantic and Gulf Railroad stockholder meeting published in *Savannah Morning News*, February 15, 1872; *Atlanta Constitution*, March 23, 24, 1872.

23. *Savannah Morning News*, March 1, 1872.

24. Screven submitted his resignation on February 19 and withdrew it on March 1, 1872. According to a later account by Hiram Roberts, the proposed lease of the road caused the issue of Screven's mayoralty to move to the background. Once the lease proposition was rejected, Screven had managed to retain both posts. *Savannah Daily Republican*, July 4, 1872; City of Savannah Mayor's Office Papers, February 28, 1872, City of Savannah Research Library and Municipal Archives; City of Savannah Council Committee to John Screven, February 29, 1872, Arnold and Screven Family Papers.

25. Screven arranged for funding on March 16, 1872. He was authorized to issue $1,500,000 in bonds secured by second mortgage and to use this money to secure a loan of $500,000 to be applied to liquidate floating indebtedness. Extracts of Atlantic and Gulf Railroad Board Meetings published in *Savannah Morning News*, June 20, 1872; Directors to John Screven, March 21, 1872, Arnold and Screven Family Papers; *Savannah Morning News*, March 22, 1872.

26. Minutes of Council, June 11, 1872; *Macon Telegraph and Messenger*, February 20, 1872.

27. Transcripts of the Atlantic and Gulf Railroad meeting published in *Savannah Morning News*, July 4, 1872; *Savannah Daily Republican*, July 4, 1872; *Bainbridge Democrat*, July 18, 1872.

28. Research has uncovered no proof of Waring's charges in Screven's journal, council minutes, or financial ledgers. However, given the errors of the financial ledgers discovered in an audit in the 1880s and the frequent mention of secret—and thus unrecorded—sessions of council, lack of proof is not surprising. The only hint that Waring's charges might be true is found in Anderson's diary. At one point Anderson, during the debate concerning investment in the Savannah and Atlanta Railroad, mentioned Screven's desire to have the city aid the Atlantic and Gulf Railroad. Waring's charges, however, would explain the mysterious evaporation of city funds. Councilmen who might have been involved would have been reluctant to make such a transgression public. Transcripts of the Atlantic and Gulf Railroad meeting published in *Savannah Morning News*, July 4, 1872; *Savannah Daily Republican*, July 4, 1872; *Bainbridge Democrat*, July 18, 1872.

29. Anderson Diary, July 2, 1872, Edward Clifford Anderson Papers; *Savannah Morning News*, July 6, 1872.

30. Both houses of the Georgia State Assembly passed the measure with fewer than five votes to spare, but Governor Bullock refused to sign the bill. He and other opponents of the bill maintained that the road was already mortgaged. This prevented the state from having a prior lien; that being the case, the constitution would not allow the state to invest. Richard Arnold to John Screven, August 12, 1872, in Arnold, *Letters of Richard D. Arnold, M.D.*, 157–58. The Georgia legislative debate is published in *Savannah Morning News*, August 13, 14, 15, 16, 27, 1872.

31. Minutes of Council, July 3, 17, 31, November 20, 1872; Gamble, *History*, 288–89.

32. *Georgia Acts*, 1872, 258–59; Minutes of Council, January 1, 1873.

33. *Savannah Morning News*, January 15, 1873; *Augusta Chronicle*, January 17, 1873.

34. *Savannah Morning News*, January 15, 20, 1873; *Augusta Chronicle*, January 17, 1873.

35. *Savannah Morning News*, January 22, 25, 1873.

36. *Savannah Morning News*, January 4, 1873; Anderson Diary, November 25, December 3, 21, 27, 1872, Edward Clifford Anderson Papers.

37. Anderson discounted the veracity of the statement, but he did not challenge Russell's declaration. *Savannah Morning News*, January 20, 1873; Anderson Diary, January 8, 9, 13, 1873, Edward Clifford Anderson Papers.

38. Anderson Diary, January 8, 14, 21, 1873, Edward Clifford Anderson Papers; Rubin, *Third to None*, 131–35; *Savannah Morning News*, January 22, 23, 1873.

39. Anderson Diary, January 21, 1873, Edward Clifford Anderson Papers; *Savannah Morning News*, January 22–23, 1873.

CHAPTER 8. "TO PROTECT THE PUBLIC CREDIT"

1. *Savannah Morning News*, January 25, 1873; Anderson Diary, February 3, 1873, Edward Clifford Anderson Papers; Minutes of Council, February 23, 1873.

2. A sinking fund is an account into which money is paid until a municipal debt is due. Griffith and Adrian, *History of American City Government*, 149–50; City of Savannah Finance Committee Papers, March 12, 1873, City of Savannah Research Library and Municipal Archives; *Savannah Morning News*, March 7, 1873; *Commercial and Financial Chronicle*, July 31, 1875.

3. Minutes of Council, March 12, April 9, 1873; Rebarer, *Rebarer's Digest*, 26–27.

4. The council did not act on the committee's suggestion for a sinking fund until the end of the year. *Savannah Morning News*, May 1, 1873; Minutes of Council, November 18, December 17–18, 1873.

5. Balleisen, *Navigating Failure*, 31.

6. For additional information on the causes and impact of the Panic of 1873, see Wicker, *Banking Panics of the Gilded Age*, 16–17; Rockoff, "Banking and Finance, 1789–1914"; *New York Times*, August 11, 1873; Hillhouse, *Municipal Bonds*, 15–17. See also Cashman, *America in the Gilded Age*, 29; Nevins, *Emergence of Modern America, 1865–1878*, 290–305; Nugent, *Money and American Society, 1865–1880*, 176–78; Wicker, *Banking Panics of the Gilded Age*. For works on Jay Cooke's actions, see Lubetkin, *Jay Cooke's Gamble*; Oberholtzer, *Jay Cooke*; Stack, *Jay Cooke Story*.

7. *Savannah Morning News*, September 19–26, 1873; Anderson Diary, September 24, 1873, Edward Clifford Anderson Papers.

8. The runs occurred at the Savannah Bank and Trust, the Freedmen's Bank, and the Southern Bank of the State of Georgia. Nothing out of the ordinary occurred at the Central Railroad, Merchants National Bank, or other private banks. The Merchants National Bank and the banking house of Edward C. Anderson Jr. continued to pay currency for all checks drawn on deposits. *Savannah Morning News*, Septem-

ber 26, 30, 1973; Anderson Diary, September 25, 26, 1873, Edward Clifford Anderson Papers.

9. Wicker, *Banking Panics in the Gilded Age*, 8, 14, 24.

10. *Savannah Morning News*, September 26, October 1, 3, 1873; Anderson Diary, September 26, 1873, Edward Clifford Anderson Papers; Wicker, *Banking Panics in the Gilded Age*, 31.

11. *Savannah Morning News*, September 26, October 1, 3, 1873; Anderson Diary, September 26, 1873, Edward Clifford Anderson Papers.

12. The city applied to the Merchants National Bank, Edward Anderson Jr., William M. Wadley (president of the Central Railroad Company), and the Central Railroad Bank for help. In 1874, bonds issued for Opelika Railroad came due. Anderson Diary, July 26, November 10–15, December 23, 1873, Edward Clifford Anderson Papers; Gamble, *History*, 209.

13. *Savannah Morning News*, March 25, 1875; Anderson Diary, January 19, 20, 1874, Edward Clifford Anderson Papers.

14. Mayor's Report, 1874.

15. *Savannah Morning News*, April 10, August 11, 13, 24, 1868; *Atlanta Constitution*, August 26, 1868; Anderson Diary, August 22, 1870, Edward Clifford Anderson Papers; Echols, *Georgia's General Assembly of 1878*, 28–29. In September 1868, Republicans joined Democrats in the Georgia General Assembly in purging African Americans elected to that body. See Drago, *Black Politicians and Reconstruction in Georgia*, 48–52.

16. *Savannah Morning News*, January 2–20, 1875; Anderson Diary, January 7, 12, 1875, Edward Clifford Anderson Papers.

17. *Savannah Morning News*, January 16, 18, 19, 1875.

18. The *Advertiser* received the contract for city printing over the *Savannah Morning News* in January 1874. Only sporadic editions of the *Advertiser* have survived. Anderson Diary, January 28, 1874, January 17, 1875, Edward Clifford Anderson Papers.

19. *Savannah Morning News*, January 18, 19, 1875.

20. Letter to the editor published in the *Savannah Advertiser* is found in the Keith M. Read Collection, MS 648, Georgia Historical Society, Savannah; Anderson Diary, January 12, 19, 21, 26, 1875, Edward Clifford Anderson Papers.

21. *Savannah Morning News*, January 11, 13, 1875; Minutes of Council, January 13, 1875; Anderson Diary, January 12, 1875, Edward Clifford Anderson Papers.

22. *Savannah Morning News*, January 11, 13, 14, 1875; Minutes of Council, January 13, 1875; Anderson Diary, January 12, 18, 20, 21, 1875, Edward Clifford Anderson Papers.

23. *Savannah Morning News*, January 19, 20, 21, 1875.

CHAPTER 9. ANDERSON'S PRAETORIAN GUARD

1. Minutes of Council, February–March 1875.

2. Wallenstein, *From Slave South to New South*, 24, 32, 51, 170, 184, 193; DeBats, "Uncertain Arena," 427.

3. In 1868, the finance committee had reported unfavorably on a petition to grant a

street railroad to carry freight because the city would lose approximately $21,000 from drayage badges and business. Minutes of Council, September 16, 1868; City of Savannah Letterbooks, February 11, 1875, City of Savannah Research Library and Municipal Archives; *Savannah Morning News* February 9, 12, 13, 1875.

4. *Savannah Morning News*, February 16, 1875.

5. *Savannah Morning News*, March 1, 1875; Report of Superior Court action of March 9, 1875, in *Savannah Morning News*, March 10, 1875. The Supreme Court of Georgia ultimately ruled in favor of the city. *Mayor and Aldermen of Savannah v. James K. Hines*, 53 *Georgia Reports* 617 (S.C. 1875).

6. Rufus Lester served as LaRoche's attorney. Report of Superior Court action of March 20, 1875 in *Savannah Morning News*, March 4, 22, 1875.

7. Minutes of Council, March 29, 1875; City of Savannah Finance Committee Papers, April 7, 1875, City of Savannah Research Library and Municipal Archives.

8. In June 1875, the city council passed an ordinance repealing the tax on gross sales. However, to make up the difference, it imposed a tax on retailers based on the value of their goods. Minutes of Council, March 24, April 7, 1875, May 19, June 16, 1875; City of Savannah Finance Committee Petitions, April 1875, City of Savannah Research Library and Municipal Archives; *Savannah Morning News*, March 25, 1875.

9. *Savannah Morning News*, February 17, April 15, 1875.

10. "Municipal Indebtedness," 7; Robert, "Municipal Debt of the United States," 399.

11. Minutes of Council, May 5, June 3, 17, 21, 30, July 14, 1875; Anderson Diary, June 3, 1875, Edward Clifford Anderson Papers; *Savannah Morning News*, October 23, November 7, 1875; Mayor's Report, 1875.

12. The court recorder and assistant treasurer positions were to be eliminated. Reductions in pay applied to the city marshal, harbormaster, and waterworks supervisor. Minutes of Council, December 15, 1875, December 29, 1876; City of Savannah Mayor's Office Papers, December 29, 1875.

13. Most indignation was reserved for the elimination of the office of recorder, a position filled by William Fleming, a law partner of Rufus Lester. Complaining that the office provided for such a small amount that it really would not make a difference in the city's finances, "Citizen" pointed to the coincidental increase in the mayor's salary since the mayor would be assuming the recorder's duties. "Citizen" maintained that the purpose of the office was to give Judge Fleming a job rather than a pension, and now that had been taken away. *Savannah Morning News*, January 1, 1876.

14. *Savannah Morning News*, January 5, 1876. Mayor Screven had proposed that the city lots be included in the city's property assessment but not taxed. Mayor's Report, 1871, published in *Savannah Morning News*, October 9, 1871.

15. *Henry C. Wayne v. the Mayor and Aldermen of the City of Savannah*, 56 *Georgia Reports*, 448–53 (1876); *Savannah Morning News*, May 23, 1876.

16. Minutes of Council, June 1, July 12, 1876.

17. *Savannah Morning News*, August 22, 1876; *S. P. Goodwin v. Mayor and Aldermen of the City of Savannah*, 53 *Georgia Reports* 411–13 (1874).

18. *Savannah Morning News,* July 20, 26, 1876.

19. Anderson issued over $147,000 in mayors' notes. Gamble, *History,* 291.

20. Minutes of Council, August 9, 1876; *Savannah Morning News,* August 10, 1876.

21. *Savannah Morning News,* July 20, August 22, 1876.

22. *Savannah Morning News,* September 2, 1876.

23. *Augusta Chronicle,* August 12, 1875; Alexander R. Lawton to Sarah Lawton, August 30, 1876, in Alexander Robert Lawton Papers, no. 415, Southern Historical Collection, Wilson Library, University of North Carolina at Chapel Hill; Mother to Eugenia, September 12, 1876, Phillips and Meyers Family Papers, no. 596, Southern Historical Collection, University of North Carolina, Chapel Hill.

24. Sarah Alexander Cunningham Collection, Georgia Historical Society, Savannah.

25. Adam Short Papers, MS 1141, Georgia Historical Society, Savannah.

26. Usinger, "Yellow Fever from the Viewpoint of Savannah."

27. Alexander R. Lawton to T. M. Cunningham, September 14, 1876, Alexander Robert Lawton Papers; Harriet Cumming to Emma Barnett, October 15, 1876, in Alexander and Boggs, *Alexander Letters, 1787–1900,* 322–23.

28. When Dr. E. U. White, a physician from New York, arrived in October, he backed Falligant's claim. *Savannah Morning News,* August 27, October 2, 1876; Alexander R. Lawton to T. M. Cunningham, September 14, 1876, Alexander Robert Lawton Papers.

29. Humphreys, *Yellow Fever and the South,* 18–35. Regarding the effects of yellow fever on the public health movement in the New South, see John H. Ellis, *Yellow Fever and Public Health in the New South.*

30. Scrapbook of Sarah G. Alexander Lawton, June 6–19, July 12, 1876, Sarah Alexander Cunningham Collection; *Savannah Morning News,* September 15, 1876; Minutes of Council, September 20, 1976; James Johnston Waring, *Epidemic at Savannah, 1876,* 17, 23.

31. *Savannah Morning News,* October 19–November 2, 1876; Scrapbook, in DeRenne Family Papers, 1735–1916, MS 1064a, Hargrett Rare Book and Manuscript Library, University of Georgia Libraries, Athens; James Waring to Mary Waring, October 20, 1876, Joseph Frederick Waring Letters and Diary, MS 837, Georgia Historical Society, Savannah; Humphreys, *Yellow Fever and the New South,* 19.

32. Farley, "Mighty Monarch of the South," 56–70; John Mannerlyn to John Screven, September 4, 19, 1876, Arnold and Screven Family Papers.

33. Mayor's Reports, 1873–76.

34. *Savannah Morning News,* January 11, 1877.

35. Letter to Mrs. J. F. Gilmer, November 10, 1876, Jeremy Francis Gilmer Papers, no. 276, Southern Historical Collection, Wilson Library, University of North Carolina, Chapel Hill.

CHAPTER 10. "PRESENT EMBARRASSMENTS"

1. Minutes of Council, November 1, 1876. These estimates were slightly higher than those provided by Screven in his 1872 report. *Savannah Morning News*, January 15, 1873.

2. Minutes of Council, November 1, December 13, 1876, January 24, 1877; *Commercial and Financial Chronicle*, November 4, 1876; Mayor's Reports 1876–77; *Savannah Morning News*, January 18, 1877.

3. *Savannah Morning News*, January 1, 1877.

4. *Savannah Morning News*, January 5, 1877.

5. *Savannah Morning News*, January 9, 1877.

6. *Savannah Morning News*, January 9, 11, 1877.

7. *Savannah Morning News*, January 9, 11, 1877.

8. *Savannah Morning News*, January 11–13, 1877.

9. Five out of twelve had served as aldermen since 1865. *Savannah Morning News*, January 11–13, 1877.

10. Freyer, *Producers versus Capitalists*, 86.

11. Minutes of Council, January 24, February 7, June 13, 1877.

12. Minutes of Council, January 24, 1877; City of Savannah Mayor's Office Papers, February 6, 1877, City of Savannah Research Library and Municipal Archives; Mayor's Reports, 1869–75, *Savannah Morning News*, June 1, 1877.

13. Bowden, *Two Hundred Years of Education in Savannah*, 268; *Savannah Morning News*, October 5, 6, 1875.

14. *Savannah Morning News*, July 15, 1876; Thompson, "Progressive Education and the Savannah Public School System," 80–81.

15. Mayor's Office Papers, February 6, 1877; Anderson Diary, January 30, 1877, Edward Clifford Anderson Papers; Minutes of Council, January 24, 1877; *Savannah Morning News*, June 1, 1877; Mayor's Report, 1878; Furrer, "Development of the Public School System in Savannah and Chatham County," 97.

16. Minutes of Council, January 24, 1877.

17. Statistics presented by Waring: floating debt, $4 million; real estate value, $8 million; city assets, $500,000; expected city income, $250,000; outstanding debt, $300,000; bonds due, $198,000. Minutes of Council, February 21, 1877.

18. Waring produced a letter from Judge Henry Tompkins to the city's attorney citing him for delaying the legal process. Minutes of Council, February 21, 1877.

19. Funded debt (bonded debt) is a debt acquired from selling interest-bearing bonds that mature after one year, usually a long-term loan. Steiss, *Local Government Finance*, 108–10; Minutes of Council, March 7, 1877; Anderson Diary, April 11, 1877, Edward Clifford Anderson Papers; *Savannah Morning News*, April 13, 1877.

20. Minutes of Council, March 7, 1877.

21. *Savannah Morning News*, March 22, 1877.

22. Wheaton later denied he had attempted to compromise the debt. Minutes of Council, February 19, 1879; *Charleston News and Courier*, reprint in *Savannah Morning News*, March 12, 1877; *Augusta Chronicle*, March 10, April 24, 1877; *New York World*, reprint in *Savannah Morning News*, May 26, 1877.

23. The gas company increased moonlight exemptions from five nights to nine nights monthly. Minutes of Council, March 7, 21, 23, April 4, 1877. They mayor maintained that it would be against basic common sense to reduce the police force further and argued that if citizens in default would pay their taxes, it would not be a problem. *Savannah Morning News*, March 23, 1877.

24. Creditors were aware that attempting to recover the principal interest on loans to cities in default would be expensive and time-consuming. Bensel, *Political Economy of American Industrialization, 1877–1900*, 65.

25. Balliesen, *Navigating Failure*, 18, 86.

26. Balliesen, *Navigating Failure*, 73, 81–82; Freyer, "Debt Failure and the Development of American Capitalism," 748; Picker and McConnell, "When Cities Go Broke," 448. Because municipal bonds were not secured by property liens, it was essentially a "lien upon nothing, not even on the general revenues of the municipality issuing it." Brown, *Municipal Bonds*, 13. A bondholder establishes the validity of one's claims by filing a suit to receive judgment. Burhans, *Law of Municipal Bonds*, 58. Creditors knew that if they did not act quickly, others would beat them to the punch. Balliesen, *Navigating Failure*, 85.

27. Curry obtained judgments in May, which the city subsequently appealed to the Superior Court. Merchants National Bank sought to recover payment for mayors' notes. *Savannah Morning News*, July 10, 1877.

28. Fryer, "Debt Failure," 748; Balliesen, *Navigating Failure*, 85, 138; Hillhouse, *Municipal Bonds*, 29.

29. Eisenberg, "Creditors' Remedies in Municipal Default," 1369.

30. Balliesen, *Navigating Failure*, 85.

31. Balliesen, *Navigating Failure*, 84; Picker and McConnell, "When Cities Go Broke," 434; Eisenberg, "Creditors' Remedies in Municipal Default," 1369.

32. Hillhouse, *Municipal Bonds*, 51–53, 56–60.

33. *Savannah Morning News*, April 21, 1877. Some economic historians contend that as wealth increased in stocks and bonds, assessors could not adequately assess it; thus real estate owners bore the greater tax burden. As a result, "the crisis of the property tax began in the economic and political maelstrom of the 1870s." Mintz et al., *Fundamentals of Municipal Finance*, 12.

34. W. H. Tison to J. B. Manning, April 7, 1877, in *New York World*, reprinted in *Savannah Morning News*, May 26, 1877.

35. Minutes of Council, May 2, 16, 1877; John F. Wheaton to H. H. DeLeon in Charleston, May 7, 1877, and G. W. Garaway to John F. Wheaton, May 14, 1877, City of Savannah Finance Committee Papers, City of Savannah Research Library and Municipal Archives.

CHAPTER 11. A "MONSTER AND HERMAPHRODITE"

1. *New York World*, reprinted in *Savannah Morning News*, May 26, 1877.
2. The City of Savannah's debt in 1877 was $4,185,000. *Commercial and Financial*

Chronicle, May 26, 1877; *New York World*, reprinted in *Savannah Morning News*, May 29, 1877; *New York Times*, reprinted in *Savannah Morning News*, May 30, 1877.

3. *Commercial and Financial Chronicle*, May 26, 1877; *New York World*, reprinted in *Savannah Morning News*, May 29, 1877; *New York Times*, reprinted in *Savannah Morning News*, May 30, 1877.

4. *New York Times*, July 31, 1877; *Independent* (New York City), August 16, 1877.

5. "Repudiated Municipal Debts," *Nation*, February 28, 1878, 150–51. Freyer notes that these efforts at bond repudiation took place "in a climate of strong local resistance to out-of-state business." Freyer, *Forums of Order*, 105.

6. Hillhouse, *Municipal Bonds*, 39; "Repudiation as an Epidemic," *Independent*, August 16, 1877.

7. Eisenberg, "Creditors' Remedies in Municipal Default," 1370–75; Picker and McConnell, "When Cities Go Broke," 427.

8. Ratified in 1794, the Eleventh Amendment created an umbrella under which states have protection from suits by citizens of other states and foreigners. Ironically, the case that evolved into the Eleventh Amendment emanated from Georgia. For discussion as it relates to defaulting entities, see introduction to Waibel, *Sovereign Defaults before International Courts and Tribunals*, 3–14, and Orth, *Judicial Power of the United States*, 4–7. By 1884, states had repudiated debts of $300 million. Hume, "Are We a Nation of Rascals?," 128. For discussion of legal status of cities, see Frug, "City as a Legal Concept," 1096–1116.

9. This compromise was not binding except for those acceding to it.

10. *Commercial and Financial Chronicle*, May 26, 1877; *New York World*, reprinted in *Savannah Morning News*, May 29, 1877; *New York Times*, reprinted in *Savannah Morning News*, May 30, 1877.

11. Minutes of Council, May 31, 1877.

12. Claims pressed for judgment totaled over $945,000. *Savannah Morning News*, June 1, 4, 1877.

13. *Savannah Morning News*, June 6, 7, 9, 1877.

14. *Savannah Morning News*, May 6–7, 1877; *Commercial and Financial Chronicle*, June 9, 1877.

15. The committee was scheduled to present its findings in November 1877. *Savannah Morning News*, June 7, 1877; *Commercial and Financial Chronicle*, July 28, 1877.

16. *Savannah Morning News*, June 11, 1877.

17. Nimmo, *Report on the Internal Commerce of the United States*, 38, 94, 145.

18. *Savannah Morning News*, July 10, 1877; *Augusta Chronicle*, July 11, 12, 1877,

19. *Savannah Morning News*, July 10, 20, 1877; *Augusta Chronicle*, July 11, 1877; *Commercial and Financial Chronicle*, July 14, 1877.

20. *Augusta Chronicle*, July 12, 1877; *Charleston News and Courier*, reprinted in *Savannah Morning News*, July 13, 1877.

21. Hillhouse, *Municipal Bonds*, 160–66.

22. Lehmann, "Federal Municipal Bankruptcy Act," 241–42.

23. "Western Credit," *New York Times*, June 8, 1877. In the 1920s, Henry Lehmann

bemoaned the lack of any "orderly procedure of debt adjustment" for defaulting cities. Lehmann, "Federal Municipal Bankruptcy Act," 241. Municipalities were expressly excluded from federal bankruptcy procedures. Hempel, "Evaluation of Municipal 'Bankruptcy' Laws and Procedures," 1340.

24. By the time the injunction case came before the judge, more petitioners had joined the first list. Many of these were bondholders believed their bonds to be "legally issued and valid." In the testimony that followed, neither the Merchants National Bank nor the Savannah Bank and Trust Company nor George Curry accepted the assertions that the city was unable to pay its debts. They further denied that any negotiations were taking place between the city and its creditors, that notes had been issued illegally, and that current and future suits would do "irreparable injury" to the city. *Savannah Morning News,* July 31, 1877.

25. The transcripts do not explain the legal basis of Tompkins's decision. *Savannah Morning News,* July 21, 1877.

26. *New York Nation,* reprinted in *Savannah Morning News,* July 31, 1877.

27. Letter from J. B. Manning, published in the *Savannah Morning News,* October 24, 1877; *Commercial and Finance Chronicle,* October 20, 1877. Memphis first defaulted in 1873. In 1874, when compromise negotiations began, there was popular support for further scaling back the debt or outright repudiation. Reflecting this feeling, a citizens' committee offered payment on a 50 percent basis. The compromise, reached in 1877, failed to end the crisis because the taxes instituted to cover the debt remained uncollected. The following year, a citizens meeting hatched a plan to abolish the city's charter, and the Tennessee legislature cooperated. The exasperated creditors turned to the federal courts, and the case dragged on until 1883. Hillhouse, *Municipal Bonds,* 56–60; Wrenn, *Crisis and Commission Government in Memphis,* 26.

28. Though scheduled for November, the committee did not report their findings until December. *Savannah Morning News,* December 13, 1877; *Commercial and Financial Chronicle,* December 15, 1877.

29. For any compromise to go into effect, the General Assembly would have had to sanction it. *Savannah Morning News,* December 15, 1877.

30. Ratchford, *American State Debts,* 185–86. The unpaid taxes amounted to $118,547, and the interest owed as of October was $33,480. By this point 25 percent of the city's budget was devoted to servicing its debt. *Charleston Post and Courier,* September 20, October 11, 1877; Fraser, *Charleston! Charleston!,* 296.

31. *New York Times,* December 4, 1878, February 3, 1879.

32. Minutes of Council, December 26, 1877; *Commercial and Financial Chronicle,* January 5, 1878; City of Savannah Ordinance Papers, February 28, March 6, 1878, City of Savannah Research Library and Municipal Archives.

33. *Savannah Morning News,* March 14, 1878. The ordinance passed in July. *Savannah Morning News* July 26, 1878; Minutes of Council, July 24, 1878. Waring was the only dissenting vote. The council elected sinking fund commissioners in December. Minutes of Council, December 28, 1878; Rebarer, *Rebarer's Digest,* 28–41.

34. *Macon Telegraph,* March 13, 1878; *Savannah Morning News,* March 14, 20, 1878.

35. Reprint of letter from Adams to Curry in *Savannah Morning News*, March 20, 1878; *Commercial and Financial Chronicle*, April 6, 1878; Mayor's Report, 1878.

36. *Savannah Morning News*, June 15, 1878.

37. *Commercial and Financial Chronicle*, June 22, 1878; Robert Toombs to Alexander Lawton, June 21, 1878, reprinted in *Savannah Morning News*, June 26, 1878.

38. At the council meeting following the publication of the compromise in the newspapers, aldermen considered an unambiguous resolution stating that they would not consider any new proposals. The resolution divided the council. Members who opposed the resolution had concluded that there was little likelihood of a settlement in the near future, and the city faced the prospect of mounting costs associated with "interminable litigation." Minutes of Council, July 10, 1878; Minutes of Council, July 10, 1878.

39. Waring voted against the compromise. Minutes of Council, July 10, 24, 26, 1878; Mayor's Reports, 1878–79; *Commercial and Financial Chronicle*, July 27, 1878; Gamble, *History*, 297–98.

40. *Commercial and Financial Chronicle*, August 3, 1878.

41. Minutes of Council, October 16, 1878; *Georgia Acts*, 1878–79, 85–86; *Savannah Morning News*, December 14, 1878; City of Savannah Ordinance Papers, December 17, 1878; Minutes of Council, December 17, 28, 1878.

42. *Weekly Sumter Republican*, April 27, 1877.

43. *Macon Telegraph*, June 22, 1877. Similar articles in the appeared in this newspaper on April 11 and April 28, 1877.

44. *Macon Telegraph*, April 11, 1877

45. *Macon Telegraph*, April 28, June 22, 1877; Orth, *Judicial Power of the United States*, 118.

46. *Georgia Weekly Telegraph*, September 4, 1877.

47. Georgia Constitution of 1877, article 7, section 7, paragraphs 1 and 2.

48. The Atlantic and Gulf Railroad, due to the Panic of 1873, was already a part of the larger Plant System under the name Savannah, Florida, and Western Railway. Henry Plant continued to add to the railroad's mileage in the direction of Florida and Alabama. In 1902, after his death, this line became a part of the even larger Atlantic Coast Line Railroad. Mayor's Report, 1879.

49. Minutes of Council, January 8, March 5, 1879.

50. The transcripts do not contain an explanation of the attorney's opinion. Minutes of Council, January 8, March 5, June 11, 1879; Burhans, *Law of Municipal Bonds*, 19.

51. Minutes of Council, March 19, July 9, 1879; Mayor's Report, 1879.

52. *Mayor and Aldermen of the City of Savannah v. Eugene Kelly* 108 US 296–698 (1883); Minutes of Council, May 9, May 23, July 4, 1883; Mayor's Report, 1883; Gamble, *History*, 200.

53. Scott, *Repudiation of State Debts*, 97–103.

54. Transcripts of Woods's decision in *Savannah Morning News*, November 26, 27, 1879; *Savannah Morning News*, March 23, 1883. Immediate costs demanded by the court: $23,912.50. Mayor's Reports, 1879–84; Gamble, *History*, 299.

55. *Mayor and Aldermen of the City of Savannah v. Eugene Kelly* 108 US 296–698 (1883); Minutes of Council May 9, May 23, July 4, 1883; Mayor's Report, 1883; Gamble, *History*, 200.

56. Mayor's Reports, 1883–85.

57. Mayor's Reports, 1880–88; Gamble, *History*, 340–341.

58. Anderson, $500,825; Screven, $2,680,543; Wheaton, $607,674. Gamble, *History*, 340–41.

59. *Savannah Morning News*, September 10–11, 1878.

60. *Savannah Morning News*, June 2, 1881.

61. *Savannah Morning News*, September 4, 1880.

CONCLUSION

1. Woodman, "Decline of Cotton Factorage after the Civil War."

2. Harley, *Southward Ho!*, 5, 37.

3. Harley, *Southward Ho!*, 46, 53.

BIBLIOGRAPHY

———•●•———

PERIODICALS

Albany (Ga.) News
Albany (Ga.) Patriot
American Railroad Journal
American Railway Times
Atlanta Constitution
Augusta Chronicle
Augusta Courier
Bainbridge (Ga.) Argus
Bainbridge (Ga.) Democrat
Central Georgian (Sandersville)
Charleston (S.C.) News and Courier
Charleston (S.C.) Post and Courier
Columbian Museum (Savannah)
Columbus (Ga.) Daily Sun
Columbus (Ga.) Enquirer
Columbus (Ga.) Tri-Weekly Enquirer
Commercial and Financial Chronicle
Congressional Globe
Congressional Record
Daily Morning News (Savannah)
Daily News and Herald (Savannah)
Daily Savannah Republican
DeBow's Review
Eufaula (Ala.) News
Federal Union (Milledgeville, Ga.)
Georgia Gazette (Savannah)
Georgia Reports
Georgia Telegraph (Macon)
Independent (New York City)
Macon Messenger
Macon Telegraph
Macon Weekly Telegraph
Milledgeville (Ga.) Federal Union
Nation

New Jersey Emporium and True American
New York Daily Times
New York Evening Post
New York Nation
New York Times
Niles' Weekly Register
Philadelphia Register and National Recorder
Savannah Advertiser
Savannah Daily Georgian
Savannah Daily Herald
Savannah Daily Republican
Savannah Georgian
Savannah Morning News
Savannah Republican
Southern Banner (Athens)
Southern Recorder (Milledgeville, Ga.)
Sumter Republican (Americus, Ga.)
Thomasville (Ga.) Times
Weekly Sumter Republican (Americus, Ga.)

MANUSCRIPT COLLECTIONS
BAKER LIBRARY HISTORICAL COLLECTIONS, HARVARD BUSINESS SCHOOL, CAMBRIDGE, MASSACHUSETTS

Thomas Gibbons Business Papers

CITY OF SAVANNAH RESEARCH LIBRARY AND MUNICIPAL ARCHIVES, SAVANNAH, GEORGIA

City of Savannah Cash Ledgers
City of Savannah Finance Committee Papers
City of Savannah Finance Committee Petitions
City of Savannah Harbor and Wharf Committee Papers
City of Savannah Letterbooks
City of Savannah Market Committee Papers
City of Savannah Mayor's Office Papers
City of Savannah Minutes of Council
City of Savannah Mayor's Reports
City of Savannah Ordinance Papers
City of Savannah Sewer Committee Papers
City of Savannah Tax Digests

GEORGIA HISTORICAL SOCIETY, SAVANNAH

Adam Short Papers
Central of Georgia Railway Company, Central Railroad and Banking Company of
  Georgia
City of Savannah Municipal Reports (Mayor's Reports)
Collection on William Harris Crawford
Gordon Family Papers
Joseph Frederick Waring Letters and Diary
Joseph Frederick Waring II Papers
Keith M. Read Collection
King and Wilder Family Papers
Macon and Western Railroad Minute Books
Sarah Alexander Cunningham Collection
William Wiseham Paine Papers

HARGRETT RARE BOOK AND MANUSCRIPT LIBRARY, UNIVERSITY OF GEORGIA LIBRARIES, ATHENS

Charles Green Papers
DeRenne Family Papers

KAYE KOLE GENEALOGY AND LOCAL HISTORY ROOM, LIVE OAK PUBLIC LIBRARIES, SAVANNAH, GEORGIA

Thomas Gamble Collection

RARE BOOK, MANUSCRIPT, AND SPECIAL COLLECTIONS LIBRARY, DUKE UNIVERSITY, DURHAM, NORTH CAROLINA

Aaron Wilbur Papers

SOUTH CAROLINA HISTORICAL SOCIETY, CHARLESTON

Alston Family Papers

SOUTHERN HISTORICAL COLLECTION, WILSON LIBRARY, UNIVERSITY OF NORTH CAROLINA, CHAPEL HILL

Alexander and Hillhouse Family Papers
Alexander Robert Lawton Papers
Arnold and Screven Family Papers
Diary of George Anderson Mercer
Edward Clifford Anderson Papers
Henry Stevens Haines Books
Gordon Family Papers
Jeremy Francis Gilmer Papers
Phillips and Meyers Family Papers
Richard D. Arnold Papers
William Harris Garland Papers

BOOKS, ARTICLES, DISSERTATIONS, THESES, AND WEBSITES

Abbot, William W. "The Structure of Politics in Georgia: 1782–1789." *William and Mary Quarterly* 14 (January 1957): 47–65.

Abbott, Carl. *Boosters and Businessmen: Popular Economic Thought and Urban Growth in the Antebellum Middle West*. Westport, Conn.: Greenwood Press, 1981.

Abbott, Richard H. "The Republican Party Press in Reconstruction Georgia, 1867–1874." *Journal of Southern History* 61 (November 1995): 725–60.

Acts of the General Assembly of the State of Georgia, Passed in Milledgeville at an Annual Session in November and December 1862; Also Extra Session of 1863. Milledgeville: Confederate Union Office (Broughton, Nisbet, & Barnes, State Printers), 1863.

Adams, John. *Risk*. London: UCL Press, 1995.

Alexander, Marion, and George J. Baldwin Boggs, eds. *The Alexander Letters, 1787–1900*. Savannah: Privately printed for G. J. Baldwin, 1910.

Allinson, Edward P. *Ground Rents in Philadelphia*. Philadelphia: University of Pennsylvania Press, 1888.

Amdursky, Robert S., and Clayton P. Gillette. *Municipal Debt Finance Law: Theory and Practice*. Boston: Little, Brown, 1992.

Anderson, Edward Clifford. *Florida Territory in 1844: The Diary of Master Edward C. Anderson, United States Navy*. Edited by William Stanley Hoole. Tuscaloosa: University of Alabama Press, 2004.

Anderson, John E. *Public Finance: Principles and Policy*. Boston: Houghton Mifflin, 2003.

Armroyd, George. *A Connected View of the Whole Internal Navigation of the United States, Natural and Artificial, Present and Prospective, with Maps*. Philadelphia: H. C. Carey & I. Lea, 1826.

Arnold, Richard D. *Letters of Richard D. Arnold, M.D., 1808–1876, Mayor of Savannah, Georgia, First Secretary of the American Medical Association*. Edited by Richard Harrison Shryock. Durham, N.C.: Duke University Press, 1929.

Aronson, J. Richard, John L. Hilley, and James Ackley Maxwell. *Financing State and Local Governments*. Washington D.C.: Brookings Institution, 1986.

Bailey, Anne J. *War and Ruin: William T. Sherman and the Savannah Campaign*. American Crisis series, 10. Wilmington, Del.: Scholarly Resources, 2003.

Balleisen, Edward J. *Navigating Failure: Bankruptcy and Commercial Society in Antebellum America*. Chapel Hill: University of North Carolina Press, 2001.

Barber, Henry E., and Allen R. Gann. *A History of the Savannah District, U.S. Army Corps of Engineers*. Savannah: The District, 1989.

Barney, William L., ed. *A Companion to 19th-Century America*. Malden, Mass.: Blackwell, 2001.

Bartley, Numan V. *The Creation of Modern Georgia*. Athens: University of Georgia Press, 1983.

———. "In Search of the New South: Southern Politics after Reconstruction." *Reviews in American History* 10, no. 4 (December 1982): 150–63.

Belcher, Wyatt Winton. *The Economic Rivalry between St. Louis and Chicago, 1850–1880*. New York: Columbia University Press, 1947.

Bell, Karen B. "The 'Ogeechee Troubles': Federal Land Restoration and the 'Lived Realities' of Temporary Proprietors, 1865–1868." *Georgia Historical Quarterly* 85 (Fall 2001): 375–97.

Bellows, Barbara L. "Tempering the Wind: The Southern Response to Urban Poverty, 1850–1865." PhD diss., University of South Carolina, 1983.

Bensel, Richard. *The Political Economy of American Industrialization, 1877–1900*. Cambridge, UK: Cambridge University Press, 2000.

Bernstein, Peter L. *Wedding of the Waters: The Erie Canal and the Making of a Great Nation*. New York: W. W. Norton, 2005.

Berry, Stephen W. "The South: From Old to New." In *A Companion to 19th-Century America*, edited by William L. Barney, 257–71. Malden, Mass.: Blackwell, 2001.

Bickel, William. "The Life of William W. Gordon." Student paper, Armstrong State College, 1989. Location: Lane Library, Georgia Southern University, Savannah.

Billings, Dwight B. *Planters and the Making of a "New South": Class, Politics, and Development in North Carolina, 1865–1900*. Chapel Hill: University of North Carolina Press, 1979.

Billington, Monroe Lee. *The American South: A Brief History*. New York: Scribner, 1971.

Bingham, Richard D., John P. Blair, University of Wisconsin–Milwaukee, and Urban Research Center. *Urban Economic Development*, vol. 27. Beverly Hills, Calif.: Sage, 1984.

Biographical Directory of the United States Congress: 1774–Present. http://bioguide.congress.gov/.

Blassingame, John W. "Before the Ghetto: The Making of the Black Community in Savannah, Georgia, 1865–1880." *Journal of Social History* 6 (Summer 1973): 463–88.

Blight, David. *Race and Reunion: The Civil War in American Memory*. Cambridge, Mass.: Belknap Press of Harvard University Press, 2001.

Bloom, Charles G. "The Georgia Election of April 1868: A Re-Examination of the Politics of Georgia Reconstruction." Master's thesis, University of Chicago, 1963.

Blouin, Francis X. *The Boston Region, 1810–1850: A Study of Urbanization*. Ann Arbor, Mich.: UMI Research Press, 1978.

Bolding, Gary. "Change, Continuity, and Commercial Identity of a Southern City: New Orleans, 1850–1950." *Louisiana Studies* 14 (Summer 1975): 161–78.

Boles, John B., ed. *A Companion to the American South*. Malden, Mass.: Blackwell, 2002.

Boles, John B., and Bethany L. Johnson, eds. *Origins of the New South Fifty Years Later: The Continuing Influence of a Historical Classic*. Baton Rouge: Louisiana State University Press, 2003.

Bonner, James Calvin. *A History of Georgia Agriculture, 1732–1860*. Athens, University of Georgia Press, 1964.

Botume, Elizabeth Hude. *First amongst the Contrabands*. New York: Arno Press, 1968.

Bowden, Haygood Samuel. *Two Hundred Years of Education in Savannah*. Richmond, Va.: Press of the Dietz Printing Company, 1932.

Brandfon, Robert L. *Cotton Kingdom of the New South: A History of the Yazoo Mississippi Delta from Reconstruction to the Twentieth Century*. Cambridge, Mass.: Harvard University Press, 1967.

Braynard, Frank O. *S.S. Savannah, the Elegant Steam Ship*. Athens: University of Georgia Press, 2008.

Brown, Fraser. *Municipal Bonds: A Statement of the Principles of Law and Custom Governing the Issue of American Municipal Bonds*. New York: Prentice-Hall, 1922.

Brownell, Blaine A. "The Commercial Civic Elite and City Planning in Atlanta, Memphis, and New Orleans in the 1920s." *Journal of Southern History* 41 (August 1975): 339–68.

———. "The Idea of the City in Southern History," in *The Pursuit of Urban History*, edited by Derek Fraser and Anthony Sutcliffe, 146–48. London: E. Arnold, 1983.

———. "If You've Seen One, You Haven't Seen Them All: Recent Trends in Southern Urban History." *Houston Review* 1 (Fall 1979): 63–80.

Brownell, Blaine A., and David R. Goldfield. *The City in Southern History: The Growth of Urban Civilization in the South*. New York: National University Publications, 1977.

"Brunswick and Florida Railroad Company." *American Railroad Journal* 11 (May 26, 1855): 330.

Bulloch, Joseph Gaston Baillie. *A History and Genealogy of the Habersham Family*. Columbia, S.C.: R. L. Bryan, 1901.

Burhans, James Audubon. *The Law of Municipal Bonds, including a Digest of Statutory Laws relating to Their Issue, to Which Is Added a Digest of the Statutory Laws Governing the Investment of Corporate and Trust Funds, by Savings Banks, Insurance Companies, Guardians, Executors, and Other Corporations and Trustees*. New York: S. A. Kean, 1889.

Byrne, William A. "The Burden and Heat of the Day: Slavery and Servitude in Savannah, 1733–1865." PhD diss., Florida State University, 1979.

———. "'Uncle Billy' Sherman Comes to Town: The Free Winter of Black Savannah." *Georgia Historical Quarterly* 79 (Spring 1995): 91–116.

Cairns, James P. "The Response of New Orleans to the Diversion of Trade from the Mississippi River 1845–60." PhD diss., Columbia University, 1950.

Canady, Hoyt Paul. "Internal Improvements in Georgia in the Pre-Railroad Era, 1817–1833." Master's thesis, Georgia Southern University, 1970.

Carlson, Leonard A. "FYI—Banking in Georgia, 1865–1929." *Economic Review* 77 (November 1992): 28–37.

Carnes, Lon M. "The Georgia Deepwater Ports and Their Role in the Economy of the State." PhD diss., Georgia State University, 1972.

Carter, Dan. *When the War Was Over: The Failure of Self Reconstruction in the South, 1865–67*. Baton Rouge: Louisiana State University Press, 1984.

Carter, Oberlin M. "History of Past Work: Improvement of the Savannah River and Harbor." In U.S. Congress, House, 50th Cong. 2nd sess., *Executive Document 1*, vol. 2, pt. 2 (Washington D.C.: Government Printing Office, 1888), 1013–1021.

Cashman, Sean Dennis. *America in the Gilded Age: From the Death of Lincoln to the Rise of Theodore Roosevelt.* New York: New York University Press, 1984.

Cates, Gerald. "A Medical History of Georgia in the First Hundred Years, 1733–1833." PhD diss., University of Georgia, 1976.

Cecil. "On Municipal Subscriptions to the Stock of Railroad Companies. Remarks on the Opinion of Black, C. J., in the Case of Sharpless, et al., vs. the Mayor, &c., of Philadelphia." *American Law Register* 2, no. 1 (November 1853): 1–20.

Central Rail Road and Banking Company of Georgia. *Report of the Presidents, Engineers-in-Chief and Superintendents of the Central Rail-Road and Banking Company of Georgia.* Savannah: J. M. Cooper, 1854.

Chesson, Michael B. *Richmond after the War: 1865–1890.* Richmond: Virginia State Library, 1981.

Chudacoff, Howard P. *The Evolution of American Urban Society.* Englewood Cliffs, N.J.: Prentice-Hall, 1975.

Cimbala, Paul A. "The Freedmen's Bureau, the Freedmen, and Sherman's Grant in Reconstruction Georgia, 1865–1867." *Journal of Southern History* 55 (November 1989): 597–632.

———. *The Great Task Remaining before Us: Reconstruction as America's Continuing Civil War.* New York: Fordham University Press, 2010.

———. *Under the Guardianship of a Nation: Freedmen's Bureau and Reconstruction in Georgia, 1865–1870.* Athens: University of Georgia Press, 1999.

Cleveland, Frederick. *Railroad Promotion and Capitalization in the United States.* New York: Longmans, Green, 1909.

Cobb, James C. "Beyond Planters and Industrialists: A New Perspective on the New South." *Journal of Southern History* 54, no. 1 (February 1988): 45–68.

Coddington, Edwin B. "The Activities and Attitudes of a Confederate Business Man: Gazaway B. Lamar." *Journal of Southern History* 9 (February 1943): 3–36.

Coffin, Charles C. *Four Years of Fighting.* Boston: Ticknor and Fields, 1866.

Coleman, Kenneth. *The American Revolution in Georgia, 1763–1789.* Athens: University of Georgia Press, 1958.

"Colloquy with Colored Ministers." *Journal of Negro History* 16 (January 1931): 88–94.

Cotterill, R. S. "Southern Railroads and Western Trade, 1840–1850." *Mississippi Valley Historical Review* 3 (March 1917): 427–41.

Coulter, E. Merton. "Aaron Alpeoria Bradley, Georgia Negro Politician during Reconstruction Times, Parts 1, 2 and 3"." *Georgia Historical Quarterly* 51 (September 1967): 15–41, 154–74, 264–306.

———. "The Great Savannah Fire of 1820." *Georgia Historical Quarterly* 23 (March 1939): 1–27.

———. "The Nullification Movement in Georgia." *Georgia Historical Quarterly* 5 (March 1921): 3–39.

Cox, Thomas H. *Gibbons v. Ogden, Law, and Society in the Early Republic.* Athens: Ohio University Press, 2009.

Cozzens, Peter. *General John Pope: A Life for a Nation.* Urbana: University of Illinois Press, 2000.

Cumming, Joseph. B. *The Life and Labors of William M. Wadley: With an Account of the Wadley Memorial Association and the Ceremony of Unveiling the Statue.* Savannah: Morning News Steam Printing House, 1885.

Currie-McDaniel, Ruth. *Carpetbagger of Conscience: A Biography of John Emory Bryant.* Athens: University of Georgia Press, 1987.

Curry, Leonard P. "Urbanization and Urbanism in the Old South: A Comparative View." *Journal of Southern History* 40 (February 1974): 43–60.

Cutler, David M., and Grant Miller. *Water, Water, Everywhere: Municipal Finance and Water Supply in American Cities.* Cambridge, Mass.: National Bureau of Economic Research, 2005.

Davis, David Brion. *Inhuman Bondage: The Rise and Fall of Slavery in the New World.* New York: Oxford University Press, 2006.

Davis, John. *Travels of Four Years and a Half in the United States of America: During 1798, 1799, 1800, 1801, and 1802.* New York: R. Edwards, 1803.

Davis, Lance E., and John Legler. "The Government in the American Economy." *Journal of Economic History* 26, no. 4 (December 1966): 514–53.

DeBats, Donald A. "An Uncertain Arena: The Georgia House of Representatives, 1806–1861." *Journal of Southern History* 56 (August 1990): 428–37.

Debow, James Dunwoody Brownson. *The Seventh Census of the United States: 1850: Embracing a Statistical View of Each of the States and Territories*, vol. 2. Washington, D.C.: R. Armstrong, 1853.

DeCredico, Mary A. *Patriots for Profit: Georgia's Entrepreneurs and Confederate Mobilization, 1847–1873.* Chapel Hill: University of North Carolina Press, 1986.

Desai, Hatel D. "A Biographical Sketch of Edward Clifford Anderson, Sr." Student paper, Armstrong State College, 1991. Location: Lane Library, Georgia Southern University, Savannah.

Dillon, John. *Commentaries on the Law of Municipal Corporations.* 3rd ed. Boston: Little, Brown, 1881.

———. *The Law of Municipal Bonds.* St. Louis: G. I. Jones, 1876.

Dixon, Jefferson Max. "The Central Railroad of Georgia, 1833–1892." PhD diss., Georgia Peabody College for Teachers, 1953.

———. "Georgia Railroad Growth and Consolidation, 1860–1917." Master's thesis, Emory University, 1949.

Dorsey, Jennifer Hull. *Hirelings: African American Workers and Free Labor in Early Maryland.* Ithaca: Cornell University Press, 2011.

Downey, Tom. *Planting a Capitalist South: Masters, Merchants, and Manufacturers in the Southern Interior, 1790–1860.* Baton Rouge: Louisiana State University Press, 2006.

Downs, Alan C. *Sherman's March to the Sea.* Westport, Conn.: Praeger, 2014.

Downs, Gregory P. *Declarations of Dependence: The Long Reconstruction of Popular Politics in the South, 1861–1908.* Chapel Hill: University of North Carolina Press, 2011.

Doyle, Don Harrison. *New Men, New Cities, New South: Atlanta, Nashville, Charleston, Mobile, 1860–1910.* Chapel Hill: University of North Carolina Press, 1990.

Drago, Edmund. *Black Politicians and Reconstruction in Georgia: A Splendid Failure.* Athens: University of Georgia Press, 1992.

————. "Georgia's First Black Voter Registrars during Reconstruction." *Georgia Historical Quarterly* 78 (Winter 1994): 760–93.

Duffy, John. *The Sanitarians: A History of American Public Health.* Urbana: University of Illinois Press, 1990.

Durham, Roger. *Guardian of Savannah: Fort McAllister, Georgia, in the Civil War and Beyond.* Columbia: University of South Carolina Press, 2008.

Dyer, John P. "Northern Relief for Savannah during Sherman's Occupation." *Journal of Southern History* 19 (November 1953): 457–72.

Echols, Samuel A. *Georgia's General Assembly of 1878.* Atlanta: J. P. Harrison, 1878.

The Edinburgh Gazetteer, or Geographical Dictionary, Accompanied by an Atlas. Edinburgh: A. Constable, 1822.

Edwards, Laura F. "Southern History as U.S. History." *Journal of Southern History* 75, no. 3 (August 2009): 533–64.

Eisenberg, David M. "Creditors' Remedies in Municipal Default." *Duke Law Journal* 1976 (January 1977): 1363–95.

Eisterhold, John A. "Savannah: Lumber Center of the South Atlantic." *Georgia Historical Quarterly* 57 (Winter 1973): 526–43.

Ellis, John H. *Yellow Fever and Public Health in the New South.* Lexington: University Press of Kentucky, 1992.

Ellis, Richard E. "Market Revolution and the Transformation of American Politics, 1801–1837." In *The Market Revolution in America: Social, Political, and Religious Expressions, 1800–1880,* edited by Melvyn Stokes and Stephen Conway, 149–76. Charlottesville: University Press of Virginia, 1996.

————. *The Union at Risk: Jacksonian Democracy, States' Rights, and the Nullification Crisis.* New York: Oxford University Press, 1987.

"Enforcing Payment of Municipal Securities after Judgment." *Central Law Journal* 1 (April 2, 1874): 159–60.

Engerman, Stanley L., and Robert E. Gallman, eds. *The Cambridge Economic History of the United States: The Long Nineteenth Century,* vol. 2. Cambridge: Cambridge University Press, 2000.

Ewert, George. "The New South Era in Mobile, 1875–1900." In *Mobile: The New History of Alabama's First City,* edited by Michael V. R. Thomason, 128–53. Tuscaloosa: University of Alabama Press, 2001.

Ezell, John Samuel. *The South since 1865.* 2nd ed. Norman: University of Oklahoma Press, 1978.

Farley, M. Foster. "The Mighty Monarch of the South: Yellow Fever in Charleston and Savannah." *Georgia Review* 27 (Spring 1973): 56–70.

Federal Reporter, vol. 206. St. Paul: West Publishing Company, 1913.

Filante, Ronald W. "A Note on the Economic Viability of the Erie Canal, 1825–1860." *Business History Review* 48, no. 1 (April 1974): 95–102.

Finlay, Mark. "Panic in Savannah: The Yellow Fever Era." *Coastal Current Insight* (Coastal Heritage Society), n.d., n.p.

Fish, Carl Russell. *The Restoration of Southern Railroads.* University of Wisconsin Studies in the Social Sciences and History. Madison: University of Wisconsin Press, 1917.

Fitzgerald, Michael W. *Urban Emancipation: Popular Politics in Reconstruction Mobile, 1860–1890.* Baton Rouge: Louisiana State University Press, 2002.

Folsom, Burton W. *Urban Capitalists: Entrepreneurs and City Growth in Pennsylvania's Lackawanna and Lehigh Regions, 1800–1920.* Baltimore: Johns Hopkins University Press, 1981.

Foner, Eric. *Free Soil, Free Labor, Free Men: The Ideology of the Republican Party before the Civil War.* New York: Oxford University Press, 1970.

———. *Reconstruction: America's Unfinished Revolution, 1863–1877.* New York: Harper & Row, 1988.

Ford, Lacy K. *Origins of Southern Radicalism: The South Carolina Upcountry, 1800–1860.* New York: Oxford University Press, 1988.

Formwalt, Lee W. "The Camilla Massacre of 1868: Racial Violence as Political Propaganda." *Georgia Historical Quarterly* 21, no. 3 (Fall 1987): 399–426.

Fornell, Earl W. "The Civil War Comes to Savannah." *Georgia Historical Quarterly* 43 (June 1959): 248–60.

Fraser, Derek, and Anthony Sutcliffe, eds. *The Pursuit of Urban History.* London: E. Arnold, 1983.

Fraser, Walter J. *Charleston! Charleston! The History of a Southern City.* Columbia, S.C.: University of South Carolina Press, 1991.

———. *Savannah in the Old South.* Athens: University of Georgia Press, 2003.

Fraser, Walter J., and Winfred B. Moore, eds. *From the Old South to the New: Essays on the Transitional South.* Westport, Conn.: Greenwood Press, 1981.

Freehling, William W. *Prelude to Civil War: The Nullification Controversy in South Carolina, 1816–1836.* New York: Harper & Row, 1966.

———. *The Road to Disunion,* vol. 1, *Secessionists at Bay, 1779–1854.* New York: Oxford University Press, 1990.

———. *The Road to Disunion,* vol. 2, *Secessionists Triumphant, 1854–1861.* New York: Oxford University Press, 2007.

Freyer, Tony Allan. "Debt Failure and the Development of American Capitalism: Bruce Mann's Pro-Debtor Republic." *Law and Social Inquiry* 30 (October 2005): 739–62.

———. *Forums of Order: The Federal Courts and Business in American History.* Greenwich, Conn.: JAI Press, 1979.

———. *Producers versus Capitalists: Constitutional Conflict in Antebellum America.* Charlottesville: University Press of Virginia, 1994.

Frug, Gerald E. "The City as a Legal Concept." *Harvard Law Review* 93 (April 1980): 1062–1138.

Furrer, Marie Margaretta. "Development of the Public School System in Savannah and Chatham County." Master's thesis, University of Georgia, 1933.

Gamble, Thomas. *History of the City Government of Savannah, Ga., from 1790 to 1901.* Savannah: n.p., 1900.

Georgia General Assembly. *Acts of the General Assembly of the State of Georgia,* 1828–1885. Cited throughout as *Georgia Acts.*

Georgia Writers' Project and Federal Writers' Project. *Savannah River Plantations.* Savannah: Georgia Historical Society, 1947.

Georgia. State Board of Health. *Report of the Board of Health of the State of Georgia for 1876 with Appendix and Mortuary Record of the Epidemic in Savannah in 1876.* Savannah: Morning News Office, J. H. Estill, 1877.

Gerstner, Francis Anthony Chevalier de (Franz Anton von Gerstner). "Letters from the United States of North America on Internal Improvements Steam Navigation Banking, Written . . . during His Sojourn in the United States in 1839." *Journal of the Franklin Institute of the State of Pennsylvania and Mechanics Register* 26 (December 1840): 28–73.

Gibson, Campbell. *Population of the 100 Largest Cities and Other Urban Places in the United States: 1790 to 1990.* Washington, D.C.: Population Division, U.S. Bureau of the Census, 1998. https://www.census.gov/population/www/documentation/twps0027/twps0027.html.

Gillespie, Michele. "Artisans and Mechanics in the Political Economy of Georgia 1790–1860." PhD diss., Princeton University, 1990.

———. *Free Labor in an Unfree World: White Artisans in Slaveholding Georgia, 1789–1860.* Athens: University of Georgia Press, 2000.

Gillette, Howard, Jr., and Zane Miller, eds. *American Urbanism: A Historiographical Review.* New York: Greenwood Press, 1987.

Gleeson, David T. *Irish in the South, 1815–1877.* Chapel Hill: University of North Carolina Press, 2001.

Goff, John H. "The Steamboat Period in Georgia." *Georgia Historical Quarterly* 12 (September 1928): 236–54.

Going, Allen Johnston. *Bourbon Democracy in Alabama, 1874–1890.* Westport, Conn.: Greenwood Press, 1972.

Goldfield, David R. *Cotton Fields and Skyscrapers: Southern City and Region, 1607–1980.* Baton Rouge: Louisiana State University Press, 1982.

———. *Region, Race and Cities: Interpreting the Urban South.* Baton Rouge: Louisiana State University Press, 1997.

Golway, Terry. *Machine Made: Tammany Hall and the Creation of Modern American Politics.* W. W. Norton, 2014.

Goodrich, Carter. "The Gallatin Plan after One Hundred and Fifty Years." *Proceedings of the American Philosophical Society* 102 (October 20, 1958): 436–41.

———. "Internal Improvements Reconsidered." *Journal of Economic History* 30 (June 1, 1970): 289–311.

———. "The Virginia System of Mixed Enterprise." *Political Science Quarterly* 64 (September 1, 1949): 355–87.

Gordon, Sarah. *Passage to Union: How the Railroads Transformed American Life, 1829–1929.* Chicago: Ivan R. Dee, 1996.

Gottlieb, Manuel. "The Land Question of Georgia during Reconstruction." *Science and Society* 3 (Summer 1939): 356–88.

Gouge, William M. *The Curse of Paper-Money and Banking, or, A Short History of Banking in the United States of America.* New York: Greenwood Press, 1968.

Granger, Mary L. *A History of the Savannah District, 1829–1968.* Savannah: U.S. Army Engineer District, Savannah, 1968.

Grant, Ulysses Simpson. *The Papers of Ulysses S. Grant,* vol. 23. Edited by John Y. Simon. Carbondale: Southern Illinois University Press, 2000.

Grantham, Dewey W. *The Democratic South.* Athens: University of Georgia Press, 1965.

Green, George D. *Finance and Economic Development in the Old South: Louisiana Banking, 1804–1861.* Stanford: Stanford University Press, 1972.

Griffin, J. D. "Savannah's City Income Tax." *Georgia Historical Quarterly* 50 (June 1966): 173–76.

Griffith, Ernest S., and Charles R. Adrian. *A History of American City Government: The Formation of Traditions, 1775–1870.* Washington, D.C.: University Press of America, 1983.

Hacker, Louis M. *The Course of American Economic Growth and Development.* New York: John Wiley and Sons, 1970.

Hackney, Sheldon. "'Origins of the New South' in Retrospect." *Journal of Southern History* 38, no. 2 (May 1972): 191–216.

Hahn, Steven. *A Nation under Our Feet: Black Political Struggles in the Rural South, from Slavery to the Great Migration.* Cambridge, Mass.: Belknap Press of Harvard University Press, 2003.

———. *The Roots of Southern Populism: Yeoman Farmers and the Transformation of the Georgia Upcountry, 1850–1890.* New York: Oxford University Press, 1983.

Hair, William. *Bourbonism and Agrarian Protest: Louisiana Politics, 1877–1900.* Baton Rouge: Louisiana State University Press, 1975.

Hammond, Bray. "Long and Short Term Credit in Early American Banking." *Quarterly Journal of Economics* 49 (November 1, 1934): 79–103.

Harden, William. *A History of Savannah and South Georgia.* Chicago: Lewis Publishing, 1913.

Harley, Timothy. *Southward Ho! Notes of a Tour to and through Georgia in the Winter of 1885–1886.* London: Sampson Low, Marston, Searle and Rivington, 1886.

Harris, Leslie M., and Daina Ramey Berry, eds. *Slavery and Freedom in Savannah.* Athens: University Of Georgia Press, 2014.

Hartz, Louis. *Economic Policy and Democratic Thought: Pennsylvania, 1776–1860.* Cambridge, Mass.: Harvard University Press, 1948.

Haunton, Richard. "Law and Order in Savannah, 1850–1860." *Georgia Historical Quarterly* 56 (Spring 1972): 1–24.

———. "Savannah in the 1850s." PhD diss., Emory University, 1968.

Heath, Milton S. *Constructive Liberalism: The Role of State Economic Development in Georgia to 1860.* Cambridge: Harvard University Press, 1954.

Heilbrun, James. *Urban Economics and Public Policy.* New York: St. Martin's, 1974.

Hempel, George H. "An Evaluation of Municipal 'Bankruptcy' Laws and Procedures." *Journal of Finance* 28 (December 1973): 1339–51.

Henry, Thomas. *Digest of Railroad Laws in Georgia.* Atlanta: Franklin Printing and Publishing, 1895.

Hicks, John Donald. *The Populist Revolt: A History of the Farmers' Alliance and the People's Party.* Lincoln: University of Nebraska Press, 1956.

Higgens-Evenson, Ronald. *The Price of Progress: Public Services, Taxation, and the American Corporate State, 1877 to 1929.* Baltimore: Johns Hopkins University Press, 2003.

Hild, Matthew. *Greenbackers, Knights of Labor, and Populists: Farmer-Labor Insurgency in the Late-Nineteenth-Century South.* Athens: University of Georgia Press, 2007.

Hillhouse, A. M. *Municipal Bonds: A Century of Experience.* New York: Prentice-Hall, 1936.

Hitchcock, Henry. *Marching with Sherman.* New Haven: Yale University Press, 1927.

Holcombe, Randall G., and Donald J. Lacombe. "Factors Underlying the Growth of Local Government in the 19th Century United States." *Public Choice* 120 (September 2004): 359–77.

Hopkins, Florrie. "Thomas Gibbons, Esquire." Student paper, Armstrong State College, 1987. Location: Lane Library, Georgia Southern University, Savannah.

Howard, Oliver O. *Autobiography of Oliver Otis Howard.* New York: Baker and Taylor, 1907.

Howe, Daniel Walker. *What Hath God Wrought: The Transformation of America, 1815–1848.* New York: Oxford University Press, 2007.

Hume, John F. "Are We a Nation of Rascals?" *North American Review* 139 (August 1884): 127–44.

Humphreys, Margaret. *Yellow Fever and the South.* New Brunswick, N.J.: Rutgers University Press, 1992.

Hyman, David N. *Public Finance: A Contemporary Application of Theory to Policy.* Chicago: Dryden Press, 1983.

Inscoe, John C., ed. *The Civil War in Georgia: A New Georgia Encyclopedia Companion.* Athens: University of Georgia Press, 2011.

Jackson, Kenneth T., and Stanley K. Schultz, eds. *Cities in American History.* New York: Alfred A. Knopf, 1972.

James, Herman G. *Municipal Functions.* New York: D. Appleton, 1917.

Janes, Thomas. *Hand-Book of the State of Georgia, Accompanied by a Geological Map of the State.* Atlanta: S. W. Green Electrotyper, 1876.

Jennison, Watson W. *Cultivating Race: The Expansion of Slavery in Georgia, 1750–1860*. Lexington: University Press of Kentucky, 2012.

Johnson, Emory R. "River and Harbor Bills." *Annals of the American Academy of Political and Social Science* 2 (May 1892): 50–80.

Johnson, Whittington B. "Free Blacks in Antebellum Savannah: An Economic Profile." *Georgia Historical Quarterly* 64 (Summer 1980): 418–31.

Jones, Charles C., Jr., and Salem Dutcher. *Memorial History of Augusta, Georgia: From Its Settlement in 1735 to the Close of the Eighteenth Century*. Syracuse: D. Mason, 1890.

Jones, Charles C., Jr. *History of Savannah, Georgia: From Its Settlement to the Close of the Eighteenth Century*. Syracuse: D. Mason, 1890.

Jones, Jacqueline. *A Dreadful Deceit: The Myth of Race from the Colonial Era to Obama's America*. New York: Basic Books, 2013.

———. *Saving Savannah: The City and the Civil War*. New York: Alfred A. Knopf, 2008.

Judd, Dennis R., and Todd Swanstrom. *City Politics: Private Power and Public Policy*. New York: HarperCollins College Publishers, 1994.

Kearns, Mary Pinckney. "Secession Diplomacy: A Study of Thomas Butler King, Commissioner of Georgia to Europe, 1861." Master's thesis, Georgia Southern University, 2006.

Kennedy, Joseph C. G. *Population of the United States in 1860, Compiled from the Original Returns of the Eighth Census*, vol. 1. Washington D.C.: Government Printing Office, 1864.

Kirwan, Albert Dennis. *Revolt of the Rednecks: Mississippi Politics, 1876–1925*. Lexington: University of Kentucky Press, 1951.

Klein, Maury. *The Great Richmond Terminal: A Study in Businessmen and Business Strategy*. Charlottesville: Eleutherian Mills-Hagley Foundation/University Press of Virginia, 1970.

———. *History of the Louisville and Nashville Railroad*. New York: Macmillan, 1972.

———. "Southern Railroad Leaders, 1865–1893: Identities and Ideologies." *Business History Review* 42 (April 1968): 288–310.

———. "The Strategy of Southern Railroads." *American Historical Review* 73 (April 1968): 1052–68.

Knight, Lucian Lamar. *A Standard History of Georgia and Georgians*. 6 vols. New York: Lewis Publishing, 1917.

Koeppel, Gerard T. *Bond of Union: Building the Erie Canal and the American Empire*. Cambridge: Da Capo Press, 2009.

Lamar, Lucius Q. C. *A Compilation of the Laws of the State of Georgia: Passed by the Legislature since the Year 1810 to the Year 1819, Inclusive*. Augusta: T. S. Hannon, 1821.

Lambert, John. *Travels through Canada, and the United States of North America, in the Years 1806, 1807, and 1808: To Which Are Added, Biographical Notices and Anecdotes of Some of the Leading Characters in the United States*. London: Printed for C. Craddock and W. Joy, 1813.

Lane, Mills B., ed. *The Rambler in Georgia: Desultory Observations on the . . . State from the Revolution to the Civil War, Recorded by Thirteen Travellers*. Savannah: Beehive Press, 1973.

La Rochefoucauld-Liancourt, François-Alexandre-Frédéric. *Travels through the United States of North America*. London: R. Phillips, 1799.

Larsen, Lawrence Harold. *The Urban South: A History*. Lexington: University Press of Kentucky, 1990.

Larson, John Lauritz. "'Bind the Republic Together': The National Union and the Struggle for a System of Internal Improvements." *Journal of American History* 74 (September 1987): 363–87.

———. *Bonds of Enterprise: John Murray Forbes and Western Development in America's Railway Age*. Cambridge: Harvard University Press, 1984.

———. *Internal Improvement: National Public Works and the Promise of Popular Government in the Early United States*. Chapel Hill: University of North Carolina Press, 2001.

———. *The Market Revolution in America: Liberty, Ambition, and the Eclipse of the Common Good*. Cambridge: Cambridge University Press, 2010.

Lawrence, Alexander A. *A Present for Mr. Lincoln: The Story of Savannah from Secession to Sherman*. Macon: Ardivan Press, 1961.

Laws of the United States Relating to the Improvement of Rivers and Harbors from August 11, 1790 to March 4, 1913. Washington, D.C.: Government Printing Office, 1913.

Lawton, Alexander R. "An Address by Alexander R. Lawton: Delivered in the City Hall, Savannah, Georgia April 21, 1919." *Georgia Historical Quarterly* 3, no. 2 (June 1919): 45–60.

Lee, F. D., and J. L. Agnew. *Historical Record of the City of Savannah*. Savannah: J. H. Estill, 1869.

Le Hardy, Julius Caesar. "Sanitary Progress in Savannah, Georgia." *Sanitarian* 37 (July 1896): 30–36.

———. *Yellow Fever: Its History, Causes, Nature, Pathology and Treatment: Considering Exclusively the Epidemic of 1876 in Savannah*. Atlanta: J. P. Harrison, 1878.

Lehmann, Henry W. "The Federal Municipal Bankruptcy Act." *Journal of Finance* 5 (September 1950): 241–56.

Leigh, Frances B. *Ten Years on a Georgia Plantation since the War*. New York: Negro University Press, 1883.

Lepler, Jessica M. *The Many Panics of 1837: People, Politics, and the Creation of a Transatlantic Financial Crisis*. New York: Cambridge University Press, 2013.

Lerski, Hanna Hryniewiecka. *William Jay, Itinerant English Architect, 1792–1837*. Lanham, Md.: University Press of America, 1983.

Lewis, David. "The Emergence of Birmingham as a Case Study of Continuity between the Antebellum Planter Class and Industrialization in the New South." *Agricultural History* 68 (Spring 1994): 62–79.

Lubetkin, M. *Jay Cooke's Gamble: The Northern Pacific Railroad, the Sioux, and the Panic of 1873*. Norman: University of Oklahoma Press, 2006.

MacKay, Robert, Eliza Anne McQueen MacKay, and Walter Charlton Hartridge. *The Letters of Robert MacKay to His Wife, Written from Ports in America and England, 1795–1816.* Athens: University of Georgia Press, 2010.

Majewski, John. *Modernizing a Slave Economy: The Economic Vision of the Confederate Nation.* Chapel Hill: University of North Carolina Press, 2011.

Mandle, Jay R. *The Roots of Black Poverty: The Southern Plantation Economy after the Civil War.* Durham, N.C.: Duke University Press, 1979.

Martin, Jonathan D. *Divided Mastery: Slave Hiring in the American South.* Cambridge, Mass.: Harvard University Press, 2004.

"Mary Telfair." Georgia Historical Society. https://georgiahistory.com/education -outreach/online-exhibits/featured-historical-figures/additional-featured-historical -figures/mary-telfair.

Matthews, John M. "Negro Republicans in the Reconstruction of Georgia." *Georgia Historical Quarterly* 60 (Summer 1976): 145–64.

May, J. Thomas. "Continuity and Change in the Labor Program of the Union Army and the Freedmen's Bureau." *Civil War History* 17 (September 1971): 245–54.

McCabe, James Dabney. *History of the Grange Movement, or, The Farmer's War against Monopolies.* New York: Franklin, 1967.

McDonald, Terrence J., and Sally K. Ward, eds. *The Politics of Urban Fiscal Policy.* Beverly Hills, Calif.: Sage Publications, 1984.

McGrane, Reginald Charles. *The Panic of 1837: Some Financial Problems of the Jacksonian Era.* Chicago: University of Chicago Press, 1966.

McGreevy, Patrick. *Stairway to Empire: Lockport, the Erie Canal, and the Shaping of America.* Albany: State University of New York Press, 2009.

McGuire, Peter S. "The Railroads of Georgia, 1860–1880." *Georgia Historical Quarterly* 16 (September 1932): 179–213.

McMath, Robert C. *Populist Vanguard: A History of the Southern Farmers' Alliance.* Chapel Hill: University of North Carolina Press, 1975.

Melish, John. *Travels through the United States of America, in the Years 1806 and 1807, and 1809, 1810, and 1811.* New York: Johnson Reprint, 1970. First published 1818.

Melosi, Martin V. *Effluent America: Cities, Industry, Energy, and the Environment.* Pittsburgh: University of Pittsburgh Press, 2001.

———. *Garbage in the Cities: Refuse, Reform, and the Environment: 1880–1980.* College Station: Texas A&M University Press, 1981.

———. *Pollution and Reform in American Cities, 1870–1930.* Austin: University of Texas Press, 1980.

———. *The Sanitary City: Urban Infrastructure in America from Colonial Times to the Present.* Baltimore: Johns Hopkins University Press, 2000.

Melton, Maurice. *The Best Station of Them All: The Savannah Squadron, 1861–1865.* Tuscaloosa: University of Alabama Press, 2012.

Miller, Randall M. "The Failure of the Colony of Georgia under the Trustees." *Georgia Historical Quarterly* 53 (March 1969): 1–17.

Miner, H. Craig. *A Most Magnificent Machine: America Adopts the Railroad, 1825–1862.* Lawrence: University Press of Kansas, 2010.

Mintz, Joel A., Ronald H. Rosenberg, Larry A. Bakken, and American Bar Association, Section of State and Local Government Law. *Fundamentals of Municipal Finance*. Chicago: American Bar Association, 2010.

Mohl, Raymond A. "A Scotsman Visits Georgia in 1811." *Georgia Historical Quarterly* 55 (Summer 1971): 259–74.

Mohr, Clarence L. *On the Threshold of Freedom: Masters and Slaves in Civil War Georgia*. Athens: University of Georgia Press, 1986.

Monkkonen, Eric H. *America Becomes Urban: The Development of U.S. Cities and Towns, 1780–1980*. Berkeley: University of California Press, 1988.

———. "Politics of Municipal Indebtedness and Default, 1850–1936." In *The Politics of Urban Fiscal Policy*, edited by McDonald and McDonald, 125–59. Beverly Hills, Calif.: Sage Publications, 1984.

Montgomery, Horace. *Cracker Parties*. Baton Rouge: Louisiana State University Press, 1950.

Moore, James Tice. "Redeemers Reconsidered: Change and Continuity in the Democratic South, 1870–1900." *Journal of Southern History* 44, no. 3 (August 1978): 357–78.

Morse, Jedidiah. *The American Geography, or, A View of the Present Situation of the United States of America: Containing Astronomical Geography—Geographical Definitions, Discovery, and General Description of America and the United States*. Dublin: Printed for J. Jones, 1792.

"Municipal Indebtedness." *Bankers' Magazine and Statistical Register* 34, no. 1 (July 1879): 7–8.

Myer, William G., United States Courts, and United States Supreme Court. *Federal Decisions; Cases Argued and Determined in the Supreme, Circuit and District Courts of the United States, Comprising the Opinions of Those Courts from the Time of Their Organization to the Present Date, Together with Extracts from the Opinions of the Court of Claims and the Attorneys-General, and the Opinions of General Importance of the Territorial Courts*. Arranged by William G. Myer. St. Louis: Gilbert Book Co., 1887.

Nathans, Elizabeth Studley. *Losing the Peace: Georgia Republicans and Reconstruction: 1868–72*. Baton Rouge: Louisiana State University Press, 1968.

Neblett, Thomas R. "Major Edward C. Anderson and the C. S. S. Fingal." *Georgia Historical Quarterly* 52 (June 1968): 132–58.

Neuteboom, Peter. *On the Rationality of Borrowers' Behaviour: Comparing Risk Attitudes of Homeowners*. Amsterdam: IOS Press, 2010.

Nevins, Allan. *The Emergence of Modern America, 1865–1878*. New York: Macmillan, 1927.

Nichols, George W. *The Story of the Great March: Diary of a Staff Officer*. New York: Harper and Brothers, 1866.

Nimmo, Joseph. *Report on the Internal Commerce of the United States*. Washington, D.C.: GPO, 1885.

Northen, William J. *Men of Mark in Georgia: A Complete and Elaborate History of the State from Its Settlement to the Present Time, Chiefly Told in Biographies and Autobi-*

ographies of the Most Eminent Men of Each Period of Georgia's Progress and Develop-ment. Atlanta: A. B. Caldwell, 1907.

Nugent, Walter T. K. *Money and American Society, 1865–1880*. New York: Free Press, 1968.

Oberholtzer, Ellis. *Jay Cooke: Financier of the Civil War*. Philadelphia: G. W. Jacobs, 1907.

O'Connell, Jeremiah Joseph. *Catholicity in the Carolinas and Georgia: Leaves of Its History, 1820–1878*. New York: D. J. Sadlier, 1879.

Orth, John V. *The Judicial Power of the United States: The Eleventh Amendment in American History*. New York: Oxford University Press, 1987.

Padgett, James A., ed. "With Sherman through Georgia and the Carolinas." *Georgia Historical Quarterly* 33 (March 1949): 49–81.

Parkman, Aubrey. *History of the Waterways of the Atlantic Coast of the United States*. Washington, D.C.: National Waterways Study, U.S. Army Engineer Water Resources Support Center, Institute for Water Resources, 1983.

Peeples, Dale Hardy. "Georgia Railroads: Civil War and Reconstruction." PhD diss., University of Miami, 1959.

Pepper, George W. *Personal Recollections of Sherman's Campaign in Georgia and the Carolinas*. Zanesville, Ohio: H. Dunne, 1866.

Perman, Michael. *The Road to Redemption: Southern Politics, 1869–1879*. Chapel Hill: University of North Carolina Press, 1984.

Phillips, U. B. *A History of Transportation in the Eastern Cotton Belt to 1860*. New York: Columbia University Press, 1908.

Picker, Randal C., and Michael W. McConnell. "When Cities Go Broke: A Conceptual Introduction to Municipal Bankruptcy." *University of Chicago Law Review* 60 (1993): 425–56.

Pitkin, Timothy. *A Statistical View of the Commerce of the United States of America*. New Haven: Durrie and Peck, 1835.

Platt, Harold L. *City Building in the New South: The Growth of Public Services in Houston, Texas, 1830–1910*. Philadelphia: Temple University Press, 1983.

Pollack, Norman. *The Populist Mind*. Indianapolis: Bobbs-Merrill, 1967.

Ponton, M. M. *Life and Times of Henry M. Turner*. Atlanta: A. B. Caldwell Publishing, 1887.

Pope, John. *Tour through the Southern and Western Territories of the United States of North-America*. New York: C. L. Woodward, 1888. First published 1792 by J. Dixon (Richmond).

Pressly, Paul M. "The Northern Roots of Savannah's Antebellum Elite, 1780s-1850s." *Georgia Historical Quarterly* 87 (Summer 2003): 157–99.

———. *On the Rim of the Caribbean: Colonial Georgia and the British Atlantic World*. Athens: University of Georgia Press, 2013.

Prince, Oliver Hillhouse. *A Digest of the Laws of the State of Georgia*. Athens: O. H. Prince, 1837.

Rabinowitz, Howard N. "Continuity and Change: Southern Urban Development,

1860–1900." In *The Pursuit of Urban History*, edited by Derek Fraser and Anthony Sutcliffe, 92–122. London: E. Arnold, 1983.

———. *The First New South, 1865–1920*. Arlington Heights, Ill.: Harlan Davidson, 1992.

———. *Southern Black Leaders of the Reconstruction Era*. Urbana: University of Illinois Press, 1982.

Rable, George C. *But There Was No Peace: The Role of Violence in the Politics of Reconstruction*. Athens: University of Georgia Press, 1984.

Ratchford, Benjamin Ulysses. *American State Debts*. Durham, N.C.: Duke University Press, 1941.

Ready, Milton. "The Georgia Concept: An Eighteenth Century Experiment in Colonization." *Georgia Historical Quarterly* 55 (July 1971): 157–72.

Rebarer, Frank E., compiler. *Rebarer's Digest: Supplement to the City Code, 1871*. Savannah: George N. Nichols, 1879.

Reid, Whitelaw. *After the War: A Southern Tour, May 1, 1865–May 1, 1866*. New York: Moore Wilstach and Baldwin, 1866.

———. *Ohio in the War: Her Statesmen, Her Generals, and Soldiers*. Cincinnati: Moore, Wilstach & Baldwin, 1868.

Reidy, Joseph P. "Aaron A. Bradley: Voice of Black Labor in the Georgia Lowcountry." In *Southern Black Leaders of the Reconstruction Era*, edited by Howard N. Rabinowitz, 281–308. Urbana: University of Illinois Press, 1982.

———. "Economic Consequences of the Civil War and Reconstruction." In *A Companion to the American South*, edited by John B. Boles, 303–20. Malden, Mass.: Blackwell, 2002.

Report of the State Commissioners Representing the Stock Held by the State in the Atlantic and Gulf Rail Road Company. Savannah: Morning News Steam-Power Press, 1872.

Reynolds, Kelly. *Henry Plant: Pioneer Empire Builder*. Cocoa: Florida Historical Society Press, 2003.

Robert, P. "The Municipal Debt of the United States." *Galaxy: A Magazine of Entertaining Reading*, September 1877, 399.

Rockoff, Hugh. "Banking and Finance, 1789–1914." In *The Cambridge Economic History of the United States: The Long Nineteenth Century*, vol. 2., edited by Stanley L. Engerman and Robert E. Gallman, 643–84. Cambridge: Cambridge University Press, 2000.

Rogers, William Warren. *A Scalawag in Georgia: Richard Whiteley and the Politics of Reconstruction*. Urbana: University of Illinois Press, 2007.

Rose, Willie Lee. *Rehearsal for Reconstruction: The Port Royal Experiment*. Indianapolis: Bobbs-Merrill, 1964.

Ross, Michael. "Resisting the New South: Commercial Crisis and Decline in New Orleans, 1865–85." *American Nineteenth Century History* 4 (Winter 2003): 59–76.

Rothbard, Murray N. *The Panic of 1819: Reactions and Policies*. Auburn, Ala.: Ludwig von Mises Institute, 2007.

Rousey, Dennis C. "From Whence They Came to Savannah: The Origins of an Urban Population in the Old South." *Georgia Historical Quarterly* 79 (Summer 1995): 305–36.

Rowland, Lawrence S., Alexander Moore, and George C. Rogers. "'Alone on the River': The Rise and Fall of the Savannah River Rice Plantations of St. Peter's Parish, South Carolina." *South Carolina Historical Magazine* 88 (July 1987): 121–50.

———. *The History of Beaufort County, South Carolina.* Columbia: University of South Carolina Press, 1996.

Rubin, Julius. "Canal or Railroad? Imitation and Innovation in the Response to the Erie Canal in Philadelphia, Baltimore, and Boston." *Transactions of the American Philosophical Society* 51 (November 1961): 1–106.

Rubin, Saul Jacob. *Third to None: The Saga of Savannah Jewry, 1733–1983.* Savannah: Congregation of Mickve Israel, 1983.

Russell, James M. *Atlanta, 1847–1890: City Building in the Old South and the New.* Baton Rouge: Louisiana State University Press, 1988.

Rutherford, John, ed. *Acts of the General Assembly of the State of Georgia, Passed in Milledgeville at a Biennial Session in November, December, January, and February 1853–4.* Savannah: Samuel T. Chapman, 1854.

Ryan, Jennifer Guthrie, and Hugh Stiles Golson. *Andrew Low and the Sign of the Buck: Trade, Triumph, Tragedy at the House of Low.* Savannah: Frederic C. Beil, 2011.

Sacher, John M. *A Perfect War of Politics: Parties, Politicians, and Democracy in Louisiana, 1824–1861.* Baton Rouge: Louisiana State University Press, 2007.

Savannah Unit, Georgia Writers' Project, Works Projects Administration in Georgia. "Whitehall Plantation, Part II." *Georgia Historical Quarterly* 26 (March 1942): 40–64.

Saye, Albert B. "The Genesis of Georgia Reviewed." *Georgia Historical Quarterly* 50 (June 1966): 153–61.

———. *New Viewpoints in Georgia History.* Athens: University of Georgia Press, 1943.

Sbragia, Alberta M. *Debt Wish: Entrepreneurial Cities, U.S. Federalism, and Economic Development.* Pittsburgh: University of Pittsburgh Press, 1996.

Schwartz, Michael. *Radical Protest and Social Structure: The Southern Farmers' Alliance and Cotton Tenancy, 1880–1890.* New York: Academic Press, 1976.

Scott, William Amasa. *The Repudiation of State Debts: A Study in the Financial History of Mississippi, Florida, Alabama, North Carolina, South Carolina, Georgia, Louisiana, Arkansas, Tennessee, Minnesota, Michigan, and Virginia.* New York: Greenwood Press, 1969.

Screven, Frank B. "The Georgia Bryans and Screvens, 1685–1861." *Georgia Historical Quarterly* 40 (December 1956): 325–48.

Seip, Terry L. *The South Returns to Congress: Men, Economic Measures, and Intersectional Relationships, 1868–1879.* Baton Rouge: Louisiana State University Press, 1983.

Sellers, Charles. *The Market Revolution: Jacksonian America, 1815–1846.* New York: Oxford University Press, 1991.

Sexton, Jay. *Debtor Diplomacy: Finance and American Foreign Relations in the Civil War Era, 1837–1873.* Oxford: Oxford University Press, 2005.

Shadgett, Olive Hall. *The Republican Party in Georgia, from Reconstruction to 1900.* Athens: University of Georgia Press, 1964.

Shaw, Ronald E. *Canals for a Nation: The Canal Era in the United States, 1790–1860.* Lexington: University Press of Kentucky, 1993.

Sherman, W. T. *General Sherman's Official Account of His Great March through Georgia and the Carolinas....* New York: Bunce & Huntington, 1865.

———. *Memoirs of General W. T. Sherman.* New York: Appleton, 1891.

Sherwood, Adiel. *A Gazetteer of the State of Georgia: Embracing a Particular Description of the Counties, Towns, Villages, Rivers, &c., and Whatsoever Is Usual in Geographies, and Minute Statistical Works, Together with a New Map of the State.* Washington City [Washington, D.C.]: P. Force, 1837.

Shoemaker, Edward M. "Strangers and Citizens: The Irish Immigrant Community of Savannah, 1837–1861." PhD diss., Emory University, 1990.

Sholes, A. E. *Chronological History of Savannah.* Savannah: Morning News Press, 1900.

Shore, Laurence. *Southern Capitalists: The Ideological Leadership of an Elite, 1832–1885.* Chapel Hill: University of North Carolina Press, 1986.

Shryock, Richard Harrison. *Georgia and the Union in 1850.* Durham: Duke University Press, 1926.

Smith, Carl S. *City Water, City Life: Water and the Infrastructure of Ideas in Urbanizing Philadelphia, Boston, and Chicago.* Chicago: University of Chicago Press, 2013.

Smith, Derek. *Civil War Savannah.* Savannah: Frederic C. Beil, 1997.

Smith, George Winston. "Cotton from Savannah in 1865." *Journal of Southern History* 21 (November 1955): 495–512.

Smith, Julia Floyd. *Slavery and Rice Culture in Low Country Georgia, 1750–1860.* Knoxville: University of Tennessee Press, 1992.

Smith, Wallace Calvin. "Georgia Gentlemen, the Habershams of Eighteenth-Century Savannah." PhD diss., University of North Carolina, 1972.

Smyth, G. Hutchinson, and George Sherwood Dickerman. *The Life of Henry Bradley Plant: Founder and President of the Plant System of Railroads and Steamships and Also of the Southern Express Company.* Whitefish, Mont.: Kessinger Publishing, 2006. First published 1898.

Snay, Mitchell. *Fenians, Freedmen, and Southern Whites: Race and Nationality in the Era of Reconstruction.* Baton Rouge: Louisiana State University Press, 2007.

"Solid Drainage in the Vicinity of Savannah, Georgia—Report of the Commissioners of the Governor." *Sanitarian* 8, no. 83 (February 1880): 85–87.

Soltow, Lee, and Aubrey C. Land. "Housing and Social Standing in Georgia, 1798." *Georgia Historical Quarterly* 64, no. 4 (Winter 1980): 448–58.

Somers, Robert. *The Southern States since the War, 1870–71.* New York: MacMillan, 1871.

South Carolina, Department of Agriculture, and Harry Hammond. *South Carolina: Resources and Population, Institutions and Industries.* Charleston: Walker, Evans, & Cogswell, 1883.

Southern Historical Association. *Memoirs of Georgia: Containing Historical Accounts of the State's Civil, Military, Industrial and Professional Interests, and Personal Sketches of Many of Its People.* Atlanta: Southern Historical Association, 1895.

Stabile, Donald. *The Origins of American Public Finance: Debates over Money, Debt, and Taxes in the Constitutional Era, 1776–1836.* Westport, Conn.: Greenwood Press, 1998.

Stack, Harry. *The Jay Cooke Story: How a Native Sanduskian Became the Nationally and Internationally Known Financier of the Civil War.* Sandusky, Ohio: Sandusky Chamber of Commerce, 1948.

Steiss, Alan Walter. *Local Government Finance: Capital Facilities Planning and Debt Administration.* Lexington: D.C. Heath, 1975.

Stewart, Dorothy Houseal. "Survival of the Fittest: William Morrill Wadley and the Central of Georgia Railroad's Coming of Age, 1866–1882." *Georgia Historical Quarterly* 78 (Spring 1994): 39–65.

Stewart, Mart A. *"What Nature Suffers to Groe": Life, Labor, and Landscape on the Georgia Coast, 1680–1920.* Athens: University of Georgia Press, 2002.

Stokes, Melvyn, and Stephen Conway, eds. *The Market Revolution in America: Social, Political, and Religious Expressions, 1800–1880.* Charlottesville: University Press of Virginia, 1996.

Strong, Paschal N. "Glimpses of Savannah, 1780–1825." *Georgia Historical Quarterly* 33, no. 1 (March 1949): 26–35.

Swint, Henry Lee, ed. *Dear Ones at Home: Letters from Contraband Camps.* Nashville: Vanderbilt University Press, 1966.

Sylla, Richard, and John Joseph Wallis. "The Anatomy of Sovereign Debt Crises: Lessons from the American State Defaults of the 1840s." *Japan and the World Economy* 10 (July 1998): 267–93.

Talbott, Page, and Telfair Museum of Art. *Classical Savannah: Fine and Decorative Arts, 1800–1840.* Savannah: Telfair Museum of Art, 1995.

Tarr, Joel A., and Josef W. Konvitz. "Patterns in the Development of the Urban Infrastructure." In *American Urbanism: A Historiographical Review,* edited by Howard Gillette Jr. and Zane Miller, 195–226. New York: Greenwood Press, 1987.

Taylor, George Rogers. *The Transportation Revolution, 1815–1860.* Economic History of the United States. New York: Rinehart, 1951.

Taylor, George Rogers, and Irene D. Neu. *The American Railroad Network, 1861–1890.* Cambridge, Mass.: Harvard University Press, 1956.

Temin, Peter. "The Post-Bellum Recovery of the South and the Cost of the Civil War." *Journal of Economic History* 36, no. 4 (December 1976): 898–907.

Testimony Taken by a Joint Committee of the Two Houses of the Legislature of Georgia upon the Condition of the Macon and Brunswick Railroad in January and February 1874. Savannah: J. H. Estill, 1875.

Thigpen, Thomas. "Aristocracy of the Heart." PhD diss., University of Georgia, 1995.

Thomas, Henry W. *Digest of the Railroad Laws of Georgia.* Atlanta: Franklin Printing and Publishing, 1895.

Thomason, Michael V. R., ed. *Mobile: The New History of Alabama's First City.* Tuscaloosa: University of Alabama Press, 2001.

Thomlinson, Ralph. *Urban Structure: The Social and Spatial Character of Cities.* New York: Random House, 1969.

Thompson, Larry James. "Progressive Education and the Savannah Public School System." PhD diss., University of Georgia, 1986.

Thornton, J. Mills. *Politics and Power in a Slave Society: Alabama, 1800–1860.* Baton Rouge: Louisiana State University Press, 2014.

Toledano, Roulhac. *The National Trust Guide to Savannah.* New York: Wiley, 1997.

Trudeau, Noah Andre. *Southern Storm: Sherman's March to the Sea.* Harper Collins, 2009.

Turner, Gregg, and Seth Bramson. *The Plant System of Railroads, Steamships and Hotels: The South's First Great Industrial Enterprise.* Laurys Station, Penn.: Garrigues House Publishers, 2004.

United States. Army. Corps of Engineers. *Annual Report of the Chief of Engineers to the Secretary of War for the Year 1872.* Washington, D.C.: U.S. Government Printing Office, 1872.

———. *Laws of the United States Relating to the Improvement of Rivers and Harbors from August 11, 1790, to March 4, 1913.* Washington, D.C.: Government Printing Office, 1913.

United States. Census Office. *Eighth Census of the United States, Population.* Washington D.C.: Government Printing Office, 1863.

———. *Ninth Census of the United States, Population.* Washington D.C.: Government Printing Office, 1872.

United States. Census Office, and J. D. B De Bow. *Statistical View of the United States: Embracing Its Territory, Population—White, Free Colored, and Slave—, Moral and Social Condition, Industry, Property, and Revenue* . . . . Washington: A. O. P. Nicholson, public printer, 1854.

United States. Congress. Joint Select Committee on the Condition of Affairs in the Late Insurrectionary States. *Report of the Joint Select Committee Appointed to Inquire into the Condition of Affairs of the Late Insurrectionary States, so Far as Regards the Execution of Laws, and the Safety of the Lives and Property of the Citizens of the United States and Testimony Taken,* vol. 3. Washington, D.C.: Government Printing Office, 1872.

United States. Department of the Treasury, and Israel De Wolf Andrews. *Communication from the Secretary of the Treasury: Transmitting in Compliance with a Resolution of the Senate of March 8, 1851, the Report of Israel D. Andrews, Consul of the United States for Canada and New Brunswick, on the Trade and Commerce of the British North American Colonies and upon the Trade of the Great Lakes and Rivers* . . . . Washington, D.C.: B. Tucker, 1854.

United States. War Department. *The War of the Rebellion. Official Records of the Union and Confederate Armies. Series I. Index to Battles, Campaigns, Etc.* Washington, D.C.: Government Printing Office, 1899.

Usinger, Robert L. "Yellow Fever from the Viewpoint of Savannah." Savannah Historical Research Association records, MS 994, Georgia Historical Society, Savannah.

Wade, Richard C. *Slavery in the Cities: The South 1820–1860*. New York: Oxford University Press, 1980.

Waibel, Michael. *Sovereign Defaults before International Courts and Tribunals*. New York: Cambridge University Press, 2011.

Wallenstein, Peter. *From Slave South to New South: Public Policy in Nineteenth-Century Georgia*. Chapel Hill: University of North Carolina Press, 1987.

Wallis, John Joseph. *What Caused the Crisis of 1839?* NBER Historical Working Paper Series. Cambridge, Mass.: National Bureau of Economic Research, 2001.

Wallis, John Joseph, Richard Eugene Sylla, Arthur Grinath, and National Bureau of Economic Research. *Sovereign Debt and Repudiation: The Emerging-Market Debt Crisis in the U.S. States, 1839–1843*. Cambridge, Mass.: National Bureau of Economic Research, 2004.

Ward, James A. "A New Look at Antebellum Southern Railroad Development." *Journal of Southern History* 39 (August 1973): 409–20.

Waring, James Johnston. *The Epidemic at Savannah, 1876: Its Causes, the Measures of Prevention Adopted by the Municipality during the Administration of Hon. J. F. Wheaton, Mayor*. Savannah: Morning News steam Printing House, 1879.

Waring, Joseph Ioor. "The Yellow Fever Epidemic of Savannah in 1820, with a Sketch of Dr. William Coffee Daniell." *Georgia Historical Quarterly* 52 (December 1968): 398–404.

Washington, George. *The Diary of George Washington, from 1789 to 1791, Embracing the Opening of the First Congress, and His Tours Through New England, Long Island, and the Southern States*. Edited by Benson John Lossing. New York: C. B. Richardson, 1860.

Watkins, Robert, and George Watkins. *A Digest of the Laws of the State of Georgia: From Its First Establishment as a British Province down to the Year 1798, Inclusive, and the Principal Acts of 1799*. Philadelphia: R. Aitken, 1800.

Weaver, David C. "Spatial Strategies in Railroad Planning in Georgia and the Carolinas, 1830–1860." *West Georgia College Studies in the Social Sciences* 18 (June 1979): 9–23.

Weaver, Herbert. "Foreigners in Antebellum Savannah." *Georgia Historical Quarterly* 37 (January 1953): 1–12.

Webb, Walter Loring. *Railroad Construction, Theory and Practice: A Text-Book for the Use of Students in Colleges and Technical Schools, and a Hand-Book for the Use of Engineers in Field and Office*. New York: John Wiley, 1917.

Welborn, James H., III, and Richard Houston. "Union Blockade and Coastal Occupation." In *The Civil War in Georgia: A New Georgia Encyclopedia Companion*, edited by John C. Inscoe, 51–55. Athens: University of Georgia Press, 2011.

Wells, Jonathan Daniel. *The Origins of the Southern Middle Class, 1800–1861*. Chapel Hill: University of North Carolina Press, 2004.

Wertenbaker, Thomas J. *Norfolk: Historic Southern Port*. Durham, N.C.: Duke University Press, 1931.

Westwood, Howard C. "Sherman Marched—and Proclaimed 'Land for the Land-less.'" *South Carolina Historical Magazine* 85 (January 1984): 33–55.

Wetherington, Mark V. *The New South Comes to Wiregrass Georgia, 1860–1910.* Knox-ville: University of Tennessee Press, 1994.

Wicker, Elmus. *Banking Panics of the Gilded Age.* Cambridge, UK: Cambridge University Press, 2000.

Wiener, Jonathan M. *Social Origins of the New South: Alabama, 1860–1885.* Baton Rouge: Louisiana State University Press, 1978.

Williams, C. Dickerman, and Peter R. Nehemkis. "Municipal Improvements as Affected by Constitutional Debt Limitations." *Columbia Law Review* 37 (February 1937): 177–211.

Williams, Thomas Harry. *Romance and Realism in Southern Politics.* Baton Rouge: Louisiana State University Press, 1966.

Wills, Jocelyn. *Boosters, Hustlers, and Speculators: Entrepreneurial Culture and the Rise of Minneapolis and St. Paul, 1849–1883.* St. Paul: Minnesota Historical Society Press, 2005.

Wilson, Adelaide. *Historic and Picturesque Savannah.* Boston: Boston Photogravure, 1889.

Wilson, Edward G. *A Digest of All the Ordinances of the City of Savannah and Various Laws of the State of Georgia, Relative to Said City, Which Were of Force on the 1st January, 1858, Together with an Appendix and Index.* Savannah: J. M. Cooper, 1858.

Wood, Betty. "Thomas Stephens and the Introduction of Black Slavery in Georgia." *Georgia Historical Quarterly* 58 (April 1974): 24–40.

———. *Women's Work, Men's Work: The Informal Slave Economies of Lowcountry Georgia.* University of Georgia Press, 1995.

Woodman, Harold D. "Class, Race, Politics, and the Modernization of the Postbellum South." *Journal of Social History* 63 (February 1997): 3–22.

———. "The Decline of Cotton Factorage after the Civil War." *American Historical Review* 71, no. 4 (July 1966): 1219–36.

———. "Itinerant Cotton Merchants of the Antebellum South." *Agricultural History* 40, no. 2 (April 1966): 79–90.

———. *King Cotton and His Retainers.* Lexington: University of Kentucky Press, 1968.

———. "The Political Economy of the New South: Retrospects and Prospects." *Journal of Southern History* 67 (November 2001): 789–810.

Woodward, C. Vann. *Origins of the New South, 1877–1913.* Baton Rouge: Louisiana State University Press, 1951.

———. *Tom Watson: Agrarian Rebel.* New York: Oxford University Press, 1963.

Wrenn, Lynette Boney. *Crisis and Commission Government in Memphis: Elite Rule in a Gilded Age City.* Knoxville: University of Tennessee Press, 1998.

Wright, Gavin. *Old South, New South: Revolutions in the Southern Economy since the Civil War.* New York: Basic Books, 1986.

————. *The Political Economy of the Cotton South: Households, Markets, and Wealth in the Nineteenth Century.* New York: Norton, 1978.

Wright, Robert E. *One Nation under Debt: Hamilton, Jefferson, and the History of What We Owe.* New York: McGraw-Hill, 2008.

————. *Origins of Commercial Banking in America, 1750–1800.* Lanham, Md.: Rowman & Littlefield, 2001.

Wynne, Lewis N., and Milly St. Julien. "The Camilla Race Riot and the Failure of Reconstruction in Georgia." *Journal of Southwest Georgia History* 5 (1987): 15–37.

Zaborney, John J. *Slaves for Hire: Renting Enslaved Laborers in Antebellum Virginia.* Baton Rouge: Louisiana State University Press, 2012.

INDEX

———•—•———

Page numbers in *italics* refer to illustrations.

Printed in the USA
CPSIA information can be obtained
at www.ICGtesting.com
LVHW091218151223
766489LV00004B/320

9 780820 363660